FIRST OVER EVEREST

THE HOUSTON-MOUNT EVEREST
EXPEDITION

LADY HOUSTON, D.B.E.

FIRST OVER
EVEREST

THE HOUSTON-MOUNT EVEREST
EXPEDITION

By
Air-Commodore P F M Fellowes, DSO,
L V stewart blacker, obe, psc,
colonel p t etherton,
and Squadron Leader the Marquess of
Douglas and Clydesdale, MP

**With 57 illustrations from photographs, diagrams
and maps**

PILGRIMS PUBLISHING
Varanasi◆Kathmandu

FIRST OVER EVEREST
P F M Fellowes, L V Stewart Blacker, P T Etherton, and
The Marquess of Douglas and Clydesdale

Published by:
PILGRIMS PUBLISHING

An imprint of:
PILGRIMS BOOK HOUSE
B 27/98 A-8, Nawabganj Road
Durga Kund, Varanasi-221010, India
Tel: 91-542-314060, 312456
E-mail: pilgrims@satyam.net.in
Website: www.pilgrimsbooks.com

Distributed in India by:
PILGRIMS BOOK HOUSE
B 27/98 A-8, Nawabganj Road
Durga Kund, Varanasi-221010, India
Tel: 91-542-314060, 312456
E-mail: pilgrims@satyam.net.in
Website: www.pilgrimsbooks.com

Distributed in Nepal by:
PILGRIMS BOOK HOUSE
P O Box 3872, Thamel,
Kathmandu, Nepal
Tel: 977-1-424942
Fax: 977-1-424943
E-mail: pilgrims@wlink.com.np

Cover Design by Sasya

ISBN: 81-7769-181-3
Rs. 235/-

Printed in India

CONTENTS

CHAPTER   PAGE

I   FIRST OVER EVEREST   I

II   PRELIMINARY STEPS IN TECHNICAL PLANNING .   18

III   OXYGEN ON THE EVEREST FLIGHT . .   34

IV   AIR PHOTOGRAPHIC SURVEY . . .   50

V   THE HUNDRED YEARS' WAR AGAINST EVEREST,
1823-1933   79

VI   STRATEGY, TACTICS AND OBJECTIVES . .   97

VII   THE FLIGHT TO INDIA   111

VIII   NEPAL   146

IX   LIFE AT PURNEA   165

X   THE FLIGHT TO EVEREST   181

XI   THE FLIGHT OVER KANGCHENJUNGA AND THE
SECOND FLIGHT TO EVEREST . . .   195

XII   DARJEELING AND THE HOMEWARD FLIGHT .   215

XIII   FILMING THE FLIGHT   232

XIV   THE AUTHORS' APPRECIATON OF THOSE WHO CON-
TRIBUTED TO THE SUCCESS OF THE EXPEDITION.   245

APPENDIX I   251

APPENDIX II   THE MOUNT EVEREST CAMERAS . .   253

APPENDIX III   THE "BRISTOL" PEGASUS S.3 ENGINE .   257

APPENDIX IV   LA SCOLTA—WELCOME . . .   259

INDEX   261

LIST OF ILLUSTRATIONS

Lady Houston, D.B.E . . . . *Frontispiece*

facing page

The Cockpit for the Pilot 32

The chief observer being fitted into his gear by Air Commodore Fellowes for a test flight at Yeovil . . 46

Darjeeling, from 14,000 feet up 58

The main instrument board in the observer's cockpit . 58

Colonel Valentine Blacker, C.B. From a painting at Carrickblacker 80

Diagram showing the triangulation of Northern India . 82

Diagram showing the flight paths of the Houston-Westland to Mount Everest 108

Diagram of portion of Everest flight 109

Hyderabad in Sind 130

The great castle at Jodhpur 130

The largest building in the world (Karachi) . . 132

Unloading the Houston-Westland from the P. & O. s.s. *Dalgoma* at Karachi on 7th March . . . 132

The Kutab Minar near Delhi 140

Imperial Delhi. The Viceroy's house from the air . . 140

Clydesdale with Blacker 142

H.E. the Viceroy with Blacker 142

H.E. the Viceroy inspects the Expedition . . . 144

Allahabad. The Mogul fort at the junction of Ganges and Jumna 144

His Highness the Maharaja of Nepal . . . 146

A main square in Khatmandu 150

Buildings are ornate in sequestered Khatmandu . . 150

The entrance to a temple in Nepal 154

Disc wheels are more in evidence than motor-cars in Nepal . 154

An aborigine of Purnea 158

Women carry loads as well as men in Nepal . . 158

As it was in the beginning : grinding corn in Nepal . 160

LIST OF ILLUSTRATIONS

facing page

At the gateway of a temple in Nepal . . . 160

A holy man of Khatmandu tells his beads . . . 162

The orchestra at the Santal dance 168

The beauty chorus at the Santal dance . . . 168

Ancient transport mingles with the modern . . 172

The members of the Expedition 176

Members of the Expedition preparing for a flight . . 178

The two pilots 178

Colonel Etherton handing up the Everest mail . . 182

A conventionalised sketch, drawn by Hashime Murayama, of the aeroplanes' track to Everest . . . 184

Flying to Everest, 3rd April, 1933 186

The Houston-Westland about two and a half minutes' flight from the summit of Everest 188-9

Looking down on to the summit of Everest for the first time 190

The western end of the Chamlang Range . . . 192

One of the great declivities of Everest . . . 194

An infra-red photograph showing the summit of Everest over the clouds. Taken from a hundred miles away . 196

Kangchenjunga, taken on infra-red plates from a hundred miles away 196

Flying towards Kangchenjunga, 4th April, 1933 . . 198

Snow slopes of Kangchenjunga 198

Kangchenjunga 200

Five photographs of Everest and Makalu taken in flight at decreasing distances 202-3

Looking steeply down on to the actual summit of Everest . 204

Makalu, 27,790 feet up, from the direction of Everest . 206

Approaching Everest on 19th April, 1933 . . . 208-9

The Houston-Westland with its wheels almost over the South Peak ("Lhotse") on 19th April . . . 210

The Everest group from the E.S.E. . . . 210

The Houston-Westland flying towards Everest on 19th April, 1933, at about 29,000 feet 212

The summit from E.N.E. and slightly above . . 212

Makalu 216

LIST OF ILLUSTRATIONS

facing page

A portion of the vertical photographs taken on 19th April
  and joined together for mapping purposes . . 218-9
An Anaglyph from vertical photographs taken over Everest.
  Made to appear in stereoscopic relief . . . 222
Flying south from Everest on 19th April, 1933 . . 226-7
Map to show the flight from Lalbalu to Everest and
  Kangchenjunga 248
A vertical photograph, taken by the Williamson camera from
  32,000 feet, of the high spurs and glaciers near Everest 254
Map to show the flight from Cairo to Purnea . . 260

B

CHRONOLOGICAL HISTORY OF THE EVEREST FLIGHT

MARCH, 1932   Headquarters of flight located at College of Aeronautical Engineering, Chelsea.

Plan for flight to Mount Everest, submitted by L. V. S. Blacker, considered by Council of Royal Geographical Society.

APRIL, 1932   Letter sent to Secretary of State for India by Council of R.G.S., intimating that in their opinion the plan is likely to produce valuable scientific results.

Air Ministry grant facilities at the Royal Aircraft Establishment, R.A.F. School of Photography, and Experimental Establishment, Martlesham.

Negotiations with Bristol Aeroplane Company for Pegasus engine.

Lord Peel and Colonel John Buchan join the Committee of the flight.

MAY, 1932   Official application made to India Office for permission to fly across Nepal.

Air Survey Plan made with Geographical Section, General Staff, War Office.

Colonel Etherton communicates with British Envoy in Nepal, a former brother officer.

British Envoy at Khatmandu intimates the flight is receiving sympathetic consideration from Nepalese Government.

Arrangements made for use of Army Department's landing-ground at Purnea.

JUNE, 1932   Decided that type I.S.3 Pegasus engine be employed for flight.

Lord Clydesdale joins the Committee and is later nominated pilot.

JULY, 1932   Master of Sempill joins Committee.

India Office approached to grant exemption from customs duties, to loan reserve pilot, and various other ranks of R.A.F. in India.

Arrangements made for supply of petrol, oil, etc.

Special concessions accorded by P. & O. Steam Navigation Company.

Negotiations opened with Gaumont-British Picture Corporation for filming expedition.

August, 1932   Government of Nepal sanctions flight.

September, 1932   Lady Houston approached by Lord Clydesdale to give financial support to expedition.

Lord Lytton and Wing Commander Orlebar join Committee.

India Office grant customs exemption.

Oxygen apparatus and heated clothing selected.

G.H.Q. of Expedition transferred to Grosvenor House, W.1 (October. 1932).

October, 1932   Selection of Eagle cameras and accessories made.

Westland P.V.3. selected.

Negotiations for personnel, material, and insurance.

Lady Houston supports flight financially.

Pegasus engine ordered from Bristol.

November, 1932   Lord Burnham joins Committee as Honorary Treasurer.

Air Commodore P. F. M. Fellowes appointed chief executive officer.

Flight-Lieut. McIntyre appointed second pilot.

Defence Department, Irish Free State, offer two suitable aeroplanes, gratis, complete with Jaguar engines.

December, 1932   First acceptance test flight carried out at Yeovil.

February, 1933   Westland planes shipped to Karachi in s.s. *Dalgoma*. Three Moth aeroplanes with executive officer and pilots leave London.

March, 1933   Westland aeroplanes unloaded at Karachi.

Colonel P. T. Etherton visits Nepal.

From Karachi by air to Purnea. Inspection at Delhi by H.E. the Viceroy.

April 3, 1933   First flight over Mount Everest.

April 4, 1933   Flight over Kangchenjunga.

April 19, 1933   Second flight over Mount Everest.

CHAPTER I

FIRST OVER EVEREST

THROUGH all our own generation and that of our fathers the summit of Mount Everest has been the symbol of remote inaccessibility. Perhaps it is this very fact which inspired the long series of brave struggles to attain it, struggles which became more determined and even more gallant after man had reached both Poles and so left Everest in its solitary and inviolate majesty. In 1932 that awesome crest was still the last stronghold of Nature, her last donjon-keep into which man had never been able to look, and her last penetralia from which he had never been able to rend the veil.

Heaven knows that Everest's inaccessibility is daunting enough for any venturer's heart. The physical aspect alone of the task, the sheer height and the wild icy bastions and ramparts of iron cliff, have appalled all those who, from Jules Verne downwards, have dreamed of surmounting it.

Up till 1932 every serious expedition against the mountain had been a land one, of climbers and porters.

As we shall see later, there had been airmen with dreams and ideas of flying to the summit, but none of these were practicable, nor could they be because there was then no engine in the world which could take an aeroplane to carry the men and the instruments of an expedition to that great height.

It fell to the good fortune of one of our number to devise the first practical flight to the summit of Everest.

Blacker, at that time a major in the Regular Army, on leave from the frontier, seized on the fact that the Pegasus engine, with its supercharger, had at last brought the dream within man's grasp and that a British aeroplane might overcome the physical obstacles and win the long sought prize.

I

The first step was to work out what in Staff College language is called a sound technical plan of action, to formulate the objective, to appreciate the situation, and from it, to specify means of execution of the plan which should be within the capacity of the weapons available to those who would wield them.

Our head-quarters were established at the College of Aeronautical Engineering in Chelsea. Mr. C. H. Roberts, the principal of this "University of the Air," placed its technical and other resources at our disposal and so the plans proceeded apace. As the organisation expanded, with its resultant large increase in personnel and material, the head-quarters were removed eight months later to Grosvenor House, Park Lane.

The originator of the plan, although a soldier, had, in addition to some years of flying experience, taken his pilot's licence under the auspices of the Bristol Company's school as early as 1911, only missing being in the first hundred by ill-luck.

The co-operation of the progressive Bristol Company with their whilom pupil and his plan was generous and cordial.

At this point he was joined by a former comrade of the old war-time in France and a fellow venturer of the Russian Civil Wars. This was Colonel P. T. Etherton, a born organiser, and the administrative wizard of the expedition from Alpha to Omega.

The technical plan was well threshed out by qualified experts, who were able to say that it was sound and without flaw. Thus it seemed that the physical defences of the mountain could be overcome and the goal attained. But the obstacles of Nature, were by no means the only bar to the summit of Everest, possibly not even the greatest.

Everest lies half in Tibet and half in Nepal, and well over a hundred miles from the frontier of the nearest British territory. Tibet and Nepal are both independent states and the approach to either is fraught with diplomatic difficulties. The great influence of Lord Curzon himself had been scarcely enough to secure bare entry into Tibet even for the first land expeditions.

It was soon discovered that the hermit kingdom was very positively closed to airmen. There remained an approach through Nepal, and here diplomacy had to put its best foot forward. No European was allowed to cross Nepal; even the guests of the Maharaja had only been taken into the foothills. For some time this obstacle seemed apparently insuperable. The Government of Nepal being independent, could not be approached through the usual official channels to accord a favour which had never been granted in history, and the distance of the capital at Khatmandu made matters more difficult still. The first step towards winning over the Government was to demonstrate the value to science and geography of the plans, and of this the only arbiters were the Council of the Royal Geographical Society.

So they were laid before them, and scrutinised from every angle. The Royal Geographical Society having bestowed its blessing it was transmitted to the India Office. The Society, and especially its Secretary, Mr. A. R. Hinks, inspired and helped the expedition in the most valuable way.

The assurance from the Council to the Indian Government was a big step forward but only one of the several foundation stones of the organisation. The second had to be secured from the Air Ministry, for it was clearly essential that the Government of Nepal should entertain no misgivings as to the technical soundness of the plan presented to them, or as to the capacity of the aircraft for carrying out their formidable task with the least possible chance of mishap. None but the Air Ministry could vouch for such a matter; not only is the Air Ministry charged in Great Britain with civil aviation, but within it are to be found those technical experts whose decision on the fitness of aircraft for their tasks is not only impartial but final.

In due course the plan, with all its data, diagrams and charts, received the benediction it needed, and here again the Air Council afforded a countenance and support to the expedition, which though unofficial, was beyond price.

This was in April 1932, and the organisation was now on a

sufficiently firm footing to warrant an approach to the Government of Nepal. It was at this moment that the expedition found an old war-time friend who bridged an important gap in the approach to the Maharaja, which was necessarily unofficial.

Meanwhile, in the same month, an influential committee was formed of which the original members were Lord Peel, Lord Clydesdale, the Master of Sempill, and Colonel John Buchan.

It was not only these names which were of such value to the expedition, but the activities which each member put forth on its behalf, to tide over its many difficulties.

The Government of Nepal proved more sympathetic than we had expected, and we learned of the progressive spirit of the ruler of that remarkable country, a spirit discriminating and eclectic, which turns a ready ear to matters of real worth. The generous gestures of the Royal Geographical Society, of the Air Ministry and of the India Office, must have carried weight with the Government of Nepal, and helped to convince them that ours was a sound organisation devoted to a scientific object.

Nevertheless, we endured many weeks of anxious waiting, because the Nepal Government were bound naturally to examine the proposal from every angle. In these matters if all goes well, the tendency is to ask why so much consideration was necessary. However, those on whom falls the responsibility must consider the effects of possible mishaps. It so happened that the course we had to plan out for our aeroplanes would take us from south to north across the least developed and most inaccessible portion of a remote and primitive kingdom, where telegraphs are not, and messages are carried by foot couriers over rugged mountains.

Had any disaster occurred during the flight a relief expedition by land might have had to be sent out. The presence of this would naturally constitute a penetration of Nepalese territory, running counter to the engagements entered into by the governments concerned. The opinion of the aristocracy of Nepal was of importance, and we could not expect that all of the grandees of Eastern Nepal would be as sympathetic to modern air activities as their progressive and broad-minded ruler.

To their credit be it recorded, the Government of Nepal hearkened to us, at last, after minor points had been cleared up, the permission coveted in vain for so long by many was ours.

The official letter reached us in the middle of August, but in the meantime we had been busy with details of organisation. Clydesdale again one of the original members of the Committee, had at his own urgent request become the Chief Pilot. The expedition is indebted to him as much for his courage and foresight in taking part in what many then considered a visionary undertaking, as for his great work as pilot in the actual flights.

The details of organisation called for sheer hard work and unremitting toil; as usual in these cases, the big items are fairly easy to come upon. Once we had selected the engine, with its supercharger, and the type of aeroplane to take it, we were clear of them, and in a later chapter it will be seen how we came to pin our faith to Westland aeroplanes, with such happy results. The minor items of material equipment were legion, and their selection constituted a prolonged and arduous task. The difficulties had their root in the novelty of conditions in which everything had to operate.

The numerous cameras, the oxygen supply gear, which, in conjunction with the electrical heating installation, was vital, engine and flying instruments, all had to work not only in the rarefied air of 33,000 feet, but for the unprecedented space of two hours, and must be taken from a sun temperature of 180° F. down to where, almost in the stratosphere, there would be 120° of frost.

The reader will judge from the illustrations facing pages 32 and 46 and from Chapter II, how varied and complex was the outfit of instruments. The selection of each item called for much care and thought; nearly everything had to be modified or added to because of the strange environment in which it was to do its work. Thus added to the labours of selection were many experiments, trials and investigations, which kept us fully occupied throughout the summer and autumn of 1932. It was fortunate for the expedition that as early as the spring of 1932, the Air Ministry had generously accorded the stored up experience and technical resources of the Royal Aircraft Establishment at South Farnborough, not to mention those of the Experimental Establishment at Martlesham Heath, and of the R.A.F. School of Photography. These resources were naturally of great value. In addition firms concerned in the supply of instruments and stores were generous in exerting efforts in the interests of the flight, the list of those who did so being a long one. Similarly, our activities in India secured the use of the landing-ground required, exemption from customs duties, and other valuable facilities, including those of a meteorological nature.

By the end of September the two main obstacles to our air attack on Everest had been surmounted. The technical planning was, but for some minor items, not only achieved, but approved by experts, whilst the diplomatic or political side of the organisation had attained its goal—the permission to fly across Nepal. The last though not quite unconditional was generous and gave a free field for our objective.

The third obstacle was the financial one. In the spring this had not seemed as formidable as the others, for we found several public-spirited individuals ready to contribute to the expedition's funds, in addition to which many firms gave concessions of value were they to be expressed in terms of money, whilst others gave money and many their time, experience and resources.

As ill luck would have it, no sooner had we rounded off our organisation, secured our sanctions and permissions, and completed our technical planning, than the full force of the financial crisis of 1932 broke upon us. Those from whom we anticipated much were compelled to withdraw, and in proportion anxieties of the organisers, who had seen their goal in sight, began to increase.

We decided to approach Lady Houston, whose munificence to British aviation is famous and justly so all over the world since the victorious conclusion of the Schneider contest.

Our earlier endeavour to secure her support had been frustrated by her ill-health, but this was now happily improved.

The ambitious project appealed to Lady Houston's resolute and far-seeing mind and she realised even more rapidly than most experts the value of such a flight to the good name and credit of British aviation.

British aviators gladly acknowledge the debt they owe her, on this account. For truth to tell, since the Atlantic was flown in 1919, our country has lagged sadly behind in the gaining and exploring of geographical objectives by air.

It was due to the organising capacity and hardihood of foreign aviators that foreign aircraft flew over both the Poles, and there were unmistakable indications that both French and German airmen contemplated an attack on Mount Everest as soon as their engines and aeroplanes could be developed to the required pitch of efficiency.

Unfortunately before definite arrangements were made, it had become too late for the flight to be attempted in 1932, and thereby to take advantage of the most favourable time of the year from the point of view of weather conditions.

Lady Houston appointed Mr. R. D. Blumenfeld to represent her *vis-à-vis* the Committee and so we had the pleasure of welcoming his personality into the growing circle of those who were striving to attain the goal.

It was growing because His Highness the Maharaja Jam Sahib of Nawanagar, Lord Burnham, and later Lord Lytton, joined the committee, Lord Burnham becoming its Honorary Treasurer.

The organisation had now outgrown its original limits and called for the presence of a senior Air Force Officer to take executive charge. Feeling that a practising pilot should have this post Blacker stood aside. Precluded by the results of war injuries from actually flying a machine, it was arranged that he should become the chief observer when the expedition took the air.

So on an appropriately auspicious date, the 11th November, Air-Commodore P. F. M. Fellowes, late of the Royal Air Force, took over his new post, the arduous duties which went with it and a large share of the burden of organisation.

The expedition became a band of brothers, bound together by a mutual confidence in Fellowes, and this feeling was no small factor of the ultimate success. Meanwhile his status in matters of the air was of exceeding value to the organisation in the final phase of hard work in England.

We had already placed important orders for material, so that the months of November, December and January go down stamped in all our minds by a hectic series of detail arrangements, trials, tests and acceptances. The work seemed to get harder as the details with which we dealt became progressively smaller and smaller.

In expeditions of this nature where funds are limited an endeavour to secure supplies at preferential rates has continuously to be made. At this Etherton proved himself an artist. To hear him declaiming on the merits and prestige of the expedition was an education in itself and, as events proved, his promises were fully justified. In other respects, apart from his administrative and organising ability, Etherton proved a past-master in devising ways and means for reducing the cost of the expedition. His knowledge of the language and conditions in India, and of how best to conserve and manage our limited resources when there, was an impressive demonstration of the way experience can be utilised. It was a surprising thing to others, innocent as they are in such matters, to realise how much can be given if you only know how to ask. Securing material for an incorporate body, such as an expedition, is an art, but a pleasing feature is that once a firm has made up its mind it frequently gives more than is required and has to be restrained in its generosity.

Besides the trials of material, it was indispensable to test out the human components as we shall describe later, and to accustom each flying member to his complex and novel tasks in the air.

TRAINING FOR THE FLIGHT

Prior to leaving for India all available knowledge on the subject of instruments and their use from every aspect was absorbed by the various members concerned, especially the operation of instruments in the air. The apparatus we carried was so special that a system of training had to be devised, not only for individuals but for the pairs working together. Owing to the lack of time we were unable to follow the usual course of practical training in the air.

By the courtesy of the Air Ministry, Clydesdale, McIntyre and Blacker, received instruction at Farnborough to accustom them to the clothes they would wear when flying at extreme heights, in the use of the special apparatus, and to give them practice in strip photography and manipulation of cameras in the air. They also received instructions in the use of the apparatus on the ground. We adopted a system of setting various problems to observers and pilots when sitting on the ground in their cockpits, as to the action they would take in different eventualities in the air. It is a maxim of air training first to achieve what is possible on the ground, so that both pilot and observer may do their thinking there before attempting to carry out their aerial duties. This procedure dominated our training.

Most important of all were the tests of the two Westland aeroplanes, the Houston and the Wallace, with their Pegasus engines, which had to be carried out at Yeovil.

As invariably happens in all expeditions, there was a frantic race against time. In anything to do with aeroplanes, everything is vital, and progress usually hinges on the late arrival of some small item which holds up everything else.

We had many such trials and tribulations before the two machines were ready for their acceptance tests.

Before we were justified in shipping the machines to India, it was essential for each to be taken to a height of at least 33,000 feet with the full load of crew and instruments it would have to carry over the mountain.

The margin, as we have seen, over 29,141 feet, was called for by the fact that the mountain might take thought, and, in a meteorological sense, add a cubit suddenly to its stature. The clerk of the weather might take it into his head to make the atmosphere more tenuous to that degree, and so less of a support for the wings of aeroplanes.

In the acceptance flights the machines would be flown by the firm's test pilot, Mr. Penrose. The opportunity could not however be missed, of accustoming the observers to their tasks at those high altitudes. For truth to tell, there were no other machines but our own in which this could be done. English weather needs no comment here, and English weather is especially devilish towards the high-altitude flyer. Many times did we rush down to Yeovil, when at last the machines were ready and the complicated installation of their engines completed, to find the air of Somersetshire a mass of cloud, mist and fog. Official records show that on the average there are only nineteen days in each year, when it is possible in England to take photographs from 25,000 feet. The month was December.

In spite of all their preliminary practice, the flying-kit was so complicated that pilots and observers were overcome with gloom. It took so long to don all the items and to connect up every electrical gadget and lead that they suspected it would be dusk, on the great day before all was ready and buttoned up. However, we put lightning fasteners onto everything possible, and practised continually, so that by the time the machines were ready to test, the flyers could get dressed in twenty-five minutes. The starting of the engines and the pulling on of the suits had to be co-ordinated so that the engines should not be kept running needlessly on the ground whilst the crew were still fixing themselves up in their gear.

Fellowes was the passenger on the thrilling day of the initial test, in one machine, and Blacker in the other.

Anxiety was intense, not only because all our hopes turned on the actual result, but from the possibility that any one of a thousand hitches might happen and delay the expedition till the Indian monsoon supervened and wrecked our hopes. Hence the race against time. The excitement when the day arrived, and there was at last blue sky above Yeovil was such that all went about dazed, and as men in a dream. The actual take off from the ground of these aeroplanes looks so easy and humdrum as amount almost to bathos. So it happened, and the little crowd of experts, photographers and Press men looked at each other with blank expressions as the Houston-Westland faded from their sight in a very few minutes into the misty English sky.

The interval of waiting seemed like hours, but at last all was well. Both aeroplanes behaved admirably. Not only did they surpass the promised height by a comfortable margin, but the engines had run with the smoothness of sewing-machines. The anxious observers had watched incessantly the electrical thermometers connected to each cylinder, but the readings had not varied so much as by a degree up to where the altimeters had registered 37,500 feet, and the yard-long thermometers out on the struts had indicated the awesome temperature of minus sixty-one degrees centigrade. All went according to plan on the test flights, thanks to the Westland and Bristol Companies.

Although the machines behaved perfectly, there were a few exciting adventures for the flyers.

On one of the flights, after soaring almost despairingly through an immense blanket of cloud, for 20,000 feet, the machine at last came into the real blue of heaven, and looking down, the pilot and observer saw themselves on the borders of Kent.

As ill luck would have it, at the 29,000-foot level the pilot's oxygen mask slipped. It was one he had borrowed, the fitting had been incorrect. The observer, busy with his cameras, realised quite suddenly that the even upward progress of the machine had given way to something of a disconcerting nature. Holding on tight he tried to telephone the pilot, feeling that a crisis was imminent, and the pilot might succumb to an oxygen failure. The dual control had been removed, the pilot was out of reach, but fortunately, he had a parachute.

An observer does not care to desert his pilot without due cause, so he waited, holding on firmly, to the strongest looking struts, whilst the altimeter needle made ominous moves down its scale. At this inopportune moment, the securing catch of the hatchway or trap-door in the floor gave way, and the door blew open, offering a vista, straight downwards of some five miles, to the surface of Kent. The observer struggled blindly to kick back the door, whilst supporting himself with both hands over this space, at the same time, trying hard to obtain some sign of life from the pilot. At last, when he was deciding whether to slip himself and the parachute through the hole in the floor, to retain a lungful of oxygen and with it, enough consciousness to pull the ring of the parachute in the air, things began to happen.

The oxygen supply seemed to improve, his mind worked more freely, and at last a small voice came from the pilot. At the same time the machine levelled on to an even keel, the observer succeeded in closing the door in the floor and sat firmly upon it.

Then the pilot explained that he had managed to make secure his oxygen mask which had very insidiously slipped to one side, so that imperceptibly his mental processes had become fogged and obscured.

With the loss of height, matters put themselves right; the oxygen came freely through its pipes and all was well. On they flew up to their "ceiling," hard at work making notes, and then home. Meanwhile, the clouds had thickened and it was no easy task to find the way to the West of England. At last the long curving white line of the surf on the Chesil Beach gave the pilot his landmark, and soon they were back at Yeovil.

It was an interesting, if thrilling experience, but it held lessons for the future, which were not lost on the expedition.

The test flights were a success, for they afforded actual practice for the flyers, in the novel and difficult tasks they would have to perform over Mount Everest, such practice was not to be had elsewhere.

As soon as the tests were over, the two machines were immediately packed, in their immense cases, under the care of the experts of the Aeronautical Inspection department, and the scrutiny of the preventive men of H.M. Customs.

Then off they went on special G.W.R. trucks to the holds of the P. & O. *Dalgoma* at Tilbury.

The expedition heaved a sigh.

But there were still other problems, before the party could leave England.

In temperate weather the development and printing of photographs is comparatively easy, but it was essential to prepare for high temperatures on the ground. Consequently, we were uncertain as to how much of this work could be carried out at the base, and whether it would be essential rapidly to transport our films to Calcutta for treatment. This, and the need for preliminary reconnaissance prior to the main flight, if our precious supplies of special petrol, oil and oxygen were not to be wasted, made it necessary to have light aircraft in addition to the two large machines. Messrs. Fry, of chocolate renown, offered us the loan of their Puss Moth, and in reply to our inquiries, we learnt that a Fox Moth could be disposed of in India if we were to fly it out. In the circumstances these two machines were available at practically no cost to the expedition, and so both were taken. Clydesdale also took out his own machine, a Tiger Moth. We thus possessed three light aircraft.

Meanwhile the transport of the personnel and material to India was arranged through the generosity of the P. & O. Steam Navigation Company and of Imperial Airways. Thus with the three small aircraft our transport difficulties were solved. One of the machines was later on destroyed by a storm in India, so it was as well we had been generous in their provision.

Incidentally, prior to a flight to India six weeks warning must be given to the authorities—not that Shell-Mex would experience difficulty in providing the fuel at short notice, but to obtain the necessary permits to fly over the various countries along the route. Persia and Turkey are notoriously slow in granting these. As regards our route, it was decided for us by the insurance company, who were not anxious to insure the smaller aircraft travelling through Eastern Europe and Anatolia during the winter season. This was because of the water-logged condition of the aerodromes and the bad weather prevalent at that season. We were therefore compelled to take the longer route via Italy, Sicily, and North Africa.

The plans having now been made, the actual material ordered, personnel selected, and a multitude of letters to various authorities written and answered, it remained only to settle actual departures. These again were mainly decided for us by the dates ships were leaving England and arriving in Karachi. Following on a fine effort by the Bristol Aeroplane Company and Westland Aircraft, the second machine was shipped and reached Karachi on March 7th. This gave the time required, provided everything proceeded according to plan.

Seven weeks in India were at our disposal to disembark the aircraft, assemble and test them at Karachi, train the personnel in their use, fly them across India, carry out experimental flights in the vicinity of Purnea, and the two main flights over Everest. A formidable task, and so it proved.

The equipment of the expedition was now fairly under way, but there remained the laying out of fuel supplies along the route and at the base in India, to level and equip the base, arrange for the housing of the personnel and aircraft at Purnea, select ground personnel, formulate the final plan of action, and arrangements for supply of meteorological data.

Before laying out the fuel supplies, the requisite type had to be decided, and to this end, the advice of the Shell Anglo-Persian Oil groups, and engineering experts of the Bristol Aeroplane Company was obtained. The next step centred on the quantities of fuel and oil required for each halting-place and at the base, these being provided in the most efficient manner by the Shell Company and Wakefield's respectively.

The base at Purnea had already been selected by Blacker and Etherton. The Public Works Department took the necessary steps to prepare the aerodrome, which we found admirably adapted to our requirements. Etherton and Blacker had gained touch as related elsewhere, with our generous host, the Maharaja of Darbhanga. The R.A.F. authorities in India lent some small hangars and provided for their erection with certain other essential aerodrome gear. The local authorities took the matter so well in hand that on arrival we found the aerodrome complete with huts and hangars. Mr. Came, the District Engineer, and Mr. Dain, the Commissioner, were responsible for these efficient arrangements.

The selection of the remaining personnel was an easy matter, as everyone was anxious to join and the Royal Air Force in India had agreed to loan a reserve pilot—Flying Officer R. C. W. Ellison, together with the ground personnel—six other ranks in all—required, and in addition two ground engineers, Burnard and Pitt we had from Westland's and Bristol's. Clydesdale was now our chief pilot and after sifting all other claims McIntyre, a member of his squadron, was nominated second pilot. We had always heard that Scotsmen were thorough and determined, and any doubts we may have had as to its truth were soon dispelled.

A medical officer, Captain Bennett, was lent to the expedition by the Director-General of Medical Services in India, an ideal man for the work. The cinematograph party were headed by Geoffrey Barkas, as Director, with Bonnett and Fisher as the cinematographers. The others did the "shooting" of pictures on the ground, and superintended the technical efficiency of the extensive equipment brought out with them. Meanwhile, *The Times* had been allotted the newspaper and photographic rights of the expedition.

In settling the plan of action we had to weigh the relative claims of the cinematograph and of the oblique and vertical photographs. We therefore visited the School of Photography at Farnborough to discuss the possibilities of securing satisfactory survey in the limited time at our disposal, probably two periods of twenty minutes per aircraft, over the mountains.The geographical branch of the General Staff at the War Office, presided over by Colonel N. M. Macleod, was a staunch ally from the first. The object was to obtain two strips going towards the mountain and one coming away, secure the maximum number of obliques, and expose as much cinema film as could be carried. Broadly speaking, we decided that the vertical photograph should govern the actual courses to be taken on the way towards the mountain for both aircraft, and for one aircraft on the return journey; the time over the mountain to be devoted to changing the magazines on the vertical cameras, and to taking oblique and cinema photographs of the actual peak. It will be seen elsewhere how all this worked out under Blacker's care.

The question of meteorological data was then taken up with Dr. Norman, the Director of Meteorology in India, who arranged to supply our requirements and to that end set up special balloon stations at Darjeeling and Purnea. We asked for a forecast twenty-four hours ahead as to possible weather in the vicinity of Everest, with wind speeds and directions at heights up to 35,000 feet, to be furnished twice daily if possible.

We now determined on preliminary tests to justify our shipping the aircraft to India. It was decided that, if both machines could be flown once to the height required, 33,000 feet, with the full load on board, and provided the apparatus functioned to reasonable satisfaction, we could proceed with the shipping arrangements.

* * * * * *

The basic conception behind the Mount Everest venture was to show how flight may be one of the handmaidens of human progress. It is hardly realised that without survey and maps there can be no real modern civilisation in a country. Map making is an essential preliminary to almost every form of modern material activity, war-like or pacific, whether it be economic, as the planning of a railway, or æsthetic, such as the laying out of a park or pleasure ground. Nine-tenths of the world even in the British Empire is unmapped or very roughly depicted on maps.

Survey by air has a prominent place on its own merits as the swift and sure instrument for topographical mapping, although hitherto it has seldom, if ever, been used except at comparatively low altitudes. The desire to increase the sum of human knowledge of Nature's greatest mountain stronghold was the paramount object of the expedition.

CHAPTER II

PRELIMINARY STEPS IN TECHNICAL PLANNING

THE practicability of a serious flight—that is, one with an actual scientific object—was dependent on the possibility of securing an engine with the necessary very high standard of performance.

In June 1930, Lieutenant Soucek of the United States Army Air Corps had accomplished a world's height record at Washington, flying a Wright "Apache" biplane equipped with a Pratt and Whitney engine of 450 h.p. He took this machine to a height of 13,157 metres, or over 40,000 feet.

Needless to say, this creditable achievement was carried out with a single-seater machine over flat country of no great altitude and probably with a minimum load of oxygen. This engine would not have been capable of carrying our much greater weights to the necessary 34,000 or even 33,000 feet called for by the flight over Mount Everest.

Our flight, then, was rendered possible by the fact that under the guidance of the talented designer of the Bristol Aeroplane Company, Mr. A. R. H. Fedden, there had been produced early in 1932, the first experimental models of an engine destined to earn laurels for itself, the Pegasus.

One of the organisers as we have seen, who was responsible for technical planning, had been an old pupil, twenty-one years before, of the Bristol Flying School, and so his acquaintance with the progress of this engine was the keystone of a practicable scheme for the flight over the world's highest mountain.

The initial step was a visit to the Bristol Company's establishment at Filton, where these engines are designed and made.

The Pegasus is a development of the Jupiter, an earlier type of 9-cylinder stationary, air-cooled radial, whose success in several spheres of aviation, on the far-faring liners of Imperial Airways, as well as on the fighting aircraft of the Royal Air Force, placed the Bristol Company in the lead of the world's design.

There were reasons, of a highly technical nature, why water-cooled engines as a class were generally unsuitable for this exacting task. A leading factor against them was their greater weight in proportion to horse power, whilst the primary recommendation of the Pegasus rested in the fact that each horse power was produced with an engine weight of the low figure of 1.6 lb.

There were other difficulties in connection with water-cooling of a practical order which threatened to cause trouble in the extremes of temperature that we should meet. The Pegasus engine excelled on account of its low weight per horse power, a point of the greatest importance where every ounce had to be carried for six miles up through the air and where each ounce had a much greater detrimental effect at that altitude than near sea-level. It excelled also by virtue of the merits of its supercharger. This is a speciality of the Bristol Company, and enabled the engine to maintain much of its power where other engines would fade away.

In the spring of 1932, then, it was reasonably certain that only one engine in the world was capable of doing the work we contemplated, a British engine and a Pegasus. To express it in other words, it was the knowledge of the development which the Pegasus engine had reached that brought a scientific flight over Mount Everest into the region of practical politics.

The matter therefore came to this: the Pegasus engine was to take the expedition over the summit, and the aeroplane and all other items of gear would be subsidiary to it.

The enterprise was fortunate in that the Bristol Company themselves proposed at that time to make an attempt on the height record, and to surpass that set up by the pilot of the U.S. Army Air Corps. Naturally, the Pegasus engine was the one which they intended to employ for this. This fact turned to the advantage of the Everest expedition since many experimental difficulties were solved during these high altitude test flights. It is now a matter of history how Capt. C. F. Uwins captured the height record for Great Britain, in a Vespa with a super-charged Pegasus engine, of the same type as our own.

The supercharger, the very heart of the engine, has already been touched on, but there were a multitude of other matters, such as the investigation of the most suitable fuel called for by the exacting high compression in the cylinders. There was lubrication, for no ordinary oil would be adequate to enable such an engine to put forth the last ounce of its power. An interesting point arose in the planning of the flight regarding the type of lubricating oil to be used. It was found that a vegetable oil would be many pounds lighter in respect of the considerable amount to be carried than an oil with a mineral base, and these pounds become of the utmost importance in the upper end of the climb. It was however found impracticable on technical grounds in the design of the engine, such as piston clearances, to employ a vegetable oil. As these could not be altered in the time available a mineral oil had to be adopted.[1]

Apart from fuel and oil, there were innumerable details to consider, such as the risk of fuel freezing in the carburettor and the behaviour of magnetos at great heights. A fuel with a large proportion of benzol would be a danger since benzol freezes at about "minus" sixty degrees Centigrade. This substance had therefore to be ruled out, except in small quantity, and tetra-ethyl-lead substituted. In these matters the Bristol Company and ourselves owe much to the co-operation of Burma Shell Ltd., whose expert representatives half across the world spared no pains to assist us in overcoming our difficulties. The magnetos were liable to be suspect of a tendency to failure at great heights, traceable to a remarkable cause, that is that the air gap in the emergency spark gap is at high altitudes a much less efficient dielectric than near sea-level. For this reason the high-tension discharge has a tendency to leak across this gap

[1] Needless to say, both types were Messrs. Wakefields'.

instead of proceeding in the orthodox way to the sparking-plugs to perform its appointed task. The co-operation, however, of British-Thompson-Houston solved all difficulties in the sphere of ignition, which never gave a moment's anxiety from first to last.

In the matter of plugs we chose the K.L.G. type, and we never had any reason to regret our choice.

Both aircraft were fitted with Handley Page slots, and in view of the disturbed air conditions to be encountered at this immense altitude, we foresaw the value of these admirable accessories, for so indeed they proved.

Closely connected with the engine were such questions as the exhaust ring, the Townend ring, and the propellers. Each of these points had to be gone into in great detail, and the pros and cons thrashed out with the designers and technical experts. To eliminate the exhaust ring and piping would naturally save weight, but would have exposed the crews to deleterious and possibly dangerous exhaust fumes, and the all-important lenses of the cameras to the risks of becoming spotted with oil. It was probably this last circumstance that led us to decide on complete exhaust rings, and to avoid even the compromise of half-rings catching the exhaust from the upper cylinders only. Then again the Townend ring, one of the latest developments in aviation, is of decided value in improving the "performance" of aeroplanes equipped with air-cooled radial engines. We should perhaps explain that it is something like a very shallow cylinder mounted over the heads of the projecting cylinder heads and valve gears, with its axis coinciding with that of the engine. Its effect is to smooth out, as it were, the air rushing past the cylinder heads and which is much disturbed and rendered turbulent by them, where they project out from the smooth surface of the carefully faired fuselage. By virtue of this smoothing out of the stream of air, the resistance or "drag" of a large diameter air-cooled engine is so much reduced that it comes nearly down to that which would result from the use of a slim, compact, water-cooled engine. The Townend ring, therefore, adds much to the speed of aeroplanes with which it is fitted when flying level, and much more than compensates for its own slight extra weight.

When, however, the machine has to be made to climb to its last gasp and to the utmost possible height, naturally the weight factor tends to become increasingly important and the forward speed of the machine rather less so. But the careful calculations of our designers brought out the fact that even in the extreme conditions in which we proposed to fly, the Townend ring was worth its keep, and with a margin to spare.

Again, the oil had to be cooled after passing through the engine before it could be pumped back again for its further task of lubrication. It might be expected that at high levels the extreme cold would necessitate very little cooling surface on the oil cooler. This was correct at first sight, but, on the other hand, the air at upwards of 30,000 feet has so little mass that comparatively few molecules are available to flow against the surface of the oil cooler and carry off the extra heat. The result of the tests and experiments, more particularly those of the Bristol Company in their preparations to secure the height record, show that these two factors tended to balance each other, so that in actual flights a quite moderate oil cooler was employed. The type we used was the Vickers-Potts, it being susceptible of easy adjustment; a greater or less number of cooling elements can be employed according to circumstances.

The propeller question was gone into at a very early stage, our policy being shaped by a compromise depending on variable circumstances. We knew that the propellers would have to go through excessive variations of heat and cold, and withstand for long periods of time, the burning Indian sun. This, of course, called for an all-metal propeller, but on the other hand, wooden propellers are lighter and distinctly kinder to the engine, probably in view of their greater resiliency. The scale was tipped in favour of the wooden propellers when the designer pointed out that it would be much easier to make two or three wooden ones, the best of which could, after tests, be

22

fitted finally to the engine, rather than stake everything on a metal one which allowed little scope for experiment.

From this it will be clear that the planning and investigation of the engines and all the details necessitated a great amount of work spread over several months, but which was from first to last aided by the generously proffered advice and co-operation of the Air Ministry and the Royal Aircraft Establishment.

Closely connected with the engine were petrol pumps, starters, and the flying instruments. The starter question alone caused some tribulation. Such big engines cannot really be "swung" with any great likelihood of success. A normal method of coaxing them into motion is by the employment of the Hucks starter, which is a Ford chassis provided with a shaft and a clutch, engaging into dogs in the boss of the propeller, no engines being able to resist this persuasion. However, it was not practicable for us to take a Hucks starter to distant Purnea merely for the sake of starting two engines. An electric starter would depend on electrical power, which we did not possess in any quantity, so finally we decided on the "inertia" starter. This is an ingenious device whereby a flywheel is spun by means of gearing and a crank handle and two of the strongest men available, to a high rate of revolutions. A clutch is suddenly let in and the momentum stored up in this flywheel imparted to the engine, the while the pilot turns a hand magneto. The inertia starter worked and the engine started, but the comments of the strong men attached to it tended to show that they had some doubts as to its suitability in thirsty weather or semi-tropical temperatures.

The flying instruments, which were supplied by Messrs. Smith's Aircraft Instruments, gave no trouble whatever, but their selection involved thought and consideration. The problem being an unusual one, certain departures from the orthodox were essential or at least desirable. The revolution indicators were perhaps the only instruments strictly normal, apart from the special tests they underwent. Oil pressure gauges and oil thermometers were of vital importance for the slightest sign of excessive oil temperature would be to the pilot a valuable sign of how his engine was working, and give the earliest warning of any potential trouble.

Then again fuel consumption was a crucial point, since any excess expenditure of fuel might mean a reduction of the margin below the danger point, and a possible forced landing in mountainous, or at least hazardous, country. It was unlikely that a failure on the part of the engine, or even maladjustment of the carburettor, would lead us into trouble in this matter of consumption owing to the skill and qualifications of our ground engineers, but the stronger the winds that were to blow, the greater the tendency for the machine to deviate from its course and the greater the fuel consumption necessitated by the effort of the pilot to adhere to it. We could not govern the force and direction of the wind, and in actual flights its power proved to be a most important factor.

The selection of the aeroplanes was by no means easy, having regard to the prominent part played by the engine. At first sight it would seem that an engine like the Pegasus would pull almost any well-designed modern aeroplane of suitable characteristics to the immense height called for by the task. Investigation proved that there were not many aeroplanes suitable for the flight. Naturally, the machine had to be a two-seater, and the majority of such machines designed for water-cooled engines were ruled out, as to have installed a radial air-cooled engine would have meant months of re-design and re-building. Then again otherwise suitable aeroplanes were inadmissible owing to low under-carriages. Our machine must have a propeller of unusual diameter in order to grip the thin air, and we had to foresee the possibility of taking off from aerodromes covered with sand, gravel or small stones. Should the propeller tips come too near the ground, there was danger of their being damaged from flying fragments.

Then again an aeroplane built for high speed at low levels would be unsuitable, inasmuch as it would be deficient in climbing capacity, an essential point.

Even with all these points suitably adjusted, it was as well to have a machine with a deep and broad fuselage in which the observer could handle his numerous cameras without becoming hopelessly congested.

Our final choice rested on the Westland P.V.3, which we never regretted. This was an experimental machine built for general military purposes by Westland Aircraft for army co-operation and day bombing, and with a view to carrying a torpedo, to fold its wings for ship's stowage. It was the only one of its type in existence, since the specification to which it was built had been altered as soon as constructed. As it happened, when we had definitely decided on the Westland P.V.3[1] and a Westland-Wallace, an offer reached us from the Defence Department of the Irish Free State, placing in the most generous manner two of their Vickers-Vespas unconditionally at our disposal for the flight. Under the circumstances we were compelled to decline it, although we realised that the Vespa with Pegasus engine would have well carried out the work.

The Westland had all the necessary characteristics, a high under-carriage, engine-bearers ready to take the Pegasus engine straight away, a big wing surface and its consequent climbing capacity, and a broad deep fuselage with a cockpit so roomy that the most exacting observer could not have complained. Added to this, the machines in design and construction were worthy of the Westland Aircraft and fully justified their reputation.

Having determined on the aeroplanes, the question of how they were to be fitted up for the enterprise in front of them now demanded settlement.

After consultation with the designers, we decided that much would be gained by covering in the observer's cockpit. Much of his work was carried out with cameras pointing downwards. At the same time, the closing-in, or roofing over of the big aperture of the ordinary observer's cockpit, would add appreciably to the flying capabilities of the machine, and the

[1] Rechristened the "Houston-Westland" as a tribute to Lady Houston.

25

designer considered that by so doing a further one thousand feet would be added to the "ceiling," or altitude which it could reach.

Theoretically the ideal solution would have been an airtight cockpit for both pilot and observer, to have let oxygen directly into this, and thus to have obviated the necessity of their wearing masks and goggles. For several practical reasons, however, this was not feasible. A modern aeroplane is so complicated, with such a mass of openings for control wires, inspection panels, cameras and so on, that it would have been practically impossible except with prolonged experiment, to produce an airtight cockpit. Moreover, the complete closing in of the cockpit would have made it most difficult for the observers to handle their cameras except vertically downwards. It had from the first been recognised that oblique photographs taken in hand-held cameras over the side of the cockpit would be most valuable, even for scientific purposes.

In the same way, practical considerations of construction coupled with the pilot's natural prejudice, told against the enclosing of the pilot's cockpit, and it was accordingly left open. A large wind-screen of triplex glass was, however, provided, which tended to make matters as comfortable for him as could reasonably be expected.

The cover for the observer's cockpit consisted of two curved doors on longitudinal hinges, opening inwards and meeting when closed at a centre line of the top of the fuselage. The hinges were on each side, a few inches above the longerons. This arrangement proved of value in the actual flights. When the two flaps were closed, the fuselage presented an excellent "stream-line" form which assisted the performance of the machine, kept all draughts out of the cockpit, and enabled the observer to remain comfortably warm in his heated suit.

When he wished to take a photograph out of the cockpit, it was the work of a moment to release the catches, swing the flaps down inwards, and hook them inside the cockpit so that they were not in the way. This gave him a clear opening of working size.

Below these flaps were small windows so arranged that the observer could see fairly well ahead without exposing himself to the cold blast, and through which he could take horizontal photographs although with difficulty.

Before the machines could be adapted for our special purpose, a large number of small gadgets and war fittings had to be removed, such as gun mountings, bomb racks, bomb release gears, sights, and voice pipes. In spite of this, however, the fitting up of the cockpit, especially that of the observer, presented many problems, in the installation of the great variety of equipment and instruments necessary.

First of all we had to select a position for the Eagle Survey Camera, which in both machines, was placed in its mounting as far forward as possible. This forward position was necessary for had it been placed to the rear of the cockpit there would have been danger of the observer becoming hopelessly entangled in the numerous wires connecting him to the machine. Apart from this camera, space had to be found close at hand for its spare spool magazine. This was all-important as the observer could not get the spare magazine rapidly adjusted if he had to lift it through any considerable distance. Then positions had to be selected for the various accessories of the camera itself, the electric motor which drives it through flexible shafting and the switches for controlling it. Close by the camera, was located the drift-sight for the camera would have to be rotated horizontally through an angle corresponding to the angle of drift of the machine which the observer must measure in a prone position.

The survey camera and its accessories being satisfactorily disposed of, there remained to plan out how the other cameras would be employed. The cinema camera was probably the second most important instrument, and one to be so arranged that the observer could point it in almost any direction. Both machines had hatchways or trap-doors in the flooring of the observer's cockpit, making it fairly easy for the camera to be pointed straight downwards, a shot which would probably be very useful. However, owing to the size and bulk of the camera itself, it was impracticable to tilt it much beyond the vertical. Then again, the side windows, already referred to, enabled horizontal shots to be taken straight out to right and left, and for a certain distance to the front on either side. This would allow of pictures being taken of the other machine in flight, and possibly even of mountain-tops on approximately the same level as the aeroplane. To secure any really oblique photograph downwards or to the front, it would be necessary to open the cockpit, the same action applying to shots backwards over the tail. This opening of the cockpit had, of course, the disadvantage of letting in a terrific blast of cold air, besides being detrimental to the climbing power of the aeroplane.

However, it was the only way in which the great majority of shots could be taken. Pictures could be taken to the front from a point about 20° to port and starboard respectively of the centre line of the machine; it was also possible for the observer to lean well out and take shots down to about 45° below the horizon, and also shots straight over the tail and slightly downwards on either side.

All these possible shots with the cinema camera were eventually used, but the work of the observer was necessarily difficult, inasmuch as he had to handle this awkward object, weighing eighteen pounds, not only in the force of the slipstream with thickly gloved hands, but with the limitations imposed by the fact that the camera was covered with an electrically-heated jacket. In this there had to be small apertures through which the various focusing and re-threading controls of the camera could be reached, also for electric leads for the heating current.

Then again for the cinema cameras, mountings were provided in order to steady them during use.

Generally speaking, the same provisions which applied to the cinema camera were equally applicable to the hand-held cameras used for taking a still oblique photograph. The problems were less difficult with these cameras, partly due to their excellent design—they were specially produced by Messrs. Williamson for air work—but also because less heating was necessary and their weight was much less. Reduced heating was necessary because they used plates instead of films, and these were not liable to stiffen in the cold. However, it was still essential to employ internal resistances for warming the blind of the focal plane shutter. This being made of rubberised fabric would have become stiff if exposed to great cold, and so have completely upset the timing of the exposures.

So much then for the layout of the camera equipment, results that were not arrived at without extensive planning and trial. Given unlimited time and money to produce an aeroplane pre-eminently suitable for the work in hand, we should no doubt have specified a twin or triple-engine machine, on the lines of the Westland Wessex. Multi-engine machines were, however, impracticable in their present stage of development, as they had not at that time sufficient climbing capacity to go over Everest with the necessary margin of two or three thousand feet.

It was vital to hold out for a margin as large as this because under certain conditions of atmospheric pressure, the air might become abnormally light or thin to such an extent that another 2,500 feet of climbing power over and above the 29,000 feet of the mountain, would be called for from the machine.

With a multi-engine aeroplane it might well have been feasible to have a fuselage with no engine at all in it; this would naturally have tended largely to diminish the vibration to which the cameras would be subjected. Moreover, if the aeroplane were a high-wing monoplane like the Wessex, the observers would have had practically a clear view downwards in all directions, which could not be the case in a biplane, or in any machine with a very small fuselage.

The next step in the laying-out of the aeroplane equipment was to find space for the oxygen cylinders and instruments.

The cylinders were of considerable weight, and the designer had to find positions for them where they would neither be in the way of the crew nor upset the trim of the machine. Finally, in the P.V.3, they were placed in racks in rear of the observer's cockpit, and in the Wallace between the pilot and observer, almost straight below the pilot's seat.

Following on this was the decision as to how the oxygen pipes were to be anchored to the instrument boards. It was essential that the tribulations of the observer should not be added to, for as we have seen, he had already to keep from entanglement in the flexible heating cables for the survey camera, its magazine, the ciné-camera, its spare film spools, and the "oblique" camera. He also would have his own heating and telephone leads, running from his right and left hip respectively. Finally it was decided to place the oxygen connection well forward in the cockpit to the right of both pilot and observer, a situation which proved eminently satisfactory. The instrument boards of both pilot and observer were much congested by the oxygen instruments—flowmeters, pressure gauges, electrical heaters and regulating valves, for all of which space had to be found where they could be got at, be visible and at the same time not in the way. The problem and the way it was solved can best be judged by the illustration.

Besides the oxygen gear, both pilot and observer had to have more instruments than usual.

The observers also carried out rehearsals in manipulating, reloading, and setting their cameras when actually in the cockpit. There were two vital duties devolving on them for the safety of the machines, the first being the electrical supply. It was essential to watch the voltmeter and ensure that the current did not exceed fifteen volts, a cut-out assisting the observer to guard against this. If it acted, the observer must close it and re-establish the circuit, after having first adjusted his resistance to reduce the voltage to fourteen. He had also to watch the oxygen supply, the moment indication being given that the main had failed, to turn on the auxiliary supply. Pilot and observer could operate the latter for themselves and each other, but the main supply for both was controlled entirely by the pilot. The further aims and objects of this all-important oxygen have been dealt with in another chapter.

The microphone communication between pilot and observer enabled them to converse with ease with the engine slightly throttled down, although it did not prove so efficient as was hoped, particularly at great heights. It was mainly experimental and hastily completed by the Royal Aircraft Establishment at Farnborough, but despite this it served us well. Actually, there was little need for intercommunication between pilot and observer, in view of the careful arrangements made between each pair before leaving on any of their flights. In the event of a microphone failure a message could be passed through the special aperture cut in the bulkhead separating the two cockpits.

Let us now see the clothing worn by pilots and observers for their voyage into the unknown. Each donned an electrically-heated suit connected to the aeroplane by cable at two points. To one cable came the electric circuit for heating purposes, suits, boots, gloves and goggles; through the other ran the circuit for his telephone, having separate wires for speech in and speech out. Correctly to connect up the telephones, boots, gloves and goggles, involved a vast amount of practice, and is a sidelight on the manifold preparations for flying over the world's loftiest point. Much mental training was likewise necessary to accustom the observer in the satisfactory operation of his cameras and other equipment when immersed in such a multiplicity of connections. In very truth the observer was the modern and heavily-equipped counterpart of Alice in Wonderland's White Knight. For he had not to sit and fall off his horse in comparative comfort in an equable temperature, but to manipulate his highly-complicated apparatus in temperatures ranging through 250 Fahrenheit degrees.

The result was he left terra firma in a prodigious perspiration, cooling gradually as he ascended to his working height, there to be subjected to the most intense cold under a vastly reduced air pressure. Arrived at an altitude rarely attained by man, his arteries and organs would be dilated and an unnatural pressure created all over his body, definitely reducing the efficiency of his brain and energy. Both observers, when working at full pressure, became completely breathless, despite the flow of that life-giving oxygen.

The pilot's cockpit is to the uninitiated a mass of instruments, switches and taps, apparently impossible for one man to control and operate, directing the machine at the same time. However, with the necessary drill these instruments so fix themselves in the pilot's mind that eventually their correct use becomes automatic. Let us glance at the instruments in this cockpit. On the left are the fuel air-vent cock, the petrol feed tap with four positions, engine switch, clock, air-speed indicator, altimeter, spy-hole to check the petrol flow, camera signal lamp with its starting and regulating switch, and two dials, one to show number of exposures, the other to indicate the time interval, a switch for a lamp illuminating the compass, the tail-trimming wheel, throttle, and altitude mixture control.

In the centre is the compass, above it the oxygen flow meter and boost gauge, and below it the rudder bias gear. On the right are the oxygen taps, main and reserve, oxygen pressure gauges, three heating switches for clothes, gloves and boots, two oxygen heating switches for main and reserve, a thermometer, engine starting switch, fuel gauge, fuel pressure valve, oil pressure gauge, two oil temperature dials giving temperature in and out, two dials recording revolutions per minutes, a pressure gauge, and circular resistance controlling the heat of his goggles. The pilot has to watch closely, and probably to operate, most of these on any altitude flight. He may have to do something with all of them if things go wrong, and it is much easier to think how he would act when in the quiet of the ground rather than when flying and distracted by noise.

Let us suppose the pilot has seen through his petrol spy-hole that the dark flow of the fuel has changed to a silver colour;

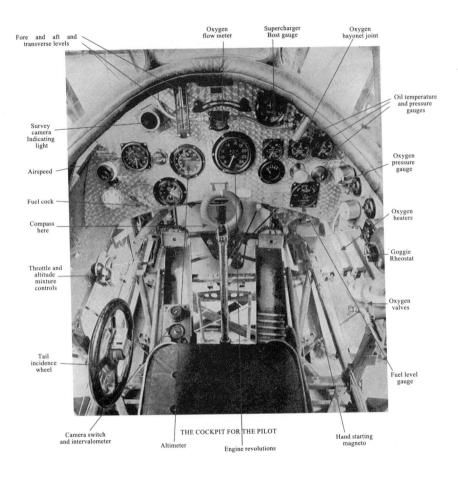

Fore and aft and transverse levels

Oxygen flow meter

Supercharger Bost gauge

Oxygen bayonet joint

Oil temperature and pressure gauges

Survey camera Indicating light

Airspeed

Oxygen pressure gauge

Fuel cock

Oxygen heaters

Compass here

Goggie Rheostat

Throttle and altitude mixture controls

Oxygen valves

Tail incidence wheel

Fuel level gauge

Camera switch and intervalometer

THE COCKPIT FOR THE PILOT

Hand starting magneto

Altimeter

Engine revolutions

something must be done. That ominous sign tells him that the supply of petrol is no longer so plentiful as to give a constant overflow from the gravity tank back to the main tank. This might be due to the exhaustion of the supply in the latter or to failure of the pump delivering the petrol to the gravity tank. The pilot must then switch off the tap to his pump, turn on to gravity only, and make for home, knowing that he has only sufficient petrol for the return, with a narrow margin for locating the aerodrome if he is not on the correct course. On the other hand, the gravity may have burst, or through an air-lock fails to deliver petrol to the engine; he would turn on the gravity flow and supply the engine direct from the pump, at the same time remembering to turn off the air vent cocks.

Constant practice is essential to think out compass bearings and to correct courses by drift-reading in the air, to visualise and apply these corrections to imaginary compass courses, and act promptly.

CHAPTER III

OXYGEN ON THE EVEREST FLIGHT

OXYGEN supply for the crews of the aircraft was taken in hand in the earliest stages of the technical organisation of the expedition.

It was clear that no flight over the mountains could possibly be carried out unless both pilot and observer were provided with an adequate and reliable supply of oxygen.

This may seem strange when it is considered that the climbing expeditions or, the assaulting portions of them, have been to over 28,000 feet, independently of oxygen, at the same time putting forth physical exertions far in excess of anything the observer of an aeroplane, let alone the pilot, would be called upon to make. This, when exposed to the bitter low temperature, without the protection of an aeroplane or of electrical warming. The explanation is that the climber's lungs are gradually accustomed by several weeks of progressive ascent to a higher altitude, whereas the pilot and observer of the aeroplane must go from sea-level to over 30,000 feet in less than three-quarters of an hour!

It was certain that no human lungs could stand such a strain, and furthermore, if the oxygen were for some reason to fail suddenly at any height over 25,000 feet, disaster would almost certainly ensue, for the pilot would lose consciousness and the aeroplane get out of control. It was not possible even to fit a dual control for the observer. Should such a failure take place during an ordinary high flight, or an attempt on the height record, carried out over low-lying country, the pilot would have a chance to tear off his mask and regain consciousness after the machine had, by itself, dived or spun down to lower levels. Several high-flying pilots have been saved in this

34

way, although just prior to our flight a French experimenter had been killed after spinning down to over 30,000 feet, apparently without regaining consciousness.

In any case, over high mountains it is evident the machine would hit the cliffs or the crags and be destroyed long before the pilot could regain consciousness and control.

So much for the vital importance of the oxygen. It remained to give effect to means which would deal adequately with the situation.

Fortunately, one of the first of the facilities generously placed at the disposal of the expedition by the Air Ministry, included access to the stored-up experience and resources of the Royal Aircraft Establishment.

It may be of interest to see how neat oxygen is obtained for the use of aviators. It is produced from air by liquefaction and rectification. The low temperatures necessary for this are obtained, in the first case, by compressing the air, then cooling and expanding it in an engine running under load. In this way work is done in overcoming the resistance afforded to increasing volume, with the result that heat is abstracted from the air and its temperature further lowered.

This cooling effect is made cumulative by the use of "heat interchangers," tubular metal devices in which the cold gases, after expansion and subsequent treatment, are made to travel in indirect contact with, and in counter-current to, the incoming cooled compressed air.

Some of the air is liquefied as such, whilst the remainder yields two separate liquids, one containing almost the whole of the oxygen, the other consisting practically of pure nitrogen.

These liquids are introduced into rectification columns in which they travel downwards through numerous plates constructed to insure intimate contact with the ascending gas, the latter being produced to the base of the column by evaporating liquid as it arrives there.

As a consequence of this counter-current between the liquid and the gas, a very pure liquid oxygen is obtained. When this is again converted into gas by evaporation, its purity is of 95.5 per cent. or even higher.

In such apparatus the resultant temperatures are extremely low, down to –190° C., so that all cold metal parts have to be well insulated to prevent, as far as possible, ingress of atmospheric heat.

Before being liquefied, the air must be thoroughly free from carbon-dioxide, since this gas, always present in the air to the extent of at least .03 volumes per hundred, becomes, at the low temperatures involved, a solid, which would rapidly choke the plant.

For a similar reason, the slightest amount of moisture present in the air would be a source of trouble, and this has to be carefully removed in the "heat interchangers."

As the warm wet air cools, the water is thrown down as a liquid until the temperature reaches 0° C. and it is then deposited as ice on the metal walls of the interchanger tubes. After traversing the length of the interchanger and being subject to still lower temperatures in the rectification columns, the oxygen which is separated from the air leaves the plant in a perfectly dry condition.

In the subsequent process of compressing this dry gas for filling cylinders, contamination with water occurs.

The compressor cylinders must be lubricated with water, for to use oil would entail combustion, or a violent explosion.

Fortunately, almost all the water is again removed from the oxygen by the act of compression, since a gas saturated with water vapour at atmospheric pressure contains only one one-twentieth of this amount when it is compressed to 120 atmospheres at the same temperature.

For flying purposes the absolute and complete elimination of moisture is essential for reasons which we shall see later on. Hence a chemical means of effecting this has to be employed.

At the working pressure of about 120 atmospheres, the oxygen is passed slowly over solid calcium-chloride which is able to reduce the water content to the very low figure of .002

grams per cubic metre, i.e., 2.5 volumes of water vapour per million volumes of oxygen.

Similarly, scrupulous care has to be exercised in the proper drying of the gas cylinders themselves before being filled. They are therefore subjected to a process of evacuation, the metal walls at the same time being heated.

So much for the preparation of oxygen. It will be seen how it was employed in the aeroplane.

The advice of the scientists was definite and unswerving. Oxygen should be inhaled from the ground up in a tiny but progressively increasing trickle until a maximum flow was reached at 35,000 feet. The reason for this is that the human lungs need to become accustomed to the breathing of pure oxygen.

The ordinary atmosphere at sea-level contains only 22 parts in a 100 of oxygen; the remainder, comprising other gases, which, however useful they may be, in the formation of picturesque sunsets and other purposes, are of no use for breathing.

The pressure of the atmosphere at sea-level is 14.7 lbs. per square inch and as is generally known pressure decreases the higher aircraft rises. Consequently the pressure of oxygen in the air decreases as the pressure of the air itself diminishes.

This decrease in atmospheric pressure calls for the additional supply of oxygen, because of the deeper breathing necessitated to take a sufficient quantity of oxygen to replace that absorbed by bodily effort.

Two other dangers are the dulling of perception and judgment and diminishing muscular strength.

The flying personnel must therefore be supplied with sufficient additional oxygen to maintain normal breathing as at sea-level.

Thus, the aviator, given an adequate supply of oxygen, need not go short of breath at all until he reaches 33,000 feet, because the shortage of oxygen in the air can be made good by giving him compressed oxygen from a steel cylinder. At the height stated there is only about a third as much air to breathe as at sea-level.

Even with ample oxygen at heights of over 33,000 feet, the aviator is slightly breathless, especially if he has work to perform, this breathlessness becoming pronounced when the 35,000 or 40,000 feet mark is passed.

Another physiological difficulty threatening the high-altitude aviator, is the air pressure which supports the small blood vessels of the body becomes so much diminished that these tend to burst. This is a real danger in the case of those past middle age, or in the case of extreme heights at any age, tending to cause unconsciousness or acute and violent pains similar to those experienced by divers, who come up to the surface too rapidly.

To meet this contingency, all the flying personnel, as related elsewhere, were tested in the great steel chamber of the Royal Aircraft Establishment.

This was the final stage. To return to the early preparations of 1932, there at once loomed the question of steel cylinders in which to carry the gas.

Few, if any, flights previously made, had necessitated keeping the aviators through as long a period as two hours, as this would, at approximately 32,000 feet. Consequently, a large amount of oxygen was necessary, especially as the rate called for at the upper end of the climb was slightly over ten litres per man per minute. The weight of the cylinders to carry all this gas was an important factor in the loading of the aeroplane, and one which definitely affected its "ceiling" or maximum attainable height. Fortunately at this stage, Messrs. Vickers Armstrong had produced cylinders of a new type made of an alloy steel known as Vibrac, without which the flight might have been impracticable. The old type of carbon steel cylinder, weighed twice as much as the Vibrac cylinder, and was considerably less safe to handle, especially under conditions of exposure to strong sunlight. Not only are the Vibrac cylinders half the weight, but they possess the additional advantage of not being liable to burst, or fly into fragments if damaged. In fact, a rifle bullet can be fired through them with no more detriment than the rapid escape of the gas contained within.

Needless to say, we kept a careful watch on the development of these cylinders.

Besides this method of carrying the gas under high pressure in steel cylinders, at least two other possibilities were considered.

One of these is the use of a portable oxygen generating plant. The development of this apparatus appears to have reached its highest form in Germany, but the resources at our disposal did not warrant the employment of these means. The method does not appear to have reached a sufficiently high standard of development to render it practicable for high-altitude use.

Another suggestion explored was that of intra-venous or intra-muscular injection of oxygen. Here again there were practical difficulties, although at some future date these means may be of value, especially because a less amount of oxygen is required. For practical purposes, therefore, the carriage of oxygen gas in high-pressure cylinders won the day.

We next decided the number of cylinders, a problem in which the Royal Aircraft Establishment came to our aid.

Should the machine fly comparatively low, and then ascend at the last possible moment to the extreme height required to surmount Everest, the amount of oxygen called for would be comparatively small, as the high rate of consumption is only demanded when the machine is at its greatest altitude. Other factors, however, prevented this course being adopted. Consideration had to be given to the survey photography, which was the main object of the flight.

If the country from about forty miles south of Everest to the summit were to be photographically mapped from a comparatively low altitude, where the ground itself was low, then much film would be required to take all the necessary strips. The film itself was heavy, each spool weighing about $4\frac{1}{2}$ lbs., and there was, in addition, the difficulty of changing the film magazines with certainty under the difficult conditions in the air. If we were to fly as low as possible, we would save on the oxygen and its weight; if, on the other hand, we flew high, we should save on the photographic gear but consume much more oxygen and take a slightly greater risk of oxygen failure. Both these variables had to be worked in to the performance of the engine and its supercharger, of which the "rated altitude" was 13,000 feet; at this altitude this particular variety of Pegasus engine, with its $7\frac{1}{2}$-inch supercharger, does its finest work in terms of fuel consumption, speed, and climb, which in turn are dependent on propeller thrust.

Much calculation and the drawing of many graphs was consequently necessary before a compromise could be arrived at, giving the greatest efficiency.

There was also a political factor involved—the necessity for crossing the Nepalese frontier at such a height that the primitive inhabitants of the outlying districts, who had never before seen an aeroplane, or probably not even heard of one, might not be unduly alarmed.

Finally, we found it possible to carry four cylinders in each aeroplane, each of 750 litres capacity, a total of 3,000; or 1,500 per person. The fourth cylinder was to be a reserve for emergency only, and used only in case of failure of the normal supply from the remaining three cylinders. To make this safeguard a reality it was decided to duplicate all the piping and instruments of the oxygen.

The oxygen cylinders were carried in racks in the fuselages of the machine, and led through valves and high-pressure copper piping to a special oxygen instrument board in the pilot's and observer's cockpits, respectively. First it passed through a pressure gauge, which indicated the pressure and atmospheres in the cylinder, and, incidentally, in the high-pressure side of the system, this conveniently giving a direct indication of the quantity of gas remaining in the cylinders.

The initial pressure was 120 atmospheres, and the cylinders would be virtually empty when the pressure dropped below thirty. From the pressure gauge the gas passed to the regulating valve, which also comprised a safety valve, its function being to reduce the pressure from the high figure of 120 atmospheres to that at which the aviator wished to breathe it. The next stage takes it through the electrical heater, a cylindrical arrangement heated by a coil of electric wire, connected to a plug and socket. In succession it comes to the flow-meter, an instrument designed to show rate of flow of the current of low-pressure gas along its piping. Contrary to expectation, this little dial is not graduated in litres per minute, but in tens of thousands of feet of altitude. The wider the handle of the regulating-valve is turned, the more gas passes through the flow-meter, and the greater height is registered by its needle. The aviator therefore needs only to adjust the regulating valve until the reading of the flow-meter corresponds to the reading of the altimeter of the aeroplane. He anticipates the reading of the altimeter and gives himself sufficient oxygen for 5,000 feet as soon as he leaves the ground, increases this to the 10,000 feet rate when he reaches 5,000 and so on successively.

From the flow-meter the gas is ready to breathe and passes to a bayonet joint mounted on the instrument board. Into this is plugged a detachable tee socket which can be easily pushed in or pulled out by the pilot or observer, as the case may be, and secured only by a quarter turn. To this is connected a flexible tubing carrying the gas to the actual mask from which he breathes it. Several varieties of tubing have been tried, one of plain rubber, but with certain disadvantages of its own; another of petroflex, excellent except for being stiff and heavy. In the case of the observer, at least, it tends for this reason to push the mask off his face. In the actual flight, we used flexible metallic tubing, four and a half feet long in the case of the pilot, and nine feet in that of the observer. This answered well, except with one of the observers, who broke his pipe by treading on it, a test it was scarcely designed to withstand. Possibly, the ideal arrangement would be that the first half of the observer's pipe, should be of flexible metallic tube, the balance of petroflex.

The object of the bayonet joint is to enable the aviator to detach himself rapidly from the aeroplane should he be under the necessity of executing a "brolly-hop" or parachute jump, as a preliminary to joining the Caterpillar Club.

We see how the gas has arrived at the mask, and the mask itself constituted one of the great afflictions which had to be borne by the fliers.

It was, in the nature of things, extremely difficult to attach satisfactorily to the human face, which has not been designed for such appendages.

Many were the adjustments of straps, and their refixing, which bound the mask to the unfortunate aviator's helmet. Final solution of the problem called for a quadruplex arrangement of metallic springs covered with leather, sewn on to the back of the helmet immediately over the crown of the head. A fibre mask of the pattern which was standard when the expedition started is distinctly uncomfortable, and projected very far to the front. It caught up in everything, more especially in the cameras which the observer had to handle, and made it almost impossible for him to look through the ordinary viewfinder. However, Messrs. Siebe Gorman have been at work on the problem, and the type they have now produced is a marked improvement and far more convenient.

An india-rubber experimental pattern produced by them, presented many advantages and was tried with success by us in some of the later high flights.

The mask fits over the lower part of the face, covers both nose, mouth and chin, but is not expected to be completely gas-tight. It has two air holes, for the individual does not breathe pure oxygen on his way up to 30,000 feet, but oxygen mixed with a decreasing quantity of air, drawn by suction from the atmosphere coming in through these holes. These holes also let out the expired air. The arrangement is somewhat unscientific, since some of the oxygen in the act of breathing is blown out and wasted. Moreover, we found it necessary to plug these holes with hastily extemporised corks when the

30,000 feet mark was passed, to ensure the observer getting his fair ration of oxygen undiluted by what in those levels passes for an atmosphere.

A minor complication in the oxygen mask was that it had to be fitted to overlap the flap of the electrically-heated goggles. Consequently there was a layer of the fur trimming belonging to these goggles interposed between the edge of the oxygen mask and the nose and cheek-bones of the user. This was to prevent oxygen coming inside the goggles and clouding them with mist.

The entire arrangement was distinctly cumbersome, and a sad hindrance to both pilot and observer. The pilots found the masks much in the way because it obscured their view downwards, and the observers were still more hampered from its preventing them getting the eye close up to the finders of the camera, or other instrument which they might be using. Finally, to surmount this trouble the oblique cameras had to be provided with special extemporised sights on the side. Forttunately, as we have seen, Messrs. Siebe Gorman have since done much to improve the situation.

In the front end of each mask was mounted the microphone for the intercommunication set, by which observer and pilot could converse. The presence of this was a troublesome necessity as it lengthened the already excessive projection of the mask to the front. Yet again the switch of the microphone had to be in such a position that it was liable to knock against the camera, and so switch itself on, to the intense indignation of the pilot, whose ears were immediately filled with buzzings and cracklings.

Thanks to the skill and experience, both of the Royal Aircraft Establishment and Siebe Gorman, the arrangement worked satisfactorily and efficiently, but oxygen gear should be redesigned before high-altitude flights of long duration, involving real mental and physical work on the part of the personnel, can be regarded as an everyday proposition. Experimental work is already being carried out to this end.

We foresee air survey being carried out at upwards of 30,000 feet, with thirty-six square miles mapped at each exposure of the camera, and ten times that amount with multi-lens cameras. This calls for an everyday routine use of oxygen.

Long-distance air liners will, in the near future traverse the stratosphere at 35,000 feet; in fact, as high as the walls of passengers' arteries can stand. The aeroplane itself, whether with fixed wings or of the autogiro type, is superior at a greater height, and moves more easily through the air, with less "drag" or parasitic resistance. The engines of to-day can be so supercharged that there will be comparatively little loss of power in the rarefied air six miles up. One factor is still lacking; the propeller with variable or controllable pitch. With its advent aeroplanes having a moderate landing speed, will fly not slower but faster as they ascend to great heights, so that machines which can take off at forty or fifty, will be able to fly at 300 or 400 miles an hour by the long-distance inter-continental air lines.

We see how this power of choosing his own height level will frequently enable the captain to find a favourable wind, where the low-flying pilot of to-day is often delayed and held up.

Before, however, that eventuates, designers must turn their attention to hermetically-sealed passenger cabins, provided with oxygen, and chemical means of absorbing the exhalations from the lungs, together with means of maintaining a positive pressure inside these closed cabins. We are only on the edge of a new world in aviation of which no man can gauge the limits.

* * * * * *

It is apparent that the lives of the aviators depended upon their oxygen supply. Further, the oxygen must be warmed on its way to the lungs of the pilots and observers.

The need for this arose from the possibility that if a minute quantity of moisture were present in the oxygen, it would freeze in its passage through the tiny orifice in the regulating valve.

44

To guard against such an eventuality the oxygen passed through an electrical heater on its way to the flyers' masks, this precaution being additional to the extreme care the makers observed in its preparation. But however careful they might be, and the skill and foresight of the British Oxygen Company seemed almost superhuman, there remained the risk of moisture becoming condensed somewhere in the installation, whether picked up from flight through humid atmosphere or a water-laden cloud. In nearly all the high flights the aviators found their masks caked and clogged with ice, proof that there was moisture in their environment.

The oxygen was therefore heated in order that any chance drop might be blown through before being given an opportunity to freeze.

The current for this was drawn from the main electrical installation of the aeroplanes. We fully realised the importance of this system and the fact that everything depended on preventing the regulating-valve from freezing up, an event entailing almost immediate fatal results.

One could not help contrasting the margins of safety in every other direction—the airframes with all possible stress calculated out and allowed for by experts; the engines with each minute portion tested by scientists again and again, duplicated magnetos and carburettors—all hanging upon our heel of Achilles, the tiny orifice in the oxygen regulating-valve, the keystone, and yet capable of being blocked up by a minute particle of ice or by a single able-bodied mosquito.

Every possible precaution was worked out, not only in the equipment itself, but in the routine and drill under which it was handled, tested, and checked.

The hearts of the big electrical installations safeguarding the oxygen were the thousand-watt dynamos, made for us by Messrs. Haslam & Newton, which performed their task to perfection.

As related elsewhere, not only were these dynamos larger than any hitherto installed in aircraft of our type, but they had to be specially driven from the engine. We devoted deep thought to the problem of finding a place for these dynamos in the highly congested interior of a fuselage in whose original design they did not figure. Finally, they were placed on their heads, as it were, immediately behind the engines in front of the pilots, and with their spindles vertical.

This position for the dynamo involved not only the manufacture of a special bevel gear, but its *ab initio* design, which the Bristol Company carried out in record time. Even were the latter unlimited, it would have been a difficult task.

The dynamos supplied current not only for the all-important oxygen heating, but for a multitude of other purposes.

Each aviator wore an elaborate one-piece suit with the lightning fastener running up the front. These admirable suits were made by Messrs. Siebe Gorman, and consisted of an outer shell of a hard wind-resisting "Everest" cloth. Beneath this was an inner suit of Kapok, quilted to a considerable thickness, and lined with twill. In this lining were sewn a galaxy of electric wires, the heating being conveyed through them all over the aviator's body, with the exception of his posterior which was thoughtfully and judiciously left unwired.

The tracery of wires was thick in front of the suits and down the arms and legs, the maze of tiny lines being connected to a single plug on a lead at the left hip. From this plug a flexible cable connected the person to a fixed electrical plug in the aeroplane cockpit.

Besides the suit, the rubber-soled flying-boots of sheepskin and the gloves were heavily wired for heating purposes, each item being connected by a short cable to the sleeve and trouser leg. To link all this up was no light task. In addition to the thick electrically-heated gauntlets, the observers wore inner gloves of silk, provided by Messrs. Gieves. These enabled them to momentarily handle their delicate instruments and cameras with the big gloves off.

The crews growled strongly about their attire, but drew comfort from the hardships of their forerunners.

The cheift observer being fitted into his gear by Air Commodore Fellowes for a
test flight at Yeovil
(Note black silk gloves)

OXYGEN ON THE EVEREST FLIGHT

An old time Alpine mountaineer thus describes his outfit for a climb up Mont Blanc: "I had on a good pair of lamb's wool stockings, two pairs of gaiters, two pairs of cloth trousers, two shirts, two waistcoats, a shooting coat and overall, a blue woolen smock frock, a night-cap, three handkerchiefs round my neck, two pairs of woollen gloves and a straw hat, from which hung a green hood. For my eyes, a pair of spectacles and a green gauze veil."

Important, too, were the electrically-heated goggles made by Messrs. James Stephens, of remarkably ingenious design. Each eyepiece has two pieces of unbreakable Triplex glass, and is only one-sixteenth of an inch thick. Each again contains two layers of glass with celluloid interposed between. A minute air space separates the two glasses in which is a fine electric filament, visible to the eye, but disposed in a ring that does not impede the vision. Through these filaments runs part of the heating current, for the Triplex glasses without precautions, would rapidly frost over with thick ice. Still another cable connected these goggles to a socket, adding to the complexity of the skein of wiring in which the fliers were involved.

The voltage of the heating current was fourteen, at which figure each suit consumed eighteen amperes. In addition to the oxygen heaters and the suits, each camera had to be warmed, together with the spare spool magazines of the survey and the spare film boxes of the Newman cine-cameras.

The voltage was, as we have seen, fourteen, but the dynamo being driven directly from the engine, this voltage tended to go up or down when the pilot increased or decreased the turning speed of his engine for climbing, or level flight at different altitudes.

It was essential that the voltage should not, in flight, rise above fifteen, since at that point the cut-out would have to operate in order to prevent short-circuiting or even burning out. If this occurred, all would go cold until the observer restored the circuit. To do this he must unscrew its lid in the air, actuate the rheostat, and then press up the contacts. On the other hand, should the voltage fall below thirteen there was a grave danger of stoppage in the survey camera motors, collapse of the heating and other calamities.

It would have been possible to produce an automatic control for the voltage, but this would have added yet more to the medley of instruments in the crowded cockpit, any of which might go wrong at a critical moment.

We decided, therefore, that the observer should control the voltage by hand. True, this added to his numerous tasks in flight and threw a considerable responsibility and strain on his vigilance, but it simplified the installation.

He was provided with a large voltmeter and a sliding rheostat (see illustration) to be adjusted from time to time by hand. It was vital to watch the voltmeter, anticipate any alteration by the pilot in the engine speed, and not allow the needle to go above the danger point of fifteen volts, nor below the equally risky thirteen volt marking.

Even with this simplification the electrical system was of necessity as complicated as that of a modern house, taking into account the provision for driving camera motors, lighting various indicating lamps, heating oxygen, suits, gloves, boots, a multitude of photographic gear, and driving a dictaphone.

A minor worry encountered in planning the electrical system was that accumulators, when exposed to very low temperatures, decline to give any appreciable current.

An accumulator was necessary in the main circuit to steady the dynamo voltage, and serve as an emergency supply to keep the vital oxygen heaters and heated goggles going in the event of a sudden breakdown of the dynamos.

The large amount of current required did not allow of the accumulators being heated, so we partially solved the problem by packing them in several layers of felt. Even so, if the dynamos for any reason gave out, the observer would have to instantly switch off the current to the clothing, camera heaters, and motors, to allow the minute supply from the battery going to the all-important goggles and oxygen heaters, and so keep the fliers alive and capable of sight. Even the dry cells of the telephones between pilot and observer were affected by the extreme cold, and for them heating arrangements had to be installed.

In truth, the telephones were never popular with the pilots, who considered the requests passed down to them by the observers distinctly tiresome, but toleration prevailed, although joy was evident when they went out of order.

It was to the skill and experience of Siebe Gorman & Co. that the expedition owed the success of the electrically-heated clothing and its satisfactory work in all the flights.

These details of organisation serve to illustrate the extent to which we were confronted by novel problems, and compelled to solve difficulties, often of an unexpected nature, calling for ingenuity and original research.

Even in an ordinary aeroplane there is little which is unnecessary; in our machines every detail was vital. A hitch in the working of any one of a hundred devices, or a failure to foresee each of a multitude of contingencies of the flight, might well have led to failure.

CHAPTER IV

AIR PHOTOGRAPHIC SURVEY

ANY expedition worthy of the name of a scientific enterprise will take steps to place its results on record by means of instruments. Instruments are the agency by which man enlarges his perceptions and widens his horizon for the benefit of science.

The most important of those we could employ in our case was clearly the camera. From the beginning, then, we realised that the primary object of the expedition must be our survey photographs. These could be of two kinds, either taken obliquely with a hand-held camera, or with a fixed one mounted in the machine and pointing vertically downwards.

The vertical photographs, taken in accordance with the technique of our survey methods, were likely to be for several reasons the most important from the scientific standpoint.

Briefly, it may be stated that our survey photography consists in linking up by a strip or series of overlapping photographs taken with the camera pointing vertically downwards, two known points on the earth's surface. By known points, are meant those whose latitude and longitude have been accurately fixed by triangulation, by having the angles to them measured with theodolites from other previously fixed points. These fixed, and accurately triangulated, constitute the foundation or skeleton of the present-day system of photographic air survey. With us the problem had its own special complications. Had we been working over reasonably flat country it would have been sufficient to take a series of photographs each sufficiently overlapping the next and then to repeat the process by taking successive strips to right and left of the original one.

When taking vertical photographs of hilly country, the tops

of the hills being nearer to the camera will appear at a larger scale than the bottoms of the valleys, and this height distortion, which prevents a vertical photograph from being a true plan, calls for special methods in plotting to eliminate it. In our case, the enormous range of height would push these distortions far beyond any previous experience, and the difficulties of plotting would be considerably increased. For these and other reasons, it was preferable to use the overlapping strip of vertical photographs mainly as a backbone, and to photograph the ground on each side by oblique photographs which, as far as possible, would be made to join on to the country depicted by the verticals.

Another obvious difficulty was that few flights could be made over the country, and thus it would be necessary to expand and augment the results of the verticals by obliques, which would cover a greater extent of country.

These considerations led us to treat the taking of the series of overlapping vertical photographs rather as the demonstration of what could be achieved given ample flying time and no other hindrances, than as an actual complete aerial survey.

Whatever our policy it was essential to have the best available cameras for vertical photography, and we accordingly selected Williamson's Automatic Eagle III Survey Cameras. These are excellent instruments in which every operation is carried out electrically by means of a small motor actuated from the main generator of the aeroplane. This motor through a flexible shaft-driven geared mechanism, which, when switched on, first turns over the film five inches wide and long enough to take one hundred and twenty exposures. This film is wound off one spool onto another in a magazine fitting detachably on top of the camera. The film being wound into position, shutters at the same time are set in readiness for the exposure. This takes place automatically after the lapse of a predetermined interval of time, it being regulated by a pointer attached to a knob moving along a scale of seconds. This is a portion of the "control box" and may be handled by either the pilot or the observer, according to the necessity of the moment. The interval between exposures can be varied by turning the knob from six or seven seconds up to a minute. This interval has to be worked out beforehand and is dependent partly on the height at which the aeroplane is flying above the ground, as well as by the speed made by the machine over the country. For instance, if it is 30,000 feet up, and flying at 120 miles an hour, it will take 30,000 feet of ground at each exposure, the amount of ground comprised within the scope of the lens being, in the case of this type, approximately equal to the height. This is equivalent to six miles which, in still air, is covered in about three minutes by a machine travelling at the speed indicated. However, such a series of photographs taken at three-minute intervals would only barely meet at the edges, even theoretically, and in practice adjoining photographs would usually not meet at all owing to tilt of the negative caused by the bumping of the machine.

It is vital that the details shown on each picture should join in accurately with that on the next, and therefore one must arrange for an overlap. Over very rough country, such as we were dealing with, an overlap of at least sixty per cent. was advisable, and in point of fact we achieved even more. An advantage of this was that it was only necessary to use for plotting the central portion of each picture which is the least distorted.

To return to the control box, we find that the camera, having had its film wound round by the electric motor, has the shutter set and then released, and exposure made at the correct time. Under these circumstances, if an exposure were contemplated for every minute, one would secure three negatives for each 30,000 feet of country passed over. Each picture would overlap the next by two-thirds of its length, thus giving the desired sixty per cent. overlap. If, on the other hand, the aeroplane is nearer the ground, the interval must be reduced in proportion, so that with the same speed and height of 10,000 feet above the ground, each picture would have to be taken every twenty seconds.

In the case of our flights the height from the ground was approximately 15,000 feet at the commencement of the photography, and became rapidly less till we were over the summit of Everest, where it would be less than 1,000 feet. This 1,000 feet would be too close to take any overlapping photographs at a speed of 120 miles an hour, and we therefore depended more on oblique photographs to give a record of the highest part of the mountain and the actual summit, and relied on the vertical photographs for the exploration of untrodden and unmapped declivities of the southern flanks of the Everest range.

Although the camera is automatic to the extent of changing its own film, and setting and releasing its shutter at the correct moment, there are still several important operations connected with a survey camera to be carried out by the hand of the observer. Once the machine is well off the ground and flying steady, he must level the apparatus by means of the bubbles provided in the camera mounting, wherein the camera itself is carried in an arrangement of jimbles.

There are two spirit-levels or bubbles, one across the machine for transverse levelling, the other fore and aft for use in a longitudinal sense. A certain amount of judgment is necessary to get the camera level, the transverse bubble being affected by wind movements which lift the wings up or down, so the observer must use his experience and judgment to know when the machine is flying really level before putting on the final adjustment to the level of the camera.

The longitudinal level has a subtlety of its own since the axis of the camera cannot be simply at right angles to the longitudinal axis of the machine, but must differ from it by the angle at which the machine is climbing. With us the designers were able to state definitely that the angle of climb at different portions of the ascent would vary from three and a half to four and a half degrees, and therefore an initial setting of about four degrees from the vertical would be correct to commence with. This had to be accurately adjusted in flight by the observer.

Another necessary adjustment was that for drift. When the machine is flying with the wind from one side or the other of any appreciable strength, the longitudinal axis of the aeroplane does not point in the direction of the object towards which it is going; it is slightly oblique, this angle being known as the drift. At the same time the camera needs to point square towards the object and at right angles in every direction with the line traversed in imagination by the machine over the ground.

This necessitates rotating the camera through the same angle in the opposite direction, in such a way that while the sides of the picture will remain parallel with the track of the machine over the ground, they will be inclined to the axis of the aeroplane by an angle corresponding to the angle of drift.

It was an important duty of the observer to measure this angle by means of an ingenious device called a drift sight, and then, having measured it, to apply the angle by rotating the camera to the same extent within its mounting.

The drift sight consists of a lens about four inches in diameter giving not magnification but minification. It is fitted in the floor of the machine so the observer can look down through it at the ground vertically beneath him. He sees conspicuous objects passing from front to rear across the lens, not necessarily parallel to the direction in which the machine is flying but usually at an angle to it. In a rotating ring are fastened parallel wires running across the diameter of the lens. The observer can rotate these wires by hand until the objects passing across the lens appear to run parallel to them. He then reads off on a scale of degrees marked on the ring the angle at which the objects appear to travel with respect to the machine, this being the angle of drift.

Still his task is not finished with the survey camera; he must set the stop and length of the exposure before leaving the ground, but in case the light should change, such as the sky being cloudy, the ground overshadowed by clouds or the country becoming snow-covered where it was previously dark and sombre, he must alter the length of exposure or vary the stop according to his own judgment.

The Williamson camera is a fine instrument, but although as automatic as it is possible almost to imagine, there are a number of tasks in the handling of it which fall, in the air, upon the pilot and the observer. The pilot has to estimate the distance between the ground and the aeroplane, and alter the predetermined interval of time so as to secure the all-essential overlap. Besides this scale on the control box, he is also provided with red and green lights, the former indicating when the film is wound ready to take an exposure, and the latter of which are lit automatically by mechanism in the control box giving him three seconds' warning of the moment when exposure is timed to take place. This gives him an opportunity to steady the aeroplane and hold it as level as possible, thereby guarding against "tilt," and the consequent distortion of the picture.

Should all go well the survey cameras would give us a series of one hundred and twenty exposures on a long film, nearly forty feet long, each overlapping at least two-thirds of the next.

The prints from these negatives can be used to provide an accurate map. Owing to the distortions of tilt and height variation, however, this cannot be done by merely pinning them together to form a mosaic. Such an attempt would reveal gross misfits along the edges. Special methods of plotting therefore have to be used, and of these the most accurate are those employing some form of stereoscope. The most complete solution is provided by an automatic plotting machine, such as a stereogoniometer. In this, successive pairs of overlapping photographs are set in the same relative angular positions as they occupied at exposure, and the stereoscopic picture thus produced is an exact small scale replica of the actual ground. A system of levers connecting this visual field to a drawing pencil then enables detail and contours to be drawn automatically.

A simpler and cheaper method employs a stereoscope in which the prints are laid flat, i.e., it is assumed that there is no tilt. In this instrument the effect is then produced artificially of a fine network of lines floating in space. This network may be raised or lowered by definite amounts as desired, and can thus be used as a reference plan for contouring by hand.

Both methods require a considerable amount of skill and experience, and the second, although it relies for its success on photographs with a minimum of tilt, was considered to offer, in this particular case, the most practical solution.

The process as described here may seem fairly simple, but a host of difficulties beset not only the two airmen, who work together in producing the vertical photographs, but also the plotter and map-maker, who converts these photographs into the map.

All these difficulties are accentuated in the case of photographs taken at the great height of 31,000 or 32,000 feet, and are increased by the presence of large mountains close under the machine.

If the work had to be done over a perfectly level country, in still air, at a reasonable temperature in good weather, and in an aeroplane specially designed to afford every facility for the photographer, the work would be comparatively simple, and the procedure briefly outlined would normally result in the production of straight strips of undistorted photographs, each square with the next, parallel to the line of flight and to the course on the ground, and each neatly overlapping onto its neighbour.

Matters were not so simple in the extremely difficult conditions with which we were confronted.

It was necessary to use a single-engine tractor aeroplane for the reason that no twin-engine machine, nor any aeroplane of the "pusher" type, possessed anything like sufficient climbing power to go over Mount Everest. The fact of the machine being a tractor added to the pilot's difficulties as it naturally made it less easy for him to see out of the cockpit vertically down onto the ground where his "ground control" was situated. The tractor also had this disadvantage that the blast of the slip-stream is considerably greater than the case of the pusher. The fact that the pilot would have to crane his head out of the cockpit to a considerable extent to see any part of the ground below, makes it difficult for him to keep the machine on the exact even keel which vertical photography demands. It is all the more so when his face and eyes are covered by an oxygen mask and a conducting-pipe is sticking out several inches in front of his nose.

The observer had his own troubles, and to overcome them was forced to attend to the survey camera in a prone position with his face through a hole in the floor, and to rise laboriously to a standing or kneeling position whenever he had to take oblique photographs through the roof of the cockpit.

The laboriousness was due to the fact that he was tied up in almost innumerable wires and leads conveying electricity to the various portions of his heated clothing and his microphone, not to mention his oxygen pipe.

The difficulties with which the camera had to contend were mainly due to the extreme cold or, more accurately, to the extremes of heat and cold to which it is subjected during its passage from 180° F. in the sun near sea-level at the Purnea landing-ground, to minus 40° or 45° C. experienced over Everest. This affected the camera in two ways. The cold made the celluloid film stiff and brittle, so that much more power had to be transmitted through the delicate mechanism to turn it at all, and when turned it was liable to fly to pieces. To overcome this it was essential to heat the camera by electrical means, no slight task, but one that was successfully surmounted after weeks of experiments by Messrs. Williamson's efforts.

The camera was almost entirely constructed of duralumin, and to prevent this radiating heat, it had to be covered with a succession of jackets, each jacket being heated by electrical resistance wires sewn into the fabric. Four of these were required for each camera, one for the body, one for the lens cone, which was necessarily separate as this cover had to be fitted on after the camera was inserted into its metal mounting ring, and two for the magazine—one for that actually on the camera, and another spare.

Each of these four jackets was provided with plugs and leads, so arranged that they would not get in the way of each other or of the numerous camera controls, nor interfere with the changing of one magazine for another in the air.

The heat imparted from these jackets did not prove sufficient, even though about eight amperes was applied to them, so in addition the heating elements of resistance wires were fixed inside each portion of the camera, the duralumin lens cone, the body and the magazine.

Here again further trouble threatened as the magazine contained no less than four pounds of celluloid film, which is nitrated and considerably more inflammable than ordinary celluloid film. There was a probability that the heating wires would become red hot in the air and the very close proximity of the red-hot wires to the inflammable, in fact explosive film, was a risk that had to be overcome.[1] Eventually, it was surrounded by a sheath of mica insulation which appears to have acted satisfactorily.

By the time the four jackets, with their plugs and sockets, were connected up to the four internal heaters, the wiring arrangements had reached a stage of no small complication, and one that had to be handled, especially in the air, with circumspection. The process of experiment was not finished without numerous tests in cold chambers in England. The aeroplanes themselves had to be shipped almost as soon as their fitting-out was ready, in fact after only one or two test flights to high altitudes, so it will be appreciated that the camera-heating arrangements had to be tested many times over and re-tested and tested again, otherwise than in actual flight. The method adopted was by enlisting the co-operation of Messrs. J. & E. Hall, leading refrigerating engineers of Dartford, who fitted

[1] This is about four times the charge for an 18-pounder field gun.

DARJEELING, FROM 14,000 FEET UP

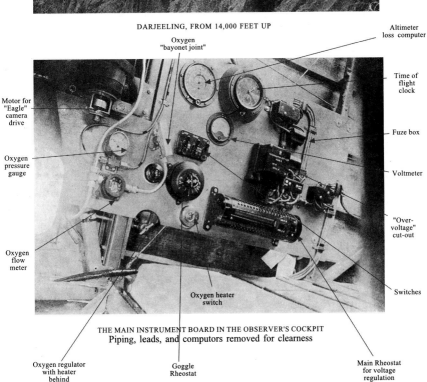

Altimeter
loss computer

Oxygen
"bayonet joint"

Time of
flight
clock

Motor for
"Eagle"
camera
drive

Fuze box

Oxygen
pressure
gauge

Voltmeter

"Over-
voltage"
cut-out

Oxygen
flow
meter

Switches

Oxygen heater
switch

THE MAIN INSTRUMENT BOARD IN THE OBSERVER'S COCKPIT
Piping, leads, and computors removed for clearness

Oxygen regulator
with heater
behind

Goggle
Rheostat

Main Rheostat
for voltage
regulation

up a special chamber which could be chilled down to minus 60° C., a temperature equivalent to 108° F. of frost. After two or three tests in this combined with a couple of runs in the air, the entire heating apparatus, for survey and ciné-cameras was operated satisfactorily, though this was not achieved without much alarm and anxiety when matters went wrong at critical points. Everything had to be done at high pressure on account of the necessity for shipping the machines early to India in order not to lose the weather.

Once the heating difficulty was surmounted and the cameras successfully installed in the machine, so that the observer could get at them and perform the various necessary tasks with reasonable facility in the air, applying the "drift" and changing the magazines, there still remained the more technical survey problems to be tackled. These were especially troublesome in our case. As already seen, if the machine can be flown in still air over the level ground in good weather, all is reasonably well, but over mountains many difficulties arise.

It is clear that the camera or, to be more precise, its vertical axis, can during flight take up a large number of positions with respect to the ground and the aeroplane. It may be at any height, or inclined at any angle to the horizontal in a transverse or in a longitudinal sense. It may be canted with respect to the aeroplane itself, also in two planes, and again so held that the edges of the negative are oblique to the track of the ground and the axis of the machine.

Our greatest difficulty was the question of height over the ground. We proposed to start photography when crossing over a ridge of 11,000 feet, with the machine at 29,000 feet. The height above the ground is, therefore, 18,000 feet or possibly less, although above the valley levels it is even more. After a few minutes' flight a peak of 18,000 would be flown over, then one of 22,000, then again the South Peak[1] of over 27,000, and finally Everest, where the margin between aeroplane and summit would be only one or two thousand feet. With 18,000 feet

"Lhotse."

59

vertical interval, over three miles, would be comprised on each exposure of the film; with two thousand less than half a mile of ground would be covered in length and breadth. The time the machine would take to fly over this distance varied therefore from one and a half minutes, down to a few seconds. The intervals between exposures had consequently to be diminished by actuating the knob on the control box at various points during the flight whilst the survey photographs were being successively taken. To allow for the sixty-six per cent. overlap, the first few photographs were taken at twenty seconds' interval, this being diminished in stages to six seconds, the shortest at which the camera would work satisfactorily, and the minimum time required for the motor to re-wind the film and re-set the shutter.

Actually, the six seconds were not short enough whilst flying over the South Peak and Everest itself, and reliance was therefore placed largely on the obliques. However, the verticals were still essential, as the foundation for the obliques to rest on. The value of the obliques was greater than it might have been over level or comparatively moderately hilly country because of the terrific steepness of the southern slopes of Everest, which meant that a camera held by hand in the ordinary way at a small angle downwards pointed almost at right angles to the slopes.

This adjustment of the intervals between exposures to the lie of the ground was successful inasmuch as it enabled a consecutive film of overlapping pictures to be taken of ground considered by some experts to be almost too difficult and steeply-pitched for an air survey, but it did not mean that the task of the plotter was rendered any easier. He necessarily had to deal with photographs of which different portions represented ground of enormously different heights.

The necessity for eliminating "drift" could be dealt with on orthodox lines, as already seen, with the aid of the Hughes Drift Sight, but to keep the machine on a level keel was a much more arduous task for the pilot than it would have been in untroubled atmosphere. As events turned out, the air was surprisingly calm at high levels until the machines reached the proximity of the mountains themselves.

An unexpected circumstance which almost entirely nullified the value of the survey photographs taken on the first flight, was the thick and well nigh impenetrable dust-haze rising from the ground to the height of 19,000 feet, and rendering the southerly "ground control" practically invisible.

On the other hand, fortune favoured our enterprise in one direction, in that the lenses, being warmed by the electrical apparatus, remained from first to last free from any trace of mist or frost.

It will be clear from the foregoing that the vertical photographs were, in the main, to be devoted to producing results of a purely scientific nature. The pictorial effects anticipated from the pictures taken by the vertical cameras would hardly be appreciated by the world in general, as the mountains and glaciers shown would be practically unrecognisable when viewed from that unaccustomed angle.

To illustrate the results of this exploration so as to catch the eye of the general world, it was necessary to take as many photographs as possible with "still" cameras.

At the same time we recognised at an early stage in the plans that these still photographs, commonly known in aviation circles as "oblique," would have a subsidiary scientific value of their own. No one appreciated this better than the secretary of the Royal Geographical Society, Mr. A. R. Hinks.

His prescience led him to consider that in view of the exceptional nature and steepness of the ground to be surveyed by photography, the orthodox vertical series of pictures would be inadequate and might, indeed, present insuperable difficulties in effective plotting. At the best, the vertical photographs would undoubtedly constitute the background and indispensable foundation of the scientific result, but it was clear that more ground could be covered, and the vertical photographs amplified, by a series of obliques taken with knowledge and foresight.

Thus the two were to a certain extent complementary, though each was practically valueless without the other. The vertical photograph, however useful scientifically, would be so dull as to hold no interest for the general public, whilst, conversely, the geographical value of the obliques by themselves could only be trivial.

Having decided on the necessity of a large series of good oblique photographs, we had to determine the type of camera to be used when taking them.

As with the vertical camera, we adhered to the products of Messrs. Williamson, and had no cause to regret this decision. Apparatus of considerable size was necessary because we foresaw that the pictures would be subject to vibration whilst being taken. However perfect the engines and their designers, we could not expect to be entirely free from vibration transmitted along the structure of the machine. Again, however calm the weather, the aeroplanes might not succeed in approaching the mountains without being thrown about by wind currents. None could say how violent such currents might be when we approached the cliffs on the south of Everest, and it was to take these photographs that we should be compelled to approach the crest as closely as possible.

We found that the smallest negative likely to give satisfactory results would be five inches by four, so decided to use Williamson's reliable P.14, a type which has won fame for itself in the Royal Air Force.

This was a plate camera, and we preferred plates, for there is little doubt that good negatives taken on them can be enlarged to a greater extent than corresponding pictures on films; but more so because the use of plates simplified the heating problem.

These cameras had also to be kept warm by electrical resistances, and their lenses prevented from misting or freezing over. Moreover, they had focal plane shutters with fabric blinds, tending to stiffen if allowed to become chilled by frost. To keep the lenses warm and blinds of the shutters flexible, called for comparatively little heating, which could be carried out by a single internal resistance in each camera, coupled with a fabric jacket sufficient to prevent heat being radiated from the duralumin body of the camera to the outer air. This involved an electrical lead to the camera, another "kinky" article for the observer to get tangled up in, but none the less indispensable. The cameras were so satisfactory that a very few tests in England convinced us of the soundness of their mechanism and they functioned splendidly from first to last.

From the beginning, however, we were much in the dark as to probable light values in the upper air of those latitudes and over snow-covered mountains of such immense height.

Here again we were involved in original research without previous experience to guide us. Every factor pointed to a superabundance of light. We knew that the flight must be done on a cloudless day, the sun would be well above the eastern horizon and blazing from a sky of perfect blue. Practically all the subjects to be photographed would be under snow, reflecting a great deal of light. Moreover, the position of the sun in the east at right angles to the course of the machines, and at its probable height between nine and ten in the morning, would, we anticipated, produce shadows creating precisely the light and shade to make the hoped-for pictures.

This was what we expected, but the scientists consulted thought cosmic rays might exert an influence, though to what extent, if any, none could say. A point in the still cameras was that we had no reason to anticipate danger from the effects of static electricity, due to the use of glass plates rather than film.

We planned to meet the unknown factors in quality and intensity of light by taking filters of different depths, mostly Alpha, K.1 and K.2. The bulk of these were gelatine filters, chosen for the facility with which they could be changed or replaced in the cameras and the minimum of trouble they gave from possible misting over, to which glass filters are liable.

As for the actual exposures, practical trial was the only way to ensure success, so numerous photographs were taken in England at various heights and in all conditions and environments in India, though naturally the results would have to be accepted with caution. We did not anticipate that a photograph, taken with a given stop and exposure at 30,000 feet on the coast of the Arabian Sea at Karachi, would necessarily bear close relation to one taken over the icy crags of the frontier between Nepal and Tibet, at the same altitude but many degrees of latitude further north. We could only work intelligently and make careful note of our results, starting from the known fact that the longest exposure we could reasonably hope to give in the air would be one-hundredth and tenth of a second. We succeeded in taking photographs with good results, using at times much longer exposures, but one could never be certain that an unexpected bump in the wind, or an imperceptible vibration, would not transmit itself to the image on the emulsion.

Apart from the judgment of light and consequent exposure and stop, manual skill was required in handling these oblique cameras in the air. Fortunately unlike the ciné-cameras, their weight did not entail distress or make an undue demand on the observer's lungs. On the other hand, whilst the photograph was actually being taken or, to be more precise, immediately after the release of the shutter, the camera had to be safeguarded and insulated by the arms and hands of the observer. This meant that he had infallibly to dispose some resilient part of his own anatomy between the camera itself and any portion of the aeroplane structure. This was simple enough with the machine at rest on the aerodrome, or supported on trestles in a hangar, but a very different proposition when a wind-blast of well over 120 miles an hour was struggling to wrench the instrument from the observer's hands. Both the latter were employed in holding the actual camera, with the forefinger of the right hand on the trigger which releases the shutter. None of the observers had more than two hands; by deduction, therefore, it follows that the individual concerned would have not only to brace himself in the cockpit against the violent push of the wind, but also to use his feet for holding on with, hooking them to any odd wire or part of the aeroplane in case he should be jerked out by a sudden violent bump, or lean over more than was desirable in the interests of gravity when actuated by the antagonistic demands of art. Fortunately, no observer fell out, which was just as well, as we found at an early period that, to save weight, the giving him a safety belt, let alone a parachute, must be abandoned.

There were so many wires and pipes already connected into the aeroplane that the addition of a safety belt might have resulted in strangling him. Moreover, it was decided to do without the parachutes and their harness, as in case of engine failure they would have been of little avail.

The operation of the cameras was planned in detail long before the machines were ready to leave the ground for their test flights. We hoped to take pictures obliquely downwards on either side, that is, east and west of the long straight strips of the survey photographs; this would have the effect of creating a fringe on either side of more or less roughly depicted mountain features, which experts could graphically join on to accurate representations secured from the vertical cameras. Besides this, there would be many photographs, as it proved, taken of the mountain-tops themselves, either close at hand or at a slight downward inclination. Mr. Hinks attached considerable value to the geographical explorations to be achieved from these, and he foreshadowed even the possibility of using pairs of these stereoscopically, should it be possible to take the two negatives of a pair with a short interval between.

There were recesses in the mountains to the south of the range on which the eye of man had never rested and certainly many more to which no one had ever penetrated. Even the hardy ground surveyors sent by the Government of Nepal immediately prior to 1929, had penetrated only as far as the monastery of Dingboche, about twelve miles from the mountain. Twelve miles, measured horizontally on a map, may not sound a great distance along, for instance, the Great North Road, but it is an immense space for human beings when it includes nearly 20,000 feet of the most formidable cliffs that could be imagined.

The policy decided on was that the leading machine, carrying the chief observer, should be equipped with two still cameras in addition to that for the survey and with one Sinclair Newman ciné-camera, the leading observer to devote most of his attention to obtaining an ample quantity of satisfactory obliques, particularly of the mountains themselves. The following, or supporting machine, carried the professional cinematographer provided with two of the same type of ciné-camera, who would devote attention to the handling of these, regarding the still camera, with which he was also provided, as supplementary.

In this way each observer had three cameras demanding full attention, beside the Eagle camera whose functioning he shared with the pilot. Further, in each case the principal camera for the observer would be carried in duplicate to guard against the work being interrupted by any of the multifarious hitches to which these delicate instruments are liable at extreme altitudes. For the chief observer we considered it unnecessary to provide a full-sized camera as the duplicate for the P.14 on account of its reliability, and so a $3\frac{1}{2}$ x $2\frac{1}{2}$ Williamson Pistol camera was used. A minor advantage was that it had an all-metallic shutter, thus obviating the necessity of heating arrangements for it.

INFRA-RED PHOTOGRAPHY

Our natural desire in the planning of the flight was to include as many scientific activities as possible in order that the world should reap the maximum benefit from the toil and money that was to be expended.

Infra-red photography had been known for many years, but had progressed very little beyond the laboratory stage until 1932, and by the summer of that year, Mr. Bloch, of Messrs. Ilford's Research Department, had brought infra-red photography to such a state of advancement that it was possible to take photographs by this method from the air.

It should be explained that Ilford's infra-red plate is one made specially sensitive to the rays from that end of the spectrum known as infra-red. To achieve these results, the incoming rays are passed through a deep-red filter or screen of special composition, this in turn passing through those rays which affect the emulsion on the special plate. The difficulty in the practical use of infra-red screens and plates has been one of exposure; in order to penetrate the deep-red filters, it has been necessary to give a very long exposure in comparison with that required for ordinary emulsion.

As all the world knows, infra-red photography has a special capacity for recording radiations which are not visible to the human eye and to which the ordinary photographic plate is completely insensitive.

However, the world owes it to Mr. Bloch and his research that these exposures have been reduced to reasonable length, and even down to such lengths as made them feasible for air photography.

As a general rule, one would have been fortunate to secure a photograph on an infra-red plate with an exposure of one-twenty-fifth of a second, but they had so improved by 1932 that results were obtained with exposures as rapid as one-sixtieth.

These achievements seemed so promising that we decided not to miss such an opportunity of taking what might prove exceptionally valuable photographs during our high flight over the mountains.

At the outset there was little prospect of achieving from the air definite results with infra-red plates and filters, for obstacles were many, but by ingenuity and resource we hoped to produce, at any rate, good pictures.

To overcome the difficulty of length of exposure necessary, we used as large an aperture lens with as long a focal length as was conveniently possible.

Fortunately, Messrs. Taylor, Taylor & Hobson had such a lens in stock and most generously lent it to the expedition.

This was a 4.5 aperture lens with a focal length of twenty-five inches. Needless to say, it weighed a good deal, In fact, it was with its mounting, as much as a man could lift with one hand. Also, another difficulty was that of heating it sufficiently to prevent frosting over. Having secured the lens, there remained to find a camera for it, and here again the resources of *The Times* and the ingenuity of Mr. Bogaerde, its Art Editor, came to the rescue.

He conjured up a camera with focal length and a suitable focal plane shutter capable of giving exposures of the length required. This camera was a somewhat rough and ready improvisation made of plywood, but in the competent hands of Mr. C. W. Williamson, it was quickly reconditioned and covered with aluminium in such a way as to give us hope of its successful working. It was not, however, in any sense of the word, an air camera, the plates, for instance, had to be carried in ordinary old-fashioned mahogany double-dark slides and secured to the camera by spring clips. The complete instrument, when put together, was three feet long, one foot high, a foot wide, and large enough to take half-plates.

It was obvious that it could not be handled as an ordinary oblique camera is handled in an aeroplane, even by a Samson, as it would be quite out of control and immediately wrenched from the hands of the observer should he venture to place it over the edge of the cockpit.

A plan had, therefore, to be evolved. As it happened, one of the uses for which the Houston-Westland had been originally designed was that of deck-landing on ships, combined with carrying a torpedo in its under-carriage, straight below the pilot and parallel to the fuselage. Swords were beaten out of ploughshares, and camera mountings improvised where torpedoes had hung.

The camera was placed horizontally below the fuselage pointing almost straight to the front. Certain calculations, and the consulting of graphs and diagrams, showed that the angle made by the axis of the fuselage with the horizontal during the climb to 25,000 feet was between three and a half and four and a half degrees. Four degrees were, therefore, taken as the amount of inclination to be given in order to point the camera at the tops of the mountains when in level flight. We added another two degrees to include rather more foreground than sky in the picture. Accordingly, the big camera was secured under the fuselage inclined at an angle of six degrees downwards, but otherwise straight to the front. Luckily this just cleared the bottom cylinder of the engine, and by manipulation it was found possible to locate the hinder end of the camera, and the retaining apparatus for its plate-holder, just where the observer's hatchway came in the floor of his cockpit. So far so good, but merely clamping it to the under side of the floor of the aeroplane was not sufficient.

Vibration was the great enemy, even with a camera and a lens of this size, and our previous experience with other improvised apparatus had shown that pads or cushions stuffed with natural horse-hair had the best shock-absorbing properties for this particular purpose. Fortunately, we had provided ourselves with small cushions of soft leather stuffed with this specially curled horse-hair, in anticipation of such a requirement, as horse-hair is unobtainable in India, strange as it may appear in such an equestrian country.

So these cushions formed a sandwich between the camera and the underside of the fuselage itself. Still this was insufficient, as it was clearly unsound to secure the camera to the air-frame by any rigid bands, and even leather would have been too unyielding. Eye-bolts were consequently secured to various portions of the machine, a rubber shock-absorber, commonly known in aerial circles as "sandow" or otherwise "bunji," being fixed to these bolts and passed criss-cross underneath the camera, forming a cradle which pressed it firmly and gently, coaxingly yet unrelentingly, against these horse-hair pads.

By turning himself upside down in a way with which long practice had made him familiar, the observer was able to put his head and hands through the floor and reach the rear frame of the camera into which he could clip, if all went well, the wooden double-dark slide. If all did not go well, it would probably be whisked out of his hands, to descend to earth without visible means of support, some six miles below. From this position the observer could also reach both the winding-knob of the shutter and release lever for the exposure.

Other provisions, however, had to be made. The lowest cylinder of the engine would probably throw out a good deal of oil, which would certainly impinge on the lens of the camera. In taking off, the wheels and propeller would throw up a certain amount of dust and this, mixing with the oil from the lowest cylinder, could be relied upon to form a thick crust over the lens, which would not have the best of influence on photographic results.

So there on the field of operations at Purnea, a flap had to be improvised by the ingenuity and resource of Burnard to cover the lens until the observer was ready to take a photograph. This flap was difficult to construct because, being nearly a foot square, the wind pressure on it was very great, and it called for no small mechanical skill to construct in such a way that the observer, unaided, could move it in the air against the force of the wind from the propeller. However, Burnard solved the problem.

Then the pilot came into the picture. The observer had to manipulate the camera and take the photographs, but as the camera was practically built into the aeroplane, the pilot was the one who had to align it onto the picture the observer wished to take.

It was easy to indicate to the pilot the picture in question, should the intercommunication telephone work satisfactorily. Otherwise, messages could be passed to him written in pencil on "Bexoid" tablets, a non-inflammable white celluloid substance. For this certain team work had to be thought out and drill improvised. It was arranged that the observer should first explain to the pilot the mountain-top or other scene to be photographed. The pilot was provided with an auxiliary sighting-line over the top of the fuselage, with the line of sight parallel to the axis of the big camera. The pilot would then steer his machine on the desired alignment. Meanwhile the observer would place himself on the floor of his cockpit, with his head through the open head trap, seize one of the big double-dark slides firmly with both hands and fit it to the camera, set the shutter, and, by means of a string, one end of which was attached to the pilot's wrist, signal by a sharp jerk that he was ready to release the shutter. The pilot would then steer with his sights in line with the object. At the precise instant, when this occurred, he would jerk the string in the converse direction and the observer would release the shutter and take the photograph.

The process appears somewhat crude, but the scheme had to be improvised on the spot after arrival at Purnea, in fact, after the principal flight over Mount Everest had been made. The reason for this was that during the limited time the aeroplane was available for flight in England before packing, we had to concentrate on the acceptance tests which might not be interfered with, least of all by the fitting of a large camera outside the handsome fuselage, the pride of its designer. Even at Purnea itself, the camera could not be fitted till the last moment, on account of its great weight and air resistance making it impracticable to carry on the very high altitude flights. Even were it possible to carry the weight and put up with the "drag," we could not have taken so bulky a camera without its freezing up, an excessive amount of current being required to keep it reasonably warm.

For this reason, then, the flights made for infra-red photography had to be subsidiary and could not be initiated, nor the machines even prepared for them, until the main flights were completed. It meant several hours of hard work to fit the big infra-red camera, and unship it after it had been fitted and carefully aligned. This prohibited the aircraft being equipped with the camera until we knew it would definitely not be required for a flight over Everest.

It was disappointing that we had no chance to take this large infra-red camera to over 30,000 feet on a clear day, and secure pictures along the Himalayas. The question of heating the camera prevented us from using it above 25,000 feet; nevertheless, we have every reason to be pleased with results. The improvised mechanism worked far better than could have been anticipated. The calculations as regards angles came out exactly, so that the centre of the picture was just where one wanted it to be on the plate. On the day available for these photographs, the weather did not favour us; in fact, both the Everest range and the Kangchenjunga group were covered with cumulus cloud. The infra-red plates penetrated the mist admirably, but not the actual clouds themselves, nor the dust rising up from the plains.

The result of infra-red photography on a cumulus cloud was to bring out the colour values remarkably well, and to emphasise the beauty of graduation of light and shade, not only on the clouds, but on the mountains themselves, in a way that was beyond the scope of other photographic art.

Of all the numerous scientific matters with which the expedition was concerned, it was apparent that meteorological and weather conditions would be of primary importance.

The weather conditions for aircraft are different to those affecting a ground expedition. The question of cold would vitally affect the climbers, but had no significance for aeroplanes —in fact, to the contrary, since there was evidence to show that the character of the air would be favourable for flight, at any rate as regards its sustaining power towards the winds, for climbing aircraft in excessive cold than in great heat.

The outstanding meteorological factors at the outset were in the first place, the presence of clouds in the valleys and over the mountains, and secondly the force of the wind.

The clouds assumed paramount importance, the expedition being essentially dependent on photography to produce the desired results, whether scientific or pictorial.

These rested on the taking of continuous strips of vertical

photographs on the south side of the ridge, strips that would be valueless were their continuity to be interrupted by clouds.

Regarding the higher peaks it did not necessarily follow that photographs of their summits, when these were wreathed in smaller clouds, would be valueless. It was, however, clear that great cloud banks around the peaks would spoil even this form of photography.

It was only possible to a very limited extent to ascertain beforehand the cloud conditions likely to be encountered by the aeroplanes. There was no regular observatory within eighty miles of the mountain, the nearest permanent one being that maintained for many years past by the Government of India at Darjeeling. Cloud conditions at Darjeeling, however, were by no means necessarily the same as those around Everest and Makalu—a hundred miles away, this being especially so owing to the Kangchenjunga group having a special affinity for attracting clouds to it.

The other observatory, in no way related to the mountain, was the minor government one at Purnea, our base, 160 miles distant, where again cloud conditions are totally different from those over Everest. In autumn and spring the records show that the skies are nearly always clear at this latter station. At the same time observers on the ground except in the autumn, were seldom able to see even the crest of the mountain owing to the thick dust-haze rising up from the plains. In short, then, there seem to be no regular systematic series of observations from either observatory towards that far-distant peak. Reliance had consequently to be placed on whatever notes could be elucidated from the records of previous expeditions supplemented by general information.

In ordinary years the second half of September, and the months of October and November, are those in which the atmosphere is strikingly clear and free from cloud, due largely to the monsoon blowing away everything, more especially the dust-haze.

However, for various reasons, we were compelled to postpone our attempt to the spring, a season which local information indicated should be nearly, though not quite as good, as the autumn. On this information was less precise for the previous climbing expeditions had for the most part collected their data in the autumn.

There was no reason, however, to expect from a careful inspection of both the meteorological records and brief notes of expeditions and travellers, that the skies would not be clear and free from cloud for the majority of days in each week.

The question of wind was an entirely different one. The modern British aeroplane makes nothing of wind qua wind whatever its power and velocity; in fact, the modern pilot prefers a strong wind to a calm day, provided that the wind is favourable in direction.

In the case of our expedition, however, there were special circumstances governing the wind.

The first was fuel consumption. As the flight had to be made from a point in British India in the closest proximity to the mountain and to return by the shortest and most direct route, it followed that the wind could not be favourable both on the outward and homeward journey.

This applies to either a head or a tail wind, whilst a wind from either beam has the effect of increasing the distance which an aeroplane must pass through the air in order to fly from point to point. For example, a strong wind coming in from the left, tends to blow the machine downwind to the right. If this were not corrected by accurate steering, the machine would proceed on a curved path to reach its destination, the curved line being as Euclid assures us, longer than the straight line between two points. To maintain a straight course in such circumstances—and straight course is, incidentally, essential for survey photography—the pilot has to incline the nose of the machine into the wind and to fly, as it were, crabwise with reference to the ground. Briefly, the centre line of his machine is not parallel to the front of starting and arrival, but inclines more or less at an oblique angle to it.

The result is that more flying has to be done than if there were no wind, the fuel consumption being proportionately increased.

The expedition's plans allowed for the machines being fully loaded with instruments and other gear in view of the exacting performance demanded from them; hence the calculation of fuel to be carried was a vital matter.

The margin of fuel permissible had to be kept strictly within bounds, otherwise its weight would have encroached upon that of cameras and scientific gear. It had to be thought out in relation not only to the safe reserve which must be retained in the tanks against unforeseen contingencies, but also to the additional flying to be done, should there be a strong wind blowing at the time.

Our calculations before leaving England were based on a wind speed of forty miles an hour throughout the flight, it being assumed that this would probably be from the west or practically at right angles to the machine's course. This figure allowed a reasonably safe margin for accidental heavier consumption on the part of the engines and also gave the pilot a reserve in hand after bringing his machine back to the landing-ground.

This figure was necessarily an arbitrary one since we knew there would be a wide difference between any wind speeds observed a few hundred feet above sea-level at Purnea and that at 30,000 feet or even of 7,000 feet at Darjeeling observatory.

In point of fact, there had been no scientific observations of the wind velocities in the upper air in that region, and by upper air one means heights of 25,000, 30,000, 35,000 and 40,000 feet.

We therefore communicated early with the Meteorological Department of the Government of India to enlist their invaluable assistance in the measurement of these wind speeds. The matter was enthusiastically taken up by the department as soon as the expedition reached India. Dr. Norman afforded the expedition the most valuable help, detaching an expert meteorologist, Mr.

S. N. Gupta, to form a special upper-air sounding station at Purnea.

He was provided with a full supply of hydrogen sounding-balloons of one metre diameter and of larger sizes in addition together with a modern theodolite and other requisite technical equipment.

We had asked the Meteorological Department to provide us with information as to the direction and velocity of the wind at 20,000, 25,000, 30,000 and 35,000 feet from 5.30 a.m. to 7.30 p.m. each day, and especially from the 15th March onwards. Further, information was asked for regarding presence and character of clouds in the area from the crest of the Mount Everest massif to a line about fifty miles south of it, in the region to the west of Kangchenjunga.

An anemometer was already installed in an observatory on the roof of the district board rest-house, where there was also a concrete pillar for the theodolite.

The procedure involved the sending up of balloons twice daily, at 0630 hours and at 1430 hours. The first time was selected as being early enough to follow the balloons up into the sky with a theodolite and also allow time for the aircraft to be prepared for flight. These small indiarubber balloons, inflated to a diameter of one metre from tubes of compressed hydrogen, are on clear days, visible through the telescope of a theodolite to a great height, often to 30,000 feet or more. On the other hand, a very small amount of murkiness in the atmosphere, whether due to prevailing dust-haze, to low-lying wisps of cloud, or even the mist due to humidity, renders them difficult to follow to any useful height. As a precaution against this, larger balloons were tried, including some coloured red, but even they were of no avail on a day of poor visibility.

In spite of all difficulties, however, observations of great accuracy and reliability were received from Mr. Gupta throughout.

The method of working is for one observer to inflate and release the balloon, while a second operator follows its course upwards through the telescope of the theodolite, using a stop-watch. Readings are taken after definite intervals of time and the result collated with a chart or graph from which the wind speeds can be read off.

For each balloon ascent then, Mr. Gupta sent to the expedition a chart carrying a code showing the wind velocity and direction observed at each height until the balloon passed out of sight. A similar procedure was carried out at Darjeeling.

In addition, every evening the weather bureau at Calcutta telegraphed us at 21.30 hours, giving information of the general weather conditions along the Himalaya, and a forecast of what might be expected in the Mount Everest region, especially as regards clouds and haze, and finally an estimate of the direction and velocity of the wind currents to be expected at various heights up to ten kilometres.

The accuracy of the information contained in these telegrams was remarkable, and made it possible to plan the flying operations next day, after they had been studied in conjunction with the balloon observations taken locally by Mr. Gupta in Purnea.

The flight to Mount Everest was carried out on this information and the results of it, particularly the drift and measurements on the drift sights, confirmed to a remarkable degree both the observations and forecasts of the meteorologists.

This held good also for various other tests and subsidiary flights that were carried out, notably in the region of Kangchen-junga, and also in the second flight to Mount Everest on April 19th.

We were anxious to make the most of our opportunities of acquiring fresh information for the benefit of science since it is seldom that aeroplanes find themselves at over 30,000 feet in the vicinity of great mountains. The environment was an entirely new one, and all experience shows that nature has surprises in store for man when he penetrates to where he has never been before.

The question of gravimetric observations naturally interested

G

us, but we were soon convinced that our aeroplanes could not carry any suitable apparatus or instruments that might assist us here.

More simple it proved, was the matter of the dip-needle. By a stroke of good fortune, Messrs. Henry Hughes, were, as we have seen, able to provide us with the first liquid dip-needle of a practical nature. It was no easy task to instal such a sensitive affair in an aeroplane, still less to secure useful readings from it. We found the best way to mount it was to suspend the complete instrument inside a wooden cage, by means of short lengths of rubber cord. This avoided vibration troubles. To counter-balance the magnetic attraction of the aeroplane, we suspended this cage in the fore and aft line of the aircraft to take readings with it on the ground pointing with its nose due north, and then when the machine had climbed to 25,000 feet or so, to point it again to the north, and so obtain comparative readings.

We hope that the results of this procedure, though rough and ready, may afford some data for the future.

The question of the accelerometer was simpler. The instrument, thanks to the technical experts of the Air Ministry, already existed, and one was generously lent to us. Its object is to measure the intensity of the shocks and from that the stresses, to which machines are subjected in the air, by reason of "bumps" and other air disturbances. We carried one on all flights and made careful note of its readings.

In the same way, we obtained the loan of two barothermographs and altitude recorders, which were fixed in the machines, and whose charts give a graphic record to the initiated of the vicissitudes of air pressures and temperatures through which they pass. Last, but not least, there was a dictaphone, which we took on several important flights, with results at once intriguing and at the same time encouraging for future use in the air.

CHAPTER V

THERE is a direct and interesting connection between the foundations of the survey of the Indian sub-continent and the triangulation which resulted first in the discovery and finally in the mapping of Mount Everest and its surroundings.

The first Surveyor-General of India, who held the office from 1823 to 1826, was Colonel Valentine Blacker, C.B., and it is fitting that his descendant should have taken part in the flight over Everest.

To use the words of the Survey of India's General Report for 1926, Colonel Valentine Blacker "fully appreciated the value of a proper basis of triangulation of a high order of accuracy for the whole survey of India, as is shown by an able paper of his on the subject, reprinted by Major-General Sir Andrew Waugh."

Lieutenant-Colonel Valentine Blacker (1778-1826), historian of the Mahratta Wars of 1817-1819, served with distinction in India and in 1810 rose to the rank of Quartermaster-General at the age of thirty-two. His career in Southern India is commemorated by "Blacker's Garden" near Madras city.

As Surveyor-General of India, he completed the map of Hindustan and initiated the first explorations of the Dihang and Dibang rivers. He was appointed a C.B. in 1818, and died at Calcutta on February 4th, 1826, apparently as a result of a duel in which both combatants were killed.

Colonel Blacker executed the first complete map of Hindustan, still preserved by his descendants at Elm Park, County Armagh. To quote the Survey of India Report:

"The projection he employed was a polyconic one, and

79

differed from that actually adopted by the geographer at the India Office in London for the Atlas of India.

"The calculations for Colonel Valentine Blacker's projection were carefully made and tabulated in a more convenient form for use than was actually the case with the Atlas projection. Moreover, his central meridian and parallel, 20° latitude, 80° longitude, were more symmetrically placed than the central parallel and meridian (24½° latitude, 76½° longitude) of the Atlas.

"The polyconic projection was thus Colonel Blacker's gift to India, though his exact projection was afterwards modified by General Walker."

In 1823 when the title of Surveyor-General was permanently established, Colonel Lambton was detailed to organise the great framework of the trigonometrical survey on the present lines, and assumed the office of Superintendent.

"In 1906, the Survey Committee abandoned the Atlas sheet projection as defective, and brought the quarter-inch to one mile maps on to the polyconic system following Colonel Blacker who had had no mathematical specialists in dealing with map projections. The officers of the Honourable Company, Lambton from the Infantry, Everest from the Artillery, and Blacker from the Cavalry, had to be their own specialists.

This Lieutenant Everest, was the disciple of Colonel Blacker, who succeeded Lambton and afterwards became Colonel Sir George Everest and Surveyor-General of India.

He carried on Blacker's work, extending his triangulation to the summit of the world's highest mountain. This triangulation, made in the days of our grandfathers and great-grandfathers, is the foundation on which the work of every subsequent exploration of Mount Everest and the region round it is based, culminating in the air survey of April 1933.

Triangulation itself is a matter which, to the uninitiated, seems remote—in fact, painfully distant—from the actual production of a map which the ordinary person can use. But without triangulation the map for the ordinary person tends

COLONEL VALENTINE BLACKER, C.B.
From a painting at Carrick blacker

to become somewhat like the charts of the Spanish Main, with the seas dotted with dolphins and spouting whales and the land with armadillos.

To triangulate, the survey party first measures with almost pedantic exactness, a straight base line several miles in length on the most level country available. From each end of this base, they measure, with the largest theodolites, the angles from either end of the base to a choice selection of prominent objects, such as mountain-tops and other irremovable landmarks.

The theodolite used by Everest's predecessor, Lambton, had a circle no less than thirty-six inches in diameter engraved with the precise accuracy of those days into degrees, minutes and seconds.

Needless to say, it was the only large theodolite in India in the 1790's and the consternation which took place when, owing to the breakage of a rope, it fell to the ground from the roof of the mosque on to which it was being hoisted, can better be imagined than described. However, Lambton managed to repair it and carried on to triangulate India. No doubt Everest used the same instrument, suitably repaired by the resourceful Indian artificer of those days, a man called Syed Mohsin of Arcot. Nowadays, however, accuracy is attainable with an instrument having engraved circles of only a few inches diameter.

Once the base is fixed, and the longitude and latitude of the points at each end accurately established, the positions in space of the other landmarks to which angles have been measured, can be worked out to the finest limits provided the necessary computers be available. The fixing of these other points is by no means just a matter of measuring the horizontal angles to them, for the vertical angles must also be measured, with equal exactness. Yet again allowance must be made for a variety of causes of error, such as refraction and even the correction due to the variation of the curvature of the earth, and for gravity. These factors become important when work is carried out in the vicinity of such a mountain mass as the Himalaya, so vast that even the waters of the Indian Ocean are, to an appreciable extent, attracted towards it.

When these triangles have been measured from the original base, a fresh set is measured on top of the original ones, and so on indefinitely, in such a way as to form a network of triangles across the country to be surveyed.

The next stage is to regard these triangles, or rather the diagram which they constitute on the triangulation chart, as the skeleton on which the actual map is based. Now come the details, that is to say, the conventional signs, the green trees and forests, the blue rivers, lakes and swamps, and the brown roads which make up the beauty of a map.

Up to a few years ago, this detail was drawn in by hand by surveyors on foot, using a form of sketching-board on three legs known as a plane-table. Naturally, it is a heavy task to sketch in meticulously all the details by hand, especially in a difficult country, such as the vast deserts of the Middle East, the labyrinthine swamps of the Ganges delta, or the high mountain crags of the Himalayas.

In these days the aeroplane is slowly but surely extending itself into the sphere of the plane-tabler, more especially over ground where he cannot tread.

However, the aeroplane, with its vertical survey camera, needs a skeleton of triangulation on to which to attach its picturesque detail, just as much as the plane-tabler. Thus it was Everest's triangulation work, in the first half of the nineteenth century, that paved the way for flying-machines, of which he probably—in spite of his contemporary Stringfellow and his monoplane—had no conception, and in whose practicability his scientific training would have compelled him to disbelieve.

Apparently the triangulation pushed on from points a few miles north of Purnea in Bihar, reached the summit of Mount Everest. The story of the Bengali computer who rushed into Sir Andrew Waugh's office about 1852, crying out: "Oh, sir,

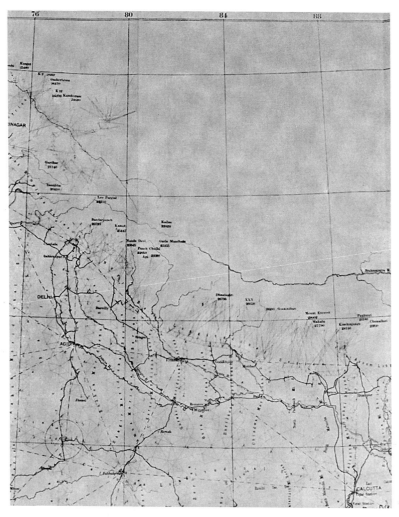

Diagram showing the triangulation of Northern India. The faint lines are the triangles

oh, sir, I have discovered the highest mountain in the world!"
is probably a subaltern's mess-room yarn, but it is good enough
to go on with.

Until the Survey of India discovered in 1852 that Mount
Everest was the highest mountain in the world, it is shown
as a black dot on a blank chart connected to India by a series
of triangles, very dry and uninteresting and labelled with a
supreme lack of imagination as Peak XV.

To fix geographically any mountain it is essential to ascertain
by observation with theodolites, the position of its summit in
regard to three dimensions of space. Its distance east of Green-
wich and north from the Equator must be determined, as also
its height above the level of the Bay of Bengal, near Calcutta.

These two measurements were of no special interest to the
expedition, since nothing short of a formidable error in the
longitude or latitude of the peak could have affected the navigation of the aeroplanes. Had the summit been found a mile
away from its position on the map, the pilot would have
ascribed the inaccuracy to an error on the part of the observer
in measuring the angle of drift, whilst the observer would
doubtless have put the blame on the pilot's steering. In any
case, a discrepancy of even a mile would have been a relatively
large one, whether due in the first instance to inaccurate
triangulation or to inexact navigation in the actual flight.

The height of the mountain was a different matter, because
it might possibly have been three or four hundred feet higher
than the 29,002 feet, with which it was credited by the observations of 1846-1849.

This three or four hundred feet might have been a factor of
sufficient importance to warrant consideration in the initial
planning of the flight, as affecting the margin with which an
aeroplane of given performance would clear the summit.

There were several original observations, taken from Jirol
Mirzapur, Joafpati, Ladnia, Harpur and Minai in 1849 and
1850; angles up from the horizontal to the top of the mountain
were measured therefrom with theodolites, the distances from

Everest varying from 108 to 113 miles. The greatest height of the mountain, calculated from the Ladnia angle, was 29,998 feet, the lowest, from Minai, being 28,990.

There is, however, a small element of possible inaccuracy connected with the "horizontal" from which these angles must be measured. In the actual theodolite is a spirit level enabling the observer to level his instrument to the horizontal before taking his angles.

Now, so immense is the mass of the Himalayas that the accuracy of this spirit-level is affected. The great quantity of earth and rock in the mountains attracts the liquid in the spirit-level towards itself to an appreciable extent, just as the moon attracts our oceans. This extent, though perceptible, is not accurately known as regards the places from which Mount Everest was measured, and hence the angles taken by these theodolites from their spirit-levels must be incorrect. This inaccuracy amounts to as much as 51 seconds at Kurseong near Darjeeling, and to 23 at Siliguri, the railway junction in the plains.

This source of inaccuracy might affect our ideas of the mountain's height by as much as 100 feet, though 60 is a more likely figure. In 1849 attraction of the spirit-level was not allowed for, hence the height would have been underestimated by this amount. So much for the gravitational attraction of the mountains.

In the period 1880-3, and again in 1902, further observations were taken from Suberkun and places near Darjeeling, such as Tiger Hill and Sandakphu, adjacent to the mountain, i.e., 87, 107 and 89 miles, and so probably more accurate, being taken with improved instruments.

In these later observations it is probable that more accurate correction was made for atmospheric refraction.

When the surveyor aligns the little telescope of his theodolite on the mountain-top, it is a ray of light reflected from the summit which passes through its lenses to his eye. This ray travels in a path curved slightly downwards with the hollow side of the curve towards the earth. This is owing to the difference in consistency of the air at the lower levels, causing the light vibrations to travel in a curved path. Hence the observer sees the mountain-top appearing as lower than it really is. Corrections must be made in the results, but, as little is known about the properties of the upper atmosphere, these corrections may themselves be inexact. Possibly the early observations were over corrected, thus making the mountain seem too low.

Sir Sidney Burrard estimated the error from this source at a probable 150 feet.

Besides these, minor possibilities of doubt exist. The theodolite itself, its telescope and graduated arcs, are not necessarily perfect. The observing surveyor may have been a trifle at fault. Such errors would result, when totalled, in a score or so of feet.

Again, suspicion rests upon the height at which the theodolite reading was taken; inaccuracy may have crept in during the process of measurement of this height from sea-level of the Bay of Bengal, and perhaps the height of the Kosi basin plain is altering at the rate of a few inches a year.

Similarly, the level of the sea itself shows a slight tendency to vary. It is, incidentally, attracted like the liquid in the spirit levels of the theodolites, and the humans of the various expeditions themselves, upwards towards Mount Everest.

Another point affecting the height at which aeroplanes might fly over Everest was that of snow on the crest.

Until the photographs were actually taken from close alongside the peak, we could not be sure that after an exceptional winter a great cornice of ice or snow might not be left clinging to the crest of the peak itself.

The additional height due to this accretion could only be guessed at, since there could be no accurate analogy from other mountains, and there were no year to year observations productive of real evidence.

The thickness of the snow bed or ice ridge would, it was

only reasonable to surmise, depend upon the wind and its effect. One uses the word "effect" advisedly, for the wind is there and possessed of immense velocity. On the other hand, the mass or weight of the air is only about a third of that at sea-level and might well have a correspondingly diminished effect in blowing snow accumulated during the winter from off the summit in spring. In any event, it was stretching the imagination to assume that there could be even as much as a hundred feet of such snow remaining in the spring.

These figures therefore added together as follows:

Error of refraction ... ... say 150 feet
Error due to gravitational attraction affecting
    the levels ... ... 60 to 100 „
Various errors possible from observation,
    inaccuracies of levels and instruments ... say 20 to 30 „
Snow possible up to ... ... 100 „

The maximum of these totals amounts to a possible 380 feet. It was, of course, highly improbable that these errors would be present and all tending in the same direction, but the figure was one large enough to warrant consideration when planning the flight.[1]

To those unacquainted with Mount Everest and the tangle of peaks of the Himalayas, it may seem a little strange that the stupendous crest, only 120 miles from the level plains, towering up for 29,000 feet almost sheer, should remain so long undiscovered. However, the lesser mountains, almost too numerous to mention, lying between it and those valleys of Sikkim and Nepal, peopled by kindly races of men, overshadowed by their nearness the great peak itself. For example, from Darjeeling, the tremendous massif of Kangchenjunga, towers up from a few miles away, whilst Makalu obtrudes itself between the traveller and Everest. Similarly, from the foothills of Nepal the impenetrable, all-pervading, dust haze rising purple from

[1] The writers are indebted for these figures, to the classic work of Sir Sidney Burrard and Sir Henry Hayden.

the plains of India for the greater part of the year, obscures the great mountain from sight. On clear days, especially in the autumn and after the monsoon rains, this dust haze is swept away, the clouds blown aside, and the majestic peak shows itself in all its splendour to the people in the west and south.

After the triangulation in the middle of the nineteenth century, a long period ensued which may be described as the phase of the native explorers. The Indian Governments were in a dynamic state. The Government of the Punjab under John Lawrence, pushed explorers far afield through the valleys of Kashmir to Imperial China and High Tartary, where the Russian Tsars were not yet known, and the governments of Bengal and Hindustan, sent their men in disguise into the no less forbidden kingdoms of Bhutan, Tibet, and Nepal.

One of the most famous of these intrepid men was officially known for many years as No. 9, though it now transpires that his actual name was Hari Ram. In these cases, it was far preferable, in the interests of long life, for these surveyors to have a number rather than a name.

In 1871, No. 9 started in the early autumn from Darjeeling, which had for some years been a European settlement, and passing through Sikkim, at length made his way into Tibet. He anticipated that, in common with all other travellers in India, he would be stopped by the frontier guard and possibly tortured, and so took measures accordingly. Before crossing the frontier onto the high plateau of the vast plain of Chang Tang, he ingratiated himself with the Lepcha chief of an important district south of the frontier whose wife happened to be ill. No. 9 had provided himself with a stock of European medicaments and under his treatment the lady became decidedly better. At last a cure was effected, although the man who had issued the pocket medicine chest from the survey department, prescribed No. 19 for her ailment, or for what Hari Ram diagnosed as her ailment. Having no No. 19 he mixed together the contents of bottles 12 and 7. In consequence of this performance, the head man treated him with great kindness of which he took advantage to press for assistance in his passage to Tibet. The head man finally consented and sent one of his own men with him.

On the march northwards there were no further interruptions beyond those which usually happen at custom houses. Luckily for him, he had concealed his instruments so well that the Tibetans never discovered them, which was fortunate, otherwise he might have had to expiate the crime on the rack. At that time it was the custom in the survey of India to construct prismatic compasses, and even pocket sextants in the form of Buddhist prayer wheels, so that the assiduous surveyor might pass for a devout mendicant.

At last Hari Ram crossed the Tipta Pass, and then the Nila Pass until he reached a monastery in the village of Shira. Here the Tibetans searched his baggage closely and put him through a third degree. It was only through the help afforded him by his Sikkim friend that he was able to get forward at all. He was subjected to much enquiry, but at last secured a pass to travel to Shigatze. He was then fairly inside Tibet and was not held up again, although one can imagine his feelings when passing by Tibetan officials and head men.

He arrived at Ramadong on the 4th September, a village of some sixty houses, and thence through cultivation and several other villages, all on or near the eastern banks of the Arun river. This is the remarkable river which bursts its way from Tibet through the main chain of the Everest range some way to the east of Makalu. Finally it joins with the Kosi of Nepal and at last reaches the Ganges in a meandering stream laced with grey sand banks, which move interminably from season to season.

On the 6th September, No. 9 crossed the Tinka Pass, and after a trying march came to a village called Tashichriang on the bank of a fine lake 20 miles long and 16 miles wide, lying at an altitude of 14,700 feet. To the explorer's surprise, the country being Tibet, he found the water clear and pure, in spite of the fact that he could discover no outlet. He was unable to go round it, so assumed there must be one some-where to the south-east.

This lake forms a portion of the frontier between Sikkim and Tibet, and here he found lofty snow peaks visible to the east and south. Marching on, he reached Ningzi on September 7th, and two days later the hot springs of Chajong, whose water is sulphurous with a medicinal reputation. The discovery he made here brings to mind the lake on the other side of Everest, straight out of its great spurs, discovered by our own flying expedition of 1933.

He marched on, first over the glacier ice of the Ragulong Pass, 15,200 feet, and then through the cultivated village of Saidjong. In turn he crossed the Daylong over snow and came again to the cultivated country past Balukoti village to the town of Shigatze on September 17th. Here he spent twelve days paying homage to the Tashi Lama of Tibet, and then marched south-westwards over the great flat plain, the Tingri Maidan. By October 2nd he had come to the immense monas-tery of Sakya, inhabited by 2,500 monks and ruled by a Lama who was regarded as a deity. With his boiling-point thermo-meter, smuggled with infinite care and precaution, from the stable courtyard where the caravans stopped, he calculated it to be 13,900 feet above the sea.

On the 3rd October he crossed another of these almost innumerable passes called the Dango, into ground within the watershed of the Arun, on the 5th reaching a village on the left bank of the Tingri river and the great western branch of the Arun. He continued westwards along the Tingri to its tributary, the Sheka, to which point the Gurkhas from Nepal had advanced when they invaded Tibet in 1854.

On October 8th, he gained the village of Tingri with 250 houses at 13,900 feet, and then, crossing the Tingri river, some miles above the junction, pushed on with renewed energy with winter threatening him over a wide level track, until reaching the Thanglang Pass on October 10th. He struggled over the ice and old-packed snow of this at 18,460 feet. With what intense feelings of relief he must have reached the town of Minam on the 11th, only to be held up by two Jongpens, Tibetan Government officials, who were ordered there two at a time so as to be a check one on the other. This is the first Tibetan town on the road from Nepal, and here his baggage was again carefully searched before being allowed to proceed further.

Now apparently the explorer was moving away from the hospitable country where the writ of the Dalai Lama runs, southwards towards the hardly less mysterious kingdom of Nepal.

From Ninam village towards Listibhansar he followed the course of the Bhotia Kosi River, and though there is only about twenty-five miles between these places he had to cross the river no less than fifteen times by means of three iron suspension bridges and eleven wooden ones, varying from twenty-four to sixty paces in length. This indicates the change in the character of the country through which he was passing. A couple of days before he was on the open stony plains of Tibet, and now was clambering and scrambling down this terrific cleft in which the river bursts through the great range of Everest itself.

At one place he found the river foaming in a gigantic chasm, the sides of which were so close to one another that it could be spanned by a bridge only twenty-four paces long. This was just south of Choksun village. Hard by this bridge the precipices on either hand were so menacing that the path had of necessity to be supported on iron pegs driven into the face of the rock. The path itself was formed by bars of iron and slabs of stone laid from peg to peg and covered with earth. In no place is it more than eighteen inches wide, and often barely half that width. It is carried for hundreds of yards at 15,000 feet above the river, which the traveller sees roaring below in its narrow bed.

Hari Ram, who had encountered much difficult country in the Himalaya, relates that he never met anything to equal this path. It is, of course, impracticable for ponies or yaks, and even sheep and goats rarely pass along it. There are other stretches of pathway between these two places which are nearly as bad, but they are fortunately not continuous.

Thus the first traveller in the British service passed from north to south along the course of the Arun, the river that sixty-two years later was to serve as a landmark by which British aeroplanes would fly to the summit of Everest itself.

This was the country on which they might have to make forced landings.

Southwards from Choksun, Hari Ram's route does not call for special comment, being much the same as in any other part of the mountains south of the great range, rugged in the extreme for a considerable distance, but becoming easier in the valleys. He, however, crossed a tributary of the Kosi, which he calls Indrawati, with five small tarns at its source in the snowy mountains to the westward. It is not easy to identify this on the present-day maps, possibly because of the change of name of the little stream. The lower ground had never previously been surveyed or even traversed by any literate person. The only landmarks were the two peaks in the neighbourhood which had been fixed from a distance by the Great Trigonometrical Survey. The results of his journey therefore formed a valuable contribution to the geography of the mountain range. In this exploration the position of the Himalayan watershed was determined in three different places.

The Survey of India considered that the actual watershed was far north of the lofty peaks visible from India, such as Everest and Kangchenjunga. The explorer went completely round Mount Everest, but his route was so hemmed in by great peaks that he never obtained even a view of the mountain itself. It was always apparently hidden by the subordinate peaks adjacent to it. He may possibly have seen it but never for any length of time continuously, or in such a way that it could be recognised and fixed by cross-bearing, as he did with the peaks of Kangchenjunga and what he considered to be Jano.

Hari Ram encountered the well-known difficulty of travellers in the mountains, that the local people have no definite name for the highest peaks. This may be explained by the fact that the very highest often look less imposing than smaller mountains close at hand. Even the Sanskrit word Himalaya itself, is never used by an educated people. The only peak for which he was given a definite name was Kangchenjunga.

All this pioneer work was carried out by this gallant explorer in imminent danger of his life. He had but a small pocket sextant concealed on him, for his latitude observations, and, to take heights nothing but a small boiling-point thermometer. In spite of that, he was fairly successful in fixing the more conspicuous peaks, and his work opened the door to investigation of the geography of nearly 30,000 square miles of largely unknown country, especially in the valley of the Arun. At the same time, he scarcely if ever approached within twenty-five miles of the summit of Everest, and the exiguous line which he left on the map represents all that was known up to 1872.

About 1880, the work was carried on by a Hindu of some account among his co-religionists, of the name of Gandarson Singh. He volunteered for the hazardous task of exploration in Tibet, and was deputed by Captain Harman from Sikkim to proceed towards the Tingri Maidan via the valley of the Tambar. This was a line of operations which would have taken him over much new ground. Instead, however, of ascending the Tambar valley, he passed on to the parallel valley of the Arun, now becoming familiar to us from Hari Ram's explorations, and which lies much closer to Mount Everest. Up this he ascended to the range called Popte, forming, so we are told, the boundary between Nepal and Tibet. Its significance is that the range must constitute a continuation of the massif of which Makalu and Everest form culminating points. He crossed this range to the Tibetan village of Kata, beyond which he was not allowed to go. His journals were far from satisfactory, and his observations few and disconnected.

In spite of everything, however, he appears to have succeeded in acquiring new information, chiefly of routes in Nepal, and to have reached a point possibly within fifteen miles of Makalu and barely eighteen or twenty from Mount Everest.

Up to 1881, then, this seems to be the nearest point to which any trained individual, even Asiatic, had penetrated towards the mountain, a state of affairs that apparently continued up to 1921.

In 1885 the bold explorer Hari Ram undertook a new journey into the forbidden land of Nepal. His plan was to go from Dagmara up the valley of the Dudh Kosi and over the Pangu Pass to Tingri in Tibet, the pass being some twenty miles west of Everest by which travellers cross from one country to another. As before, he employed the disguise of a native physician, encouraged by his former success, and took with him a stock of European and Asiatic medicines.

Owing to sickness he did not leave Dagmara till the 11th July, but crossing the frontier there, was granted a passport.

He descended into the low hills on 13th July, and a day later he and his party of four spent the night at a little village called Saria. He continued his march for several days, apparently roughly northwards, getting into increasingly high hills. On the 22nd he crossed the Sun Kosi by a ferry, where this river was three hundred paces wide and twelve or fourteen feet deep, which owing to the swift current he had difficulty in crossing. The next day, still going northwards, he struck the Dudh Kosi, crossing it some way up by a ferry. This stream is fifty paces wide and a noisy rocky torrent. From here it follows a tortuous course of several miles. Thus he continued marching day after day up and down spurs until reaching a fort called Aislu Kharka. It was held by four hundred Nepalese soldiers under a Captain whose duty it was to examine all passes held by travellers from the south. As soon as it was known that he intended proceeding northwards into Tibet, he was closely searched, kept under close surveillance for six days, and then ordered to return forthwith by the way he had come. However, by making suitable presents, and representing to the

Captain that they were inhabitants of Jumla and anxious to return by the most expeditious route, he obtained permission to proceed. Thus on the 6th August he reached the first village, where Tibetan inhabitants were met with, called Jubang; beyond which point no more Nepalese were encountered. They spent the night of the 9th August in a cave on the right bank of the Khumu Changbo, and pushing on from there came to Khumbu Dzong, the residence of the Tibetan Governor of the district. For some time this official declined to allow the party to proceed northwards by a route which he stated had never previously been traversed by anyone except Tibetans. Once again then the traveller was detained, and following his previous plan ingratiated himself with the inhabitants by treating their sick. He succeeded in curing the Governor's daughter-in-law of goitre and being taken into favour secured the sympathy of her husband. The latter was about to start on a trade expedition to the north. Here was an opportunity of which the explorer took advantage and succeeded in persuading the husband to include him in his party. So he again started on his way, after having spent six inactive weeks.

On the 22nd September they reached the village of Taran, the limit of tree vegetation, and from now onwards the track became very stony and toilsome.

On the 23rd, after wading the river, and marching through snow, they gained the rest-house of Pangji, with its image of the Horse God Takdeo on the summit of an inaccessible spur.

The place is a sacred one and out of deference to the god no ponies are allowed on the road between Taran village on the south and Keprak to the north of the Pangji pass.

Starting at daybreak on the 24th September, the explorer's party crossed the pass, which he describes as the highest and most formidable he has ever essayed. They had perforce to scramble over the dangerous snow-bed with numerous crevasses mostly covered by recently fallen snow, altogether a toilsome ascent of five or six hours before the summit was reached. The gorge up to the pass was contracted with masses of snow brought down by snow action on either side. "These are poised like capitals of pillars of frozen snow twenty or thirty feet high and thirty or forty feet in circumference." Apparently our traveller was unable to measure the height of this pass accurately owing to the breaking of his boiling-point thermometer. He estimated it, however, at over 20,000 feet, the pass being considered the boundary between Tibet and Nepal.

There followed a fatiguing march down a bed of snow lying in a narrow gorge on the north, for the power of the sun had begun to melt it. By nightfall they reached Keprak, where he was again held up by the chief village official, who declared that permission to allow them to proceed further northwards would cost him his life.

After four days' strenuous diplomacy the co-operation of the official was gained, who came with the party and even eventually secured the sanction of the Provincial Governor, the Daipon of Tingri.

Thus they marched on from Keprak, and on the northern face of the mountian-spur entered the grassy plain known as the Tingri Maidan, on the 9th October reaching the town of that name which lies at an altitude of 13,860 feet, and one of the highest towns in the world.

From Tingri Hari Ram continued into Tibet, though the remainder of his journey is not immediately concerned with this narrative. Its accomplishment had this result, that a trained traveller passed within twenty-three miles of the mountain on the western side, and so was able to take observations of a number of peaks.

Although he does not say so, he must have passed within sight of Mount Everest and probably also of Makalu, and of a peak XIV of 24,000 feet now known to us as Chamlang.[1]

No further approaches to the mountain seem to have been made until about 1903 or 1904, when a proper survey party, under Captain Ryder, who later became Surveyor-General of

[1] Reference to Vol. 8, Part II, Records of the Survey of India 1879-1892, and Map XXI.

India, went into Tibet and the Brahmaputra Valley through Sikkim.

After 1904 there is a further lapse of years when nothing actually happened, but during which Major C. G. Bruce was planning an attack upon the mountain. His intentions were repeatedly foiled by a variety of circumstances of the most diverse nature. For a number of years after the expedition to Lhasa, while the Anglo-Russian agreement was in force, the Foreign Offices did not consider it advisable for British parties to penetrate Tibet for fear of offending Russian as well as Tibetan susceptibilities. This held good from the signing of the agreement in 1907 until the outbreak of the Great War in 1914.

From August of that year onwards every man, likely to be of a suitable disposition to tackle Mount Everest, had other fish to fry, until the year 1919. This marks the inception of modern attempts against the mountain, both by land and air. In 1913 Captain J. B. Noel carried out his reconnaissance of the country to the south-east of Everest, destined to be a preliminary for operations against the great peak itself.

Came the 1924 climbing expedition with its record of valiant endeavour, and the epic heroism of Mallory and Irving. These gallant men last seen, far up, making the final ascent, had victory almost within their grasp, the toil all but achieved. Perhaps it *was* achieved and that on the summit they now rest—silent witnesses of a crowning triumph.

CHAPTER VI

STRATEGY, TACTICS AND OBJECTIVES

THE journeys of Hari Ram and Gandarson Singh completed what may be described as the early history of the advance against the defences of Mount Everest. The sequence of operations was still in the strategical stage, and it was not until much later that the attackers came face to face with the tactical problems of the conflict.

About 1882 the Survey of India secured fresh theodolite shots to the summit, presumably using more modern instruments and correcting the results by means of more exact allowances for gravitational attraction and for atmospheric refraction than was possible in 1849.

A lull ensued in the advance until 1904, when science unmasked a fresh battery, this time from a new and unattempted quarter—Tibet and the north.

Both Nepal and Tibet were, and are, forbidden lands to the European, the Russian and even to the Indian venturer, but for somewhat different reasons. Nepal, as an independent kingdom carved by chivalrous Rajput blades from the Mongol valleys south of the main range, as related elsewhere, is an ally of the British crown since 1816. Her rulers sent their sturdy battalions to the Sutlej in 1849, to the fighting, shoulder to shoulder with British and Punjabis before Delhi, in 1857, and to many campaigns which culminated in the sacrifices of the Great War, 80,000 Gurkhas shouldering rifles for the Emperor of India during the years after 1914.

Nepal remains closed because its Rajput aristocracy is none too enthusiastic about the blessings of Western penetration or of a material civilisation. Who shall blame them? It is enough

97

that Nepal retains that fidelity to a pledged word characteristic of such a knightly race.

Tibet is mainly for religious reasons a hermit kingdom. Here temporal power is exercised by two spiritual rulers, the Tashi Lama and the Dalai Lama, the "Ocean of Learning," to use the title conferred upon the latter by the former Chinese emperors.

However, prior to 1903 this Tibetan seclusion had been tampered with by Russian adventurers from the north. In the tracks of the scientists, the Prejevalskis and the Bogdanovichs, there came across the bleak uplands the more sinister figure of Dorji. The name in Tibetan signified "thunderbolt" and its bearer, either a Kalmuk or a Buriat, russified it to Dorjieff. After many ventures he established himself in what the Third International might nowadays call a "subversionary" or "diversionary" movement in Lhasa.

His presence there was not congenial to British interests in Central Asia, so in due course a military mission, under Sir Francis Younghusband marched through Sikkim over the passes to Lhasa. The Tibetans were converted to a more friendly attitude, but meanwhile the mission did not neglect the claims of science. A detachment of the ever-enterprising Survey of India, under Ryder and Rawling, not only mapped thousands of square miles of unknown country in Southern Tibet, but took observations to Mount Everest and its neighbours from the north. This work, although done from a distance of sixty miles, taught the world a great deal about the conformation of the mountain and its adjacent rivals, and substantially confirmed the earlier observations as to its height. Not only did Ryder and Rawling verify the preponderance in the height of Mount Everest over other peaks of the range, but they took further observations to the northwards, to peaks far into the interior of Tibet and proved that there, at any rate, the great mountain had no rival.

It should be said that, in spite of the rumour of legendary peaks in New Guinea and elsewhere, Ryder and Rawling satisfied the scientific world that Mount Everest was the world's highest mountain.

The operation was, however, still in the realm of strategy and nine years elapsed before the next forward step.

This was Captain Noel's reconnaissance of 1913 described in his address to the Royal Geographical Society and published in its journal of May, 1919.

Science owes this to Captain Noel, that he made the transition from strategy to tactics, by reconnoitring the position from close quarters.

His work appears to have provided at least one of the *stimuli* which led to the formation of the Mount Everest Committee, by the Alpine Club and the Royal Geographical Society.

The Great War followed, but even before its legal termination in 1921 a second reconnaissance, and more than a reconnaissance, had been sent out on the heels of Captain Noel's lone venture.

The story of the great work of 1921 has been so well told by Colonel Howard Bury, that one would not venture even to summarize it here, in the space available. The reader should consult his work to see how this major tactical reconnaissance prepared the way for the exploits of 1922 and 1924, and the glorious failure of that assault.

Up to the inception of this phase, each attacker had made his plans against the stronghold in terms of the long-range artillery of his theodolites, the close support weapons of his plane-tables and survey cameras to the fulfilment of them by the bayonetmen and bombers, the actual stormers—the climbers themselves.

Still, even in 1921, the air weapon had appeared on the horizon. General Bruce, it is true, and Captain Noel, limited by the possibilities of the D.H.9's of those days, envisaged aeroplanes rather as vehicles for the transportation of material to the intermediate depots and dumps, than as a "front line" means of attaining the objective, or of obtaining scientific results from the surmounting of the crest.

The simple Tibetans, however, who looked upon the skis of some of the climbing party of 1921, quite made up their minds that they were flying machines.

Jules Verne himself, in company with other dreamers, had visions of weird aircraft, primitive helicopters and would-be steerable balloons, flying over the summit of the world's highest peak. These dreams were followed by other projects by more practical airmen, but the overcoming of Everest from the air remained merely an impracticable idea until 1932.

Sir Alan Cobham in 1925 flew over the neighbouring mountains, but the great peaks themselves were beyond the capacity of his aircraft and engines. Again, two enterprising French flyers and at least one German, made plans for such a flight, but their dreams were not fulfilled. Later still, an American, Halliburton, in his "Flying Carpet" secured the much-coveted permission to cross the frontier of Nepal in an aeroplane and flew over the lower mountains to within sight of the culminating peak, but again, his engine was inadequate for actual surmounting.

Meanwhile came the work of the highly organised foot expeditions of 1922 and 1924. The world knows of their gallant conflict, their artistry and the racking endurance of their savage tussles with storms and snow, and their unforgettable sacrifices to the cause, but the tangible results which they handed down are apt to be forgotten. Ever in the forefront of the battle were the men of the Survey of India, with its great traditions in their hands, to be passed on enhanced and bedecked with fresh chaplets.

In 1921 the good name of that organisation rested with Morshead and Wheeler, both of the Royal Engineers, whom Science will long remember for their gifts to her. The Survey of India is accustomed to breaking records, and Morshead's party must have broken many during their work of mapping the northern, i.e., the Tibetan slopes of the mountain, its glaciers and off-shoots. Again thousands of square miles were mapped and for the first time here photographic survey methods were employed, based on Canadian precedents. These proved of definite value and added considerably to the results produced by the indefatigable plane-tablers, Lalbir Singh Thapa, Gujjar Singh, and Turubaz Khan.

Still, the work and the map were limited by the frontier line between the two states, which passes, or by a polite understanding is considered to pass, neatly through the summit itself.

Of the south side nothing was known within twenty miles, and even there only the exiguous lines made on the maps by the intrepid Hari Ram and Gandarson Singh in the 1880's, and but little on each side. The map sheets resembled the black and white geographical efforts of the preparatory schoolchild, who is induced to draw mountain ranges in the guise of hairy caterpillars, wandering irregularly over the paper.

However, this was not a final effort in the realm of ground survey.

In pursuance of its progressive policy of borrowing from the West those things of real advantage, the Government of Nepal, during the few years after 1925, carried out an up-to-date survey of the country.

Nepalese surveyors were trained in the efficient school of the Survey of India. Others were lent, and by their unremitting efforts with theodolite and plane-table, the torch of science was carried through the trackless jungles and over the myriad mountain ranges of the kingdom. Modern maps were produced and published of Nepal, up to the spurs of the main Himalaya on a scale of a quarter of an inch to the mile.

A survey party actually penetrated from the southward up to the tiny remote monastery of bleak Dingboche, to reach which it had marched through the minor ranges of Nepal, dwarfed beyond conception by the giants Everest, Makalu and the South Peak,[1] but greater than several entire Switzerlands.

Dingboche, however, is still ten miles from the foot of Everest as the aeroplane flies. All the toils of the expeditions of 1921,

[1] "Lhotse."

1922, 1924, and 1933, and the skill and vigour of the West were concentrated on struggling, and struggling in vain, over the bare two miles between the North Col and the untrodden summit.

Imagination shudders at the task confronting those who might contemplate traversing the infinitely more dreadful ten miles of the ground north-eastwards from Dingboche.

There remained the aeroplane.

It was by special favour of the Maharaja of Nepal, accorded in the spring of 1932, that the aircraft of the Houston-Everest flight were to be permitted to cross the jealously guarded border of Nepal, to show the world how the attack might be carried by air over the summit of Nature's last stronghold in the mountains.

The grant of this favour was in itself a testimony to the value of the survey work, the demonstration of mapping possibilities from the air, planned by the originators, and to which the Government of Nepal accorded due appreciation as we have seen. The benediction of the Royal Geographical Society was the foundation stone of the expedition's plans, for this drew the attention of the Air Ministry to the value of the project, the resultant combination paving the way for an approach to the Government of Nepal.

The arena was a fitting one wherein to splinter a lance for science; for from time immemorial, adventure has stamped her impress on the length and breadth of the historic kingdoms of Bengal and Oudh. Here roving blades from the heart of Asia, from Mogulistan and Ferghana, the lieutenants of Baber and of Humayun, carved for themselves principalities and satrapies. Here the bold venturers of the Honourable Company, Clive, Stringer Lawrence, the Skinners, and the Hearseys, toppled the Mogul pro-consuls from their gemmed seats of ivory, and coming from the East, pushed their own frontiers up to the marches of the veiled kingdom of Nepal.

This remote realm had, as we shall see, been the prize of generations of knightly Rajput rovers, driving down from the western deserts in their Viking-like quests for honourable advancement.

They subdued in the eighteenth century the bullet-headed Mongol clans of Gurkhas, surging up to east and north, until only the stupendous rampart of the Himalayas forced them to call a halt.

From the Euxine to the Yellow Sea runs this chain, and here in its centre, Mount Everest towers above all Nepal, and above all Asia. For the mountain forms a boundary pillar, and through its apex, on which the eye of no man, possibly the eye of no sentient being, had ever looked down, runs the frontier between two worlds. To the north lies the stark, glacial, wind-blasted plateau of Turan, stretching for many months of caravan marching up to High Tartary, Siberia and the Arctic. To the south, on the contrary, there holds sway a whole genial Olympus of cheery gods and goddesses, fairies and sprites, most benign, and full of kindly sympathy for the foibles of Aryan man, convivial and even amorous. Possibly the venture was from the first looked upon kindly by Krishna himself, that pilot of aery chariots of the old Sanskrit pantheon. So Mount Everest, unknown even by name to our ancestors, is not only the culminating pinnacle of the world, but as befits its tall majesty, marks the frontier between the two most numerous races, the two great cultures, the two great philosophies, and the two great ways of life of this planet. Thus it was indeed to the newel post of two worlds that the little band of airmen planned to convey themselves in machines, which were an epitome of the British aeroplane-maker's craft and of his scientific skill.

To reach it, they would have to pass over a zone of virtually unknown country, and over that belt of terrific declivities which no human, perhaps no animal, and certainly no surveyor, had trod.

Exactly what lay ahead no one knew, but it was clear that only by the instrumentality of the aeroplane could that great barrier be surmounted, and then only by means of a most carefully planned expedition and meticulous staff-work, could the risks be so reduced as to make them reasonably justifiable.

An attempt could, of course, have been made some years earlier in a single-seater aeroplane with good hopes of success.

However, without an observer and fully adequate photographic equipment, the flight would have been easier but mere foolish sensationalism, inasmuch as no scientific results could be expected. As the event proved, this point of view was more than justified.

One of the earliest steps had been to choose a possible aerodrome or advanced landing-ground, from which the aircraft could take off for their flight. The conditions under which sanction was given indicated some locality in Bihar, where, as it happened, a prepared landing-ground belonging to the Army Department already existed. This was conveniently situated on a railway line, with administrative facilities at hand, in the shape of a magistrate, police, a hospital, post and telegraph offices, and last, but not least, a small permanent meteorological observatory. This landing-ground was near Purnea, at a hamlet called Lalbalu.

By a quaint jape of the jesting Clio, which we took for a good omen, it came to light that it was precisely here in all the wide spaces of Bengal that the uncle of our chairman, Captain Peel, V.C., of the Royal Navy, sent a small party of his bluejackets to attack some of the 5th Irregular Cavalry of the Bengal Army, which had mutinied in 1857 on the outskirts of the aerodrome itself. The landing party of seamen from Calcutta sighted the glint of the mutinous cavalrymen's lance-heads above the low-lying mist of the early morning, and from the cover of an embankment they opened a brisk fire from their muskets, quickly routing the lancers who fled over the frontier into the jungles of Nepal, where, no doubt, they were finished off by the tribesmen. Possibly the inspiration for Mr. Kipling's story, transplanted to the north-western frontier, came from this incident.

The Army Department generously placed the Lalbalu landing-ground at our disposal, and it proved admirable for the purpose, possessing a level surface of turf remarkably good for India, if somewhat dusty. We found that little work was needed beyond an improvement of the white markings, the erection of portable hangar and tents and the sinking of one or two tube wells.

The landing-ground was ten miles east of Purnea itself, and 260 miles north of Calcutta, the dusty and not too level motor road from Purnea to Siliguri and Darjeeling running alongside it.

To reach the mountain from Lalbalu, the aeroplanes would fly almost due north for some fifty miles, first over chequer-board fields, and what in former days were exceedingly rich plantations of indigo, then over the amazing thirty-mile level stretch of turf called the Rumba. Here all the Air Forces of the world could land in safety, and this zone, unbroken by fence or ditch or anything but an infrequent tiny patch of dusty plough, runs to within a few miles of the frontier line with Nepal.

It was no doubt the temptations of this huge stretch of what men called "cavalry country" that led to the stationing there in the old days, of a brigade of cavalry.

Here and there are ruins of old indigo factories, and tumbled piles of strikingly fine brickwork which had held their boiling-vats. In the centre lie the attractive picturesque ruins of a castle-fort of the Mogul days, probably indeed earlier still, called Thakurganj.

Along the edge of the Rumba, almost due north, runs a little-used narrow-gauge railway, through Forbesganj to Jogbani, the village *entrepôt* for trade with the Nepalese villages of the plains, by goods carried on pack ponies and small ramshackle bullock carts.

After Jogbani the fields, grassy swards and cultivation of Bihar, give way to a savage wilderness of almost pathless jungle, the hunting-ground of the tiger and of the almost extinct Asian rhinoceros.

The flight over this zone, called the Terai, would, it was estimated, occupy perhaps ten minutes, though an attempt to cross it on foot would exact many days arduous marching. The machines would pass the frontier here at a height of at least 12,000 or 15,000 feet, and therefore be inaudible to those on the ground, and if visible at all, appear only as mere specks.

The Terai, though seamed with foothills and ravines, cannot be termed mountainous, and not till further north would the aircraft fly over the real Nepal.

Here is a well-ordered land of green and olive-brown mountains, rapidly increasing in height and grandeur but separated by fertile, arduously-tilled valleys, full of luxuriant rice-fields in countless terraces, hardly won from the iron slopes by human toil. The upper hill-sides, at first matted with rhodo-dendrons and sub-tropical growth, soon clothe themselves with dark pine, ilex and, in the end, with sparse birch.

The sombre green mountains become huge swelling breasts of struggling upland turf, mottled with masses of water-borne boulders, streaked with torrent beds, with stark cliff and great rock faces, and then in the high levels, overmastered by mighty glaciers.

No imagination was able to forecast the majesty of that stupendous declivity of Mount Everest's southern face, till the airmen themselves should see it at close quarters.

The actual objective of the airmen was a point in space directly over the highest summit, for it was unnecessary to go beyond the actual confines of the kingdom of Nepal, nor was there any desire to do so. Tibet was forbidden, and the aircraft might not fly there, even in the fringes of the stratosphere.

To sum up the situation in a few words.

The conditions under which the attempt would have to be made differed profoundly from those of a straightforward attack over an ordinary flat country and on a conventional height record. No meteorological expert, nor any airman, however experienced, could foretell what turmoils and tantrums would be met with in the higher air close by the mountains. The expedition secured the cordial co-operation of the Indian Meteorological Department and the dispatch of wind and weather telegrams from the permanent observatories of Khatmandu, Darjeeling and Calcutta were arranged; but the direction and velocity of the wind might change fundamentally by the time even the 25,000 foot mark was reached. In the vertical plane, again, there would be unknown maelstroms. On the leeward side of even small mountains there swirls a vast eddy with a "transverse horizontal axis" of which one side sweeps down, carrying all with it, having a force and speed scarcely to be grasped by the mind. The defences of the mountain are not merely static or passive. There is an artillery of the elements sweeping the approaches to the final stronghold vaster than gunner ever served.

Again, two physical, or physiological, dangers threaten the high-flying airman. At sea-level itself there are only twenty-one parts of oxygen in every hundred of the air we breathe, and at the relatively moderate height of 28,000 feet, human lungs take in less than one-third of the volume breathed at sea-level.

Pure oxygen then would have to be carried and inspired to enable the blood to eliminate the carbon-dioxide produced in the muscles by any sort of effort. Only so can heart and lungs sustain the labour of pumping and purifying the vitiated stream. Yet more important still is the supply of pure oxygen for the brain of the airman. Without adequate oxygen transported to the brain in the cerebral arteries the perception becomes dull, judgment is impaired, the flyer's mental processes go awry, he concentrates excessively and exclusively on one particular aspect of his task till other essentials and precautions are forgotten in a fatal oblivion, and disaster follows.

An even greater danger threatens the arteries of him who adventures into the highest levels.

These vessels tend to burst from the heart's violent pumping and such a state of affairs will, at length, cause loss of vision, a dangerous or fatal lapse into unconsciousness or hæmorrhages. The only safeguard lies in the physical fitness of the flyers themselves and in the youthful strength and elasticity of their artery walls.

This was a juncture at which the facilities so generously granted to the expedition as early as the spring of 1932, became of great value. We have described how the prospective flyers were tested in a great steel chamber of the Royal Aircraft Establishment at Farnborough, from which the air was pumped out and rarefied to a degree appropriate to an altitude of 37,000 feet.

So much for the principal and major risks, while enough has been said to show that the judgment, experience and airmanship of all the flying personnel would be severely tested. Were the oxygen to fail for even as much as thirty-five seconds, or even the warming electric current, which safeguarded any chance droplet of water in it from freezing, the crews would become unconscious. This would be hazardous enough over low-lying flat ground, with 30,000 feet of "air-room" through which the machine could swoop and dive down, until the pilot might recover consciousness and control in the less tenuous air. Over the cliffs and glaciers of the southern face of Mount Everest, the case would be different. The pilot would indeed be fortunate, as well as skilful, to secure command again over his machine in the small space available. These risks were not to be run lightly and without due cause, yet the objects of the expedition were ambitious enough to warrant its hazards.

Its scientific object consisted in a demonstration of mapping by air survey methods, of the inaccessible cliffs, glaciers and valleys of the southern side of Mount Everest. The aim was not so much to produce an extensive map of any immediate practical utility, as to demonstrate to the world, especially to the non-technical portion of it, the relative quickness and facility with which such a map might be made of a region forbidden to ground methods not only by policy, but also by the physical obstacles of the country.

The expedition planned also to supplement the vertical survey photographs taken by Williamson Eagle cameras along the direct course of the aeroplanes by a new and experimental method, suggested by the Geographical section of the General

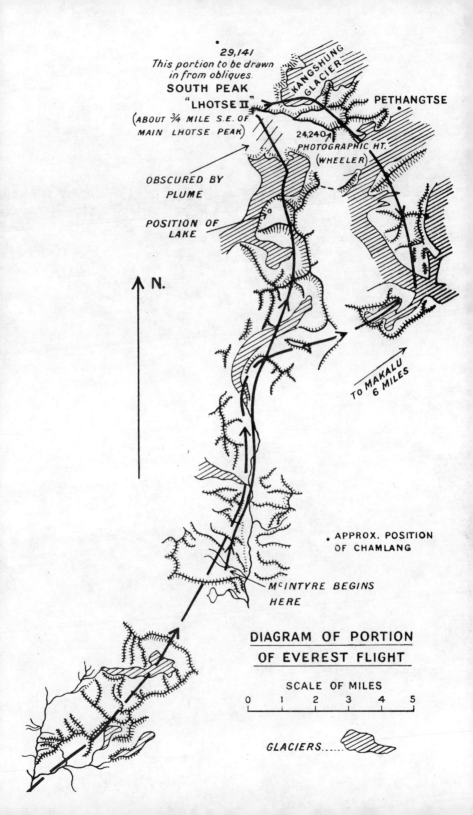

29,141
*This portion to be drawn
in from obliques.*
SOUTH PEAK
"LHOTSE II"
(ABOUT ¾ MILE S.E. OF
MAIN LHOTSE PEAK)

KANGSHUNG GLACIER

PETHANGTSE

24,240
PHOTOGRAPHIC HT.
(WHEELER)

OBSCURED BY
PLUME

POSITION OF
LAKE

↑ N.

TO MAKALU
6 MILES

APPROX. POSITION
OF CHAMLANG

MᶜINTYRE BEGINS
HERE

DIAGRAM OF PORTION
OF EVEREST FLIGHT

SCALE OF MILES

0   1   2   3   4   5

GLACIERS......

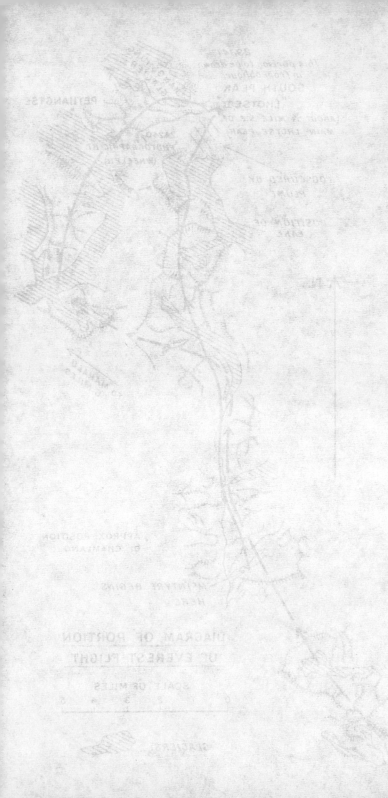

Staff at the War Office, of employing "oblique" stereoscopic photographs in pairs.

Above and beyond the actual topographical mapping, there was a definite expectation that by a close examination of the obliquely-taken as well as of the vertical photographs, geologists and physiographical experts could add to scientific knowledge. Steps were likewise taken to secure infra-red photographs as well as to investigate the aerodynamic stresses to which the aircraft might be subjected, by records from the accelerometer, an admirable instrument produced by the scientific experts of the Air Ministry.

Again, the first of Messrs. Henry Hughes' liquid dip needles was taken, with a view to experimental investigations of the earth's magnetism in the vicinity of the Himalayan masses.

Also, almost unnecessary to relate, each aeroplane was to carry either a recording barograph or a Jaumotte meteorgraph giving an automatic record on a thin sheet of smoke blacked aluminium of the minuté to minute changes in barometric pressures and in temperatures, to which the aircraft would be subjected during the stresses of their climb.

So much for the objects and the objectives. Mount Everest stood before the venturers, inviolate to man's attacks, whether by sap or by assault, for sixty-seven years. Many human lives had been spent in forging link after link in the long chain of human endeavour, while near by the summit, or even perhaps on it, lay the remains of the indomitable Mallory and Irvine.

But besides the more tangible objectives to be attained for science, there was the vital one of bringing home to the world the supremacy of British aircraft and engines. The flights would be a test not only of mere climbing power, but of airworthiness and real structural strength.

There might, too, be an economic as well as scientific value in the achievement. The air is the ocean which comes up to every man's door. The services of distribution cannot for ever confine themselves to land and water to the neglect of the air.

Transport aircraft must cross either seas or deserts or else mountain ranges. Oceans call for the building of more powerful and more able flying-boats; deserts and great jungles for the organisation of chains of landing-grounds, signals, lights and beacons; but so far the economic world has almost everywhere, except in the Andes, in New Guinea and between Kabul and Termez, shirked the real problems of mountain flying.

Everest might possibly contribute its share to the reconstruction of man's industrial life.

CHAPTER VII

THE FLIGHT TO INDIA

ON February 16th, three light aeroplanes left Heston bound for Karachi, in India. Three little Moths, a Puss, a Fox, and a Gipsy, fluttered their farewells to photographers and friends, setting out as forerunners to spy out the promised land nearly two continents away. These aircraft were the light transport scouts and maids-in-waiting to the heavier Westland machines, which, fitted with every improvement and ingenious device, were at that moment stowed safely away in the hold of the P. & O. *Dalgoma*, waiting for their mountain debut on the roof of the world.

In the first machine went Clydesdale with Shepherd, aeronautical editor of *The Times*, and Hughes, the mechanic; McIntyre flew the Gipsy Moth with most of the luggage and spares; while Fellowes, accompanied by his wife, took the Puss, the luxurious cabin-plane lent by Messrs. Fry of chocolate fame.

Just prior to departure our splendid patroness—Lady Houston —telegraphed to the Viceroy asking him to receive the members of the Flight and give them his blessing. Lord Willingdon replied, "Will gladly receive members of expedition so generously financed by you and wish them God-speed on their great adventure." Thus did the fliers set out to justify the confidence of one of the world's most notable women.

The route chosen for the party of six was the more general one taken by flyers, stretching across France, down the long shin-bone of Italy to Catania in the big toe of Sicily, then across the Mediterranean at its narrowest point to Tunis, and thence past Cairo, Baghdad and Persia to the Indus river and the mud-flats of Karachi. To the mind of most insurance companies, the route to India by Eastern Europe is considered non-insurable

III

for small aeroplanes, at this time of year, the principal reason being that Balkan aerodromes are often unfit for use under severe winter conditions. But the flyers were more than once led to doubt the wisdom of this decision, the distant danger of deep snow in the Balkans appearing a lesser evil than the pressing attentions of an eighty miles an hour contrary gale, blowing them back to Europe like the hot breath of some desert genii, when crossing from Sicily to Africa.

But they had started, which was all that really mattered. They were off at last. The busy days of scheming and preparation were finished, the anxious halts, interludes and disappointments were over. Old Man Delay with his rodeo tricks had thrown his last lasso, when they soared in formation through thin clouds into glorious sunshine. Heston aerodrome faded away as a static symbol of the past, the ground had become as dull as a stock exchange story too often told; the propellers had begun the throb and roar and whirl of their ecstatic rush—the swiftest race yet known to man. For a few moments each aeroplane seemed to its neighbour to hover and hang almost motionless as some silver bubble over the irridescent mist beneath. Only the roar of the engines gave the impression of speed and progress. In the air the infinite always lies ahead and its symbol is the sky.

Some there are who travel for the thirst of great horizons, and the fever called in Northern Europe the "Wanderlust," others take ship, or car, that they may have for companions those many fair-faced wanderers, Change and Variety; but no man or woman will ever have seen one-tenth of the earth's surface, or experienced the true height and depth of wonder unless they have taken wings and flown.

Flying can be a real love affair that gets into and occupies the mind. It is a dramatic entertainment that stretches outwards and inwards at the same time. In a curious tingling way it combines the beginning and end of movement. There are aviators, who maintain, not only that the air is the region in which it is easiest to keep awake and watchful, but that flying makes them no longer afraid of time. Of the four elements composing the human environment, air has a fourth dimensional gift, transcending the cold fatality of human limits and time-tables or the noisy insistence of mechanical clocks, and holding out already in its hand for its devotees and followers the skeleton keys that will unlock the future.

These who go up to the clouds in trips and take their travel across the sky, in the simplicity of a small aeroplane, can bear witness to much that is eternal and elemental. They can see the morning awaken and leap from the ground into a new day, they can hear the loud triumphant shout of gangster gales, feel the ghostly touch of cloud curtain and storm, and become acquainted with the fadeless duck's-egg blue of the sky, always most tender in colour when it has high mountains for a neighbour.

They thought of Alice in Wonderland as they looked down at the dancing silver ribbon of the English Channel: "the further off from England the nearer is to France," the Mock Turtle sang in his ungrammatical kind of voice. A pleasing thought to remember as the traveller contemplates the cold and chilly stare of the water. There are people, never invited to attend the Mad Hatter's tea party, who visualise aeroplanes as one day being made of rubber, able to bounce about on the earth, or float in the sea.

Be that as it may, whatever one contemplates when flying the Channel, one has to descend to earth again at Le Bourget aerodrome and come to grips with frontier formalities.

Arrangements in French territory are good and fairly expeditious compared with many foreign countries, but the red tape, restrictions and formalities employed by certain Powers are often most exasperating and out of all proportion to the speed and freedom that should accompany this form of travel. The air-minded of all nations must combine to break down the shackles of a groundling officialdom if they are to gain the full advantages of aviation. The limitations and cramping conditions of the crowded earth assume quite a different perspective to those who venture into the open sky, the irritation of petty landing-regulations being heightened by the contrast.

Heavy travel books, for instance, a necessary part of air equipment, are often an innocent source of persistent worry. In most countries on landing, these books are instantly arrested and removed by the guard, and only returned just before departure; this means that the early morning start so dear to the heart of most pilots has often to be sacrificed because the local authorities are still in bed.

The quickest landing, refuelling and "get-away" accomplished by the flyers actually occurred at Gabes in Tripoli, where a record of just under an hour was created but never broken. Generally an allowance had to be made for losing nearly three hours of valuable daylight. The constant examinations of passports, travel books and carnets, can develop into the travesty of some lower form examination in a most private and official school. On one occasion, the perfect blackboard schoolmaster appeared on the scene in the shape of a Persian doctor, who, after asking enough painstaking questions to fill a copy-book, insisted on searching the aeroplanes to make an exact tally of the stowaway rats they might be carrying.

In Italy, which the six flyers reached after a rough and windy passage over the maritime Alps, the difficulties of the party were increased by the fact that none of them knew the language. French may go down quite well, sphagetti, tactfully used, even better, but a working knowledge of Italian would on several occasions have naturally eased the situation, especially where landing in remote places is concerned. To simplify control, Shepherd was appointed Chancellor of the Exchequer and Chief Major-domo, a post in which he earned far more gratitude than is given to most Cabinet Ministers. Clydesdale's faith in loud, clear English, repeated over and over again, was frequently justified by results. As a last resort the flyers had sometimes to depend upon the histrionic ability of McIntyre. One cold night on the way to Rome, spent in pushing a bogged machine across a watery aerodrome, hot rum and lemon seemed to be the one thing needful. It was impossible to make anyone understand what was wanted until at last McIntyre began to perform the hornpipe and to posture as a sailor; while busy dancing, he swallowed off imaginary drinks. Enlightenment descended upon the waiters in a flash. In a few instants, the magic beverage appeared, proving that although sailors are reported to be happy-go-lucky folk, there is one thing they certainly do care about.

Italy keeps a careful watch on her flying visitors. The enthusiasm over the air is unbounded. A state of air-mindedness and technical knowledge are apparently maintained without difficulty; probably this high standard, in advance of nearly every other nation, is the result of Mussolini's own experiences and resolutions when himself in the Air Force. The English flyers met many different types and classes of officers among the Italian Air Force in Italy, Sicily and Northern Africa, ranging from slim, eager boys, to comparatively elderly men of domesticated appearance, aviation providing a common bond of enthusiasm for one and all. Some of the Italian aerodromes are models of efficiency and power.

Flying from Sarzana to Naples, and from Naples to Catania in Sicily, the three aeroplanes enjoyed a real Roman holiday. The aerial highway stretches along the ruler backbone of the Apennines and across little tumbling valleys that run like happy children towards the sea. The gusty winds lurking like robbers in the capacious pockets of the Alps are left behind to annoy others. The passage through the ether becomes smooth and effortless. Even the snowy crests of the mountains supply no air bumps. The air stands still. There is a luxurious well-upholstered feeling about the world. Down below, on the ground, the grape has become the spoilt child with everything done for it; terraced ranks of olive-trees stand on guard, the silver-grey legionaries of all that land. Little walled towns spring up like Jack-in-the-boxes from the plain, each set on its hill, the houses crowding and cuddling each other too much to show such prosaic sights as streets. Pisa comes as a tilted and tantalising curtain-raiser to the more opulent glories of Rome, with the final scene featuring a sudden breathless glimpse of the too-famous Bay of Naples. A view of this shapely, sunburnt town, especially from the air, will revive the discussion as to whether the man who first patented the remark: "See Naples and die," was a poet who meant what he said, or some harmless individual referring to Naples and "Mori" which happens to be an adjacent suburb.

Crossing the bay and plunging through a cloud of sulphurous smoke, the machines banked steeply to the left and there, palpitating beneath them, they could gaze down thrillingly into the glowing heart of Vesuvius. Columns of grimy smoke obscured the calm blue face of the sky, and might have been the breath of some evil spirit or ancient Cyclops dwelling amongst his infernal fires. One shuddering moment, and the aircraft darted out of this atmosphere of nightmare into the bright air again. One more circle over Vesuvius and they performed a long glide down to the aerodrome where for the first time their occupants felt the soft peach-warming glow of southern sunshine. Officers of the Italian Air Force came forward to give a friendly welcome that softened the stringent regulations they were obliged to enforce.

Cameras had to be sealed up and films were confiscated, being hurriedly developed and then returned when they proved to be under-exposed snaps of the English machines in mountainous country. As a parting gesture, the sunset gave a dramatic evening performance over the Bay of Naples with a wealth of southern glow and colour, transplendent beyond the dreams of producer or painter. It was the sort that makes even a Neapolitan ice-cream feel warmer.

To take a photograph is a fatal pastime in Naples, since the whole street, soon followed by the entire neighbourhood appear upon the scenes, demanding that a snapshot should be taken of their smiling selves. He who hesitates to beat a hurried retreat is lost.

The next day started in some uncertainty for the flyers. Excessive hotel charges raised the first signs of storm. But there was a stern Scotch strain about the party, coupled to more than a dash of fighting Irish, that proved equal to the occasion. We rejected an offending hotel bus, summoned a taxi in its stead, packed up as tightly as a sardine tin for less than half the original charge, and soon reached the aerodrome.

The next stage in the flight to India lay across the Straits of Messina to Catania, in Sicily.

The Moths nosed their way through unexpected cloud, soft-floating and billowing out in white puffs, and with grey masses of flying overcloud that brought the rain. Dodging the worst of the storm, the aircraft were soon over Sicily, the romantic land of lotus-eaters and sybarites, guarded by Scylla and Charybdis, through whose dreaded portals has passed much of the old romance and legend of classic times. Ulysses, the many-wiled, had come this way, sailing across the wine-dark sea on his return from Troy to get copy for his Odyssey; the aviators looking down at Messina from the crystal air might have been compared to some modern argonauts, in quest, not of the Golden Fleece, but of the high, white coverlet that guards the secrets of Everest.

The colours of Sicily wooed by wine and song, seem more vital and vivid than elsewhere. She has always been something of an international honey-pot and now she fills the profitable rôle of tourist trap.

The steep streets of the seaside towns were filled with the black, beetle-like figures of the devout on their way to church, reminding all that it was the Sabbath, though the summoning bells were inaudible. Houses showed up as white dots and gardens were orange groves. Dry river-beds ran down to the sea at frequent intervals, spanned by wide bridges bearing witness to the thirsty propensities of the streams that in winter and summer sign the pledge and go dry, but in spring are full of jubilant waters racing from the mountain sides. Mount Etna, cousin to Vesuvius and Stromboli, was found smoking its pipe and wearing, as usual, its hat of clouds, so that although Clydesdale climbed to an altitude of 10,000 feet, he was unable to catch a glimpse of the snow-covered crater.

At Catania, the luck of the party, which had accompanied them all along the route, now decided it was time to take a holiday. In anticipation of a sea crossing of over a hundred miles in a one-engined machine, and the reaction that comes with the thought of water instead of solid earth beneath the fuselage, the flyers had to take due precautions; and the strength and direction of the wind, visibility for navigation, petrol range, and engine efficiency were considered with more than usual care.

Before they could start, they found themselves under arrest, and at the disposal of the police for flying in all innocence over a prohibited area. By the time Naples had wired fresh instructions, the following wind had become a head gale and all hope of an easy flight to Tunis soon evaporated. Twice they were driven back to Catania by the strength of the storms that soon developed. Terrific lightning flashed and the air was full of bumps and violence. Three days of waiting followed. Finally permission was granted from Rome to move across the island to the forbidden aerodrome of Trapani, 150 miles nearer the African coast. By the time the permit had arrived, however, Trapani was declared unfit for use after the heavy rains, the risk of damaging a machine landing on a water-logged course being considered too great. No Italians were allowed to come down at Trapani; but the wheels of English aeroplanes are larger than those of Italian machines, and two of the pilots had come from Renfrew in rainy Scotland. McIntyre walked all over the Catania aerodrome, showing the layer of dirt on his boots to the Commandant. He explained that the muddy safety-line was much lower down his leg than the one employed in Scotland. Finally, after much persuasion he won the day. The three Moths battled their way to Trapani and awaited once more the verdict of the elements. The local inhabitants shook their heads and croaked like ravens. There was the poor

Signorina Angelica who left on such a day as this and failed to land the other side. There were vivid details of a reckless Italian Count who knew better than his mechanic and had never been seen again.

Storms blew up at intervals, and the wind was still a gale, but news from Tunis was better, and on the following day, waving farewell to the lugubrious guardians, the flyers sallied out over the sea. For four days the weather had acted as highwayman and held them at bay; when they dared it to delay them longer it surrendered.

The 'planes flew on a compass course between the storms; only the passing of time gave the occupants the strength of wind encountered. As the land disappeared behind, none came into view in front. There was ample time for misgiving. At last the leading machine gave a joyful waggle with its wings. McIntyre could see a crocodile-coloured shore. He was greeted by the warm breath of Africa, tropical, exotic, that fans the cheek.

North Africa is like a very old man who can do little work, but likes to sit and brood in the sun. Much of his day is devoted to sun-bathing. If he has a beard to pull, well and good, his meditations may last the longer and be the pleasanter. Africa is an ancient, many-wrinkled genie that was once, in the days of the Saracens, a genius. Yet to the aerial traveller, the arid, puckered face of the land is reminiscent not of age and decay so much as of unchangeable gigantic destiny. Like the Near East, it re-awakens the memory to flashes of old forgotten things which in a mysterious way still supply the vitality and interest for the present day.

The first impressions of low-lying shores and pointing palm trees, give more than a hint of the continent's giant frame and of the bones of empires that have flourished and turned to desert dust. It looks a land of desolate sandy wastes lost in immensity, shimmering beneath a pitiless sun; yet North Africa contains many fertile valleys and beautiful areas, and perhaps of all the continents it is most suitable for flying. Soon the Sahara, eight and a half times the size of Europe, whose sands can burn shoe-leather and whose far horizons have swallowed up whole caravans, is to be irrigated by the greatest water scheme man has ever had the boldness to conceive or put into practice. The engineers will be the same who built the Panama Canal, and the waters of the Mediterranean will be brought in from the Tunis side. This grandiose undertaking will one day not only make the desert blossom like a rose garden, but will remove much of the danger for aircraft traversing the wilderness.

Though they had left Sicily at 1.17 and the distance was only ninety-five miles, the flyers did not pass over Carthage, and land at Tunis aerodrome, until 4.27. Tunis has the most picturesque bazaars in all Africa, and its attractions had increased for the party while it was remaining an unreachable goal. Charming French officers insisted on taking the party to their mess, where their arrival was celebrated with speeches and the Entente was cordially celebrated in champagne.

The rest of the way to Cairo is desert flying, and except for short cuts follows the coast-line. It is a well-defined route, boasting far more traffic than is generally known. At one landing-ground there was a man from Nairobi making his fourteenth journey home; at another two Hungarians dropped unexpectedly out of the clouds; at yet another there was a Londoner. The arrival of English flyers is an ordinary occurrence and a bi-weekly air mail links up the Italian towns and stations in Tripoli. The aerodromes are large and fairly good. The party arrived at one landing-ground just as the setting sun illuminated the desert with a rosy floodlight, the air laden with scent from the thousand and one wild flowers that stud the Sahara after rainstorms in early spring. A be-ribboned Mayor acted as host. The machines were swiftly stored away in the big hangar by well-trained natives, and all the resources of the mess were forthcoming, including such titbits as the time from Big Ben and news from London.

An entrancing spot on the coast is Mersa Matruh, in the western desert. Some of the flyers knew this lonely bay years ago when it was quite undeveloped. It is now invested with a modern hotel and a rumour that King Fuad of Egypt contemplates building a summer palace here. History will repeat itself if Mersa Matruh becomes a monarch's home again; for it was here that in Roman days Cleopatra, Queen of charmers, entertained Mark Antony in her palace overlooking the violet and emerald waters of the bay and flanked by alluring deep blue lagoons.

The outlines of several lost cities can be seen from the air along this coast, as also the great irrigation cisterns built by the Romans in which to store the rainfall, and provide, like Joseph, for lean years. From the air, too, the division between the sandy desert and the broad strip of green, cultivated land watered by the Nile, looks as if it might have been cut by a sword.

Two days' rest in Cairo provided a welcome break in the journey. Engines as well as personnel were in need of rest and attention. Everyone made full use of their time. The Pyramids were found to retain their mystic glamour when seen from the air, the Sphinx's gaze through the distant windows of time and space remains quite unruffled by the approach of man's latest invention, but the sycamore chariots of Tutankamen encased in their gold, turn back many a page in the creaking story of transport development.

The second part of the journey, east of Egypt, brought fresh conditions and added interest. Leaving behind the friends who had showered hospitality upon them in Cairo, the aviators hurried eastward in front of a sandstorm, rose above it into clear air and were soon crossing from Africa to Asia.

Over the hills of Judah the visibility was good, affording intimate glimpses of such places as Jerusalem, Bethlehem and Nazareth.

Seen from the air, the best guide-book for Palestine becomes the Bible. The Holy Land, and the life-story of the Founder of Christianity, unfolded itself in a series of pictures that have all the mingled grandeur and simplicity of the parables. Passing swiftly across the granite hills with their amethyst shadows, the clamour of conflicting races and chattering guides, the tawdry display of man-made monuments that disfigure so many of the sacred sites upon the ground, are forgotten or remain unseen. Simplicity counts again. An aerial view of Palestine can bring a clearer sense of its religious reality and its emotional reactions, than can many days spent visiting such places in detail. Gone is the shadow of the donkey and the dragoman; in its stead there is a sense of wings.

The Holy Land can best be visualised in the air as the largest oasis in the world, saved from the clutching fingers of the encroaching desert by the Jordan river, that, rising in a cave in Mount Hermon, flows to an unknown end deep in the underworld of the Dead Sea. On one side is the fierce halation of the desert, on the other the gentler influence of the sea. But it is only in modern times that the men who go down to the sea in ships have outnumbered those who looked to the Arabian hinterland and the vanished Empires of Hittite, Egyptian and Assyrian.

Palestine to-day has few trees. This is due to the fact that the Turk once taxed trees, with the result that the needy inhabitants cut them down. Jerusalem itself, capital of Crusaders and Christians, is grey and grim, as befits a town rebuilt so many times and that has withstood so many terrible sieges. The chief work nowadays is given by earthquakes. All over this part of the world aeroplanes will be the policemen of the future.

Leaving behind the shining green dome of the mosque of Omar, the last landmark to be seen in Jerusalem, the party flew over Jericho and the mountains of Moab making for Amman, the British Air Force station at the beginning of the Baghdad route. This was the first landing at a British aerodrome since the start of the flight from Heston.

Amman is an up-to-date station full of flowers, fresh vegetables and cheerful English voices. King Abdullah, the ruler of Transjordania, an enlightened potentate, has a large white house on a hill, built for him by the British Government.

The Baghdad route was of special interest, for Fellowes had been in command of the detachment that constructed the original track in 1921, linking up the capital of the Caliphs with Cairo six hundred miles away. The old track ploughed by lorry wheels, has been straightened out, and is now well marked with signs and numbered circles, that are made still clearer by the laying of an old pipe line. How necessary these friendly guides become can be understood, when it is realised that for vast distances the ground is so similar in appearance that no matter how fast a machine is moving, it always appears to be in the same place. Without wireless, the chances of being found, if forced down in uncharted areas, are as remote as that of meeting a camel in a New York street.

A sandstorm was reported following hard upon the heels of the travellers and dogging their tracks ever since they had left Egypt. In their hurry to avoid it, they had the misfortune to run into its brother coming from the reverse direction.

Sandstorms in the Near East are the most deadly peril that can be encountered in an aeroplane. They arrive without warning and seemingly without purpose. A car or a camel can be halted, but it is difficult to land an aeroplane under blinding conditions in which ground and air are indistinguishable. Sometimes it is possible to get high up and above the storm, but often sand and dust ascend to enormous and unexpected heights, as was to be experienced later in the Himalayas. Aircraft, in fact, are not yet able to regard sandstorms with impunity, and the day when they will be able to do so is still far ahead. Enveloped in a choking yellow cloud, losing each other at frequent intervals, going backwards and forwards, flying so low that they almost touched the track, the three Moths experienced a nightmarish interlude before they were able to grope their way to the safety of the next landing-ground at Rutbah Fort.

A six-wheeler transport coach which had brought in its passengers for dinner on their way to Damascus, was parked by the side of an ancient Ford car filled to overflowing with pilgrims from Mecca, their household goods piled high upon the wings. Hard by, were three lorries loaded with police and machine-guns, guarding a party of murderers and sheep-stealers rounded up a hundred miles away; a private car, a cavalcade of camels, and the three Moths picketed outside, completed this representative collection of transport, old and new.

With the formidable exception of sandstorms, flyers over North Africa and the Near East are having matters more and more their own way. They have no spectre of thirst to torment them, nor, like the Bedouin, need they have a terror of alcohol that under those naked skies so easily leads along the path to destruction and madness. They need feel no longer that sense of alienation and hostility which men of the sea experience when first they encounter the long, flat yellow spaces of the earth, at once sinister and sensuous. It is as though they were offered tickets that it has taken four thousand years to produce, entitling them to receive, alike, the freedom of past and present.

All along this region wind the immemorial caravan routes of Bible times. Abraham, the patriarch farmer, came this way travelling with his numberless flocks journeying out of Mesopotamia; Lot pitched his tent towards Sodom and Gomorrah, now covered by the salt waters of the Dead Sea; Zenobia, Queen of Palmyra, took the yellow road, and Sheba herself bound on an embassy to Solomon the great king. Strings of camels, often led by a diminutive donkey with a jingling bell, appear over the sand-hills and vanish like a dream. Panting motor-cars overtake each other on the plain, and occasionally other aeroplanes passing by, present a striking contrast to the old order of transport. Heaven and Hell meet in the desert and the tourist sometimes finds himself on the road to nowhere.

Syria is a land better watered than Palestine, and rich in relics of a past, much of whose history has been the Bible. At the foot of the Tiger ridge of Lebanon lies Damascus, the oldest living city in the world.

In the imagination of the East the ancient capital of the Omayyad Caliphs has lingered as a legend of loveliness. Just as there are great men who centre all the genius of an epoch in their lives, so are there certain cities that by their atmosphere and association seem to symbolise the meaning of a nation. Such a city is Damascus—a story-book that characterises in its pages the heroic past of Islam, all its wars and wonderings and wanderings. The Greeks called it "beautiful," the Arabs "Pride of the Earth"; Mohammed viewing from afar this emerald in the wilderness refused to enter lest he should no longer wish to seek Paradise. Girdled in green orchards of walnut and pomegranate, rendered musical and populous by the rills of the Abana and Pharpar rivers, Damascus has played a princely part in all the ancient commerce of the East.

Laden camel caravans have passed down the Street-Called-Straight or Strait, linking up the trade routes between Babylon and Persia, Arabia, Asia and India, bringing up merchandise from Palmyra and Aleppo to the Mediterranean. By association and position the town has been the eye of Arabia, a walled city of wonder to Nomad and Ishmaelite, a lure and a magnet to almost every conqueror who has entered the debatable land that separates Asia from Africa.

Saladin, himself, the mightiest Sultan who ever lived, spent his boyhood here, and made the town his head-quarters in the war against the crusading Franks. This most chivalrous of Sultans was almost the only Oriental despot to rule his subjects by love, not fear. It must have been a strange sight to see him riding by in his simple black tunic and turban, taking out his gorgeously-clad, middle-aged ministers for exercise at the noble game of "mall," or polo, a sport he loved and which the Arabs introduced to Europe.

Damascus, like Constantinople, is still a source of inspiration for the entire Moslem East, though its importance is dwindling with the opening of Western sea and air routes. In the bazaars and booths is a polyglot humanity, Arabs and Africans, smiling Syrians, Druses, Lebanese, negroes from Nejd, and tall Bedouins with the stiff, upright walk of those who ride camels. Modern motor-cars play leap-frog over the cobbles, and little donkeys glance lazily at them as they pass in endless streams down the Burlington Arcade of the East. The perfumes of Arabia are not lacking, though gone are most of the glories of damask silk and steel. Southwards stretches a vast dusty plain to Baghdad and the southern sea. Damascus is so old that nobody will ever know its age. If Troy was built to the sound of music, Damascus was, and still is, being raised to the sound of running water, the talisman of the town.

In the air all angles of approach tend to become fresh ones. Yet in this cradle-land of civilisation the past still manages to be the present, and to be out of date, or before the time of dates. It is just another synonym for being important, and the traveller cannot help sometimes reversing the process of thought and wondering what would have been the influence of an aeroplane on antiquity.

What would Elijah have said had two aeroplanes suddenly appeared to feed him in place of the two ravens? What would the plague of locusts have done had they found themselves subdued by a flight of enormous mechanical birds? What would have been the cry of the Israelites when fleeing from Egypt, if proud Pharaoh had suddenly stepped from his chariot into his secret bomber and taken up the pursuit?

But the Near East is still a grave and contemplative place, bearded with benevolence, slow moving, where the wanderer comes face to face with Destiny, and with himself—so that iests when made are generally personal ones.

Before reaching Baghdad, the flyers passed over the territory of the Akhwan tribe, perhaps the most enthusiastic in their attitude towards aviation of any of the wandering Bedouins. They are constantly on the move and carrying out raids on their neighbours, which are governed by the strictest rules of conduct. One day they are rich and the next deprived of all they possess. Like most Arabs, they are chivalrous to those whom they admire. When on the march, the Akhwan tribe has a strange custom, for one man goes ahead to throw a mantle over a bush to reserve the site for the camp. Although other wayfarers may pass, no one will dream of trespassing on this ground however attractive and desirable it may look.

If Damascus is the father of cities, Baghdad can be described as its prodigal son. Once the historic capital of Haroun al Raschid, immortalised by the greatest story book of all time, a centre of trade, and a home of mystery, learning and romance, the Baghdad of to-day is not the Baghdad of the Arabian Nights. Palaces, gardens and courtiers have gone, and in their place is a dejected-looking collection of modern hovels and mud houses feeding on the dole of past greatness. Gradually, it is being transformed into a city of the West. Baghdad is on the Tigris, the Euphrates flowing thirty miles to the east, and the country is flat, desolate and devoid of the glamour of Palestine and Syria.

The Everest fliers were forewarned about Baghdad and knew that not a trace of the ancient city of enchantment remains, so were spared the disillusionment that awaits those who arrive dreaming of the romantic beauties conjured up by its legendary name. Some writers say that Baghdad's romance and mystery are still revealed to those who woo her assiduously and penetrate beneath the sordid dirty exterior of the modern town. This time Baghdad showed no favours. She barred entrance by a veil of sand, held our party against their will when the day was propitious, and, when we did escape, sent out after us a yellow cloud of darkness.

The city was left in an atmosphere of whirling sand, but after receiving a report that Shaiba was clear, a sandstorm engulfed the little aerial fleet, which was flying in close formation in the hope of keeping together. Acting on advice, they clung to the railway line, the three machines creeping along a few hundred feet above the ground. For an hour and a half they felt their way through the gloom growing ever worse and worse, till at length the leading machine signalled that it was about to turn. The others followed suit, but in the instant of turning vanished from sight. Nothing could be seen but the dense yellow fog and dim outline of the railway line below.

To search for other machines in such conditions is futile and may easily lead to collision. Fellowes turned his machine again convinced that he could get out quicker that way and, still clinging to the railway, groped his way again towards Shaiba. Fortune favours the resolute, and within a few minutes came a perceptible lessening in the density of the sand. A dim white circle on the ground outlined itself, showing they were over an aerodrome, but holding on to his course they emerged into clear atmosphere, at least thirty miles of visibility and good clean air to breathe. Only those who have flown can realise the relief at emerging from the sand and darkness into the clear blue sky, but the pleasure was marred by the thought that the others were still entangled in that foul yellow cloud. The impossibility of letting them know how near they were to the edge of the sandstorm was galling and induced a mental gloom that was almost as perceptible as that of the sand.

However, three hours later news came in that both Clydesdale and McIntyre had landed safely, first on flat ground near a railway station and later at the Ur aerodrome, and would come on to Shaiba the next morning. With Clydesdale in the Fox Moth were Shepherd and Hughes, the latter suffering from stomach trouble, a pleasure neither to himself nor to his companions. All three spent the night in the railway station, a record one for discomfort.

This adventure and its worries resulted from being held up in Baghdad for the whole of the previous day—a perfect one for flying. The permits to fly through Persia, due to meet us on arrival, were not forthcoming. It was Friday, the Iraqi Sabbath, government offices were closed, and the Iraqi official brains, even when sought in their homes, were unable to function. No trace of the missing permits could be found. Nothing could be done except to wire Teheran and hope for action in reply without too much of the delay common to Persia. The following morning the permits were produced from a pigeon hole in Baghdad, where they had been resting for at least a fortnight.

THE FLIGHT TO INDIA

The flyers, who had not been beguiled by the faded charms of Baghdad, now began to think of the end of the journey and the prospects of arriving ahead of time. A certain uneasiness began to appear for the first time. Persian officials have been known to force unwanted hospitality upon passers-by, holding them up for days while they investigated some trifling omission in permits. Consciences were not quite clear. Medical permits were on the doubtful side, and there was a distinct vagueness about McIntyre in the official permit. For him the inside of a Persian prison and a long siesta upon a Persian carpet seemed a quite possible fate. McIntyre, one of the most courageous of mortals, refused to take any interest in the journey extending beyond Persia, in spite of the ingenious schemes that were put forward for his rescue should the worst occur. All went well, however, the residents proved most hospitable folk, and no difficulties arose with the officials.

The flight along the Persian Gulf was rendered enthralling and interesting by the pranks played upon the eyesight by different formations of sand and rock. Often whole cathedrals and fortresses would leap into view, seemingly the work of giants, and it was difficult to believe that these effects had had for architects the fantastic force of wind and storm.

This geological strata continues down most of the shores or the piratical coast, where the main occupation of the inhabitants has always been gun-running and slave-dealing. Even now, despite the constant attentions of British gun-boats from Aden and Perim, the old game is still continued, to a lesser extent, with the old gamble of profit and loss, and shares invested in human beings. Slaves are usually rounded up in Somaliland and the highlands of Abyssinia and shipped across the Arabian Sea when it is hoped no one is looking.

Curiously enough, African girls, in many cases, are said to welcome with eagerness the arrival of the Arab slaver, much as English boys will run away to sea for the sake of adventure; it gives her a chance of seeing the world, and if she is lucky, ending up in the luxury of some rich Mussulman's town house.

But for the men and boys, the future is a most unpleasant thought. The slavers no longer deal in large consignments of misery; they ferry over a few people in a small boat, limiting their haul to small and select quantities, after the manner of a cracksman who knows the police are watching the "Fences."

From the Persian Gulf, the next stepping-stone in the chain of travel was Mekran. The flyers found a rest-house at Gwadar in Baluchistan, if four mud walls, a leaking roof and two wild-looking hillmen can be called anything so western. It was a decided change after the standards of comfort supplied by the Imperial Airways desert houses. But food in the east is often produced like a conjuring trick out of anywhere. In four hours' time, thanks to an obliging telephone that answered in English, the flyers were sitting down to a six-course dinner in a neighbouring town, on the outskirts of the British Empire in Asia. Hospitality is not easily defeated in the East.

Close to Sind there is an arid, waterless belt of country, without grass or vegetation, that has been nicknamed, "the frying-pan of the world!" Only camels and aeroplanes can tackle this inferno.

A few hours' flight in the cool morning air above layers of fleecy clouds, a drive downwards into the damp hot atmosphere of Sind, and the welcoming houses of Karachi came into view. Behind, unwinding like the reel of a cinema, in which operators and actors are one, lay 6,000 miles of travel and adventure. The beauties and variety, the comfort, discomfort and contrasts of a journey by air across Europe, Africa and part of Asia, remained; and above all the comradeship of experiences shared on a high adventure.

*　　*　　*　　*　　*　　*

Blacker was the first of the expedition to reach Karachi. He had flown out from Croydon on the same day that the Moths left Heston, going in the comfortable modern liners of Imperial Airways and arriving a fortnight before the other flyers, some time therefore elapsed before he was able to impress on them

HYDERABAD IN SIND

THE GREAT CASTLE AT JODHPUR

how much quicker and more comfortable his choice had been than theirs.

In those days, Imperial Airways came to an abrupt and anticlimatic end at Karachi, so he was forced to perform the long journey across India by train.

First, however, there were details to be arranged at Karachi, where the Aircraft Depot had so kindly consented to erect and test our aeroplanes, in their usual prompt and efficient way. So admirable is the organisation at Karachi that the explanations were short and simple and the chief observer travelled on to Delhi. Here again the Royal Air Force not only proffered every assistance but indicated how efficiently that assistance was going to be given.

After a brief sojourn in the hospitality of New Delhi he hurried on to Purnea by way of Bhagalpur. The latter town is easily reached from the main line of rail, but from there onward to Purnea, the land journey becomes almost an adventure.

The distance is but forty miles in a direct line, but it takes ten hours or more to get there.

At one phase in the journey, after some travel on narrow-gauge lines, the voyager finds himself on a smart well holystoned paddle steamer, of uncertain age, on the broad expanse of Mother Ganges. At night, with feeble lights blinking on the dim sandbank shores, the voyage seems mysterious and unending, as the paddle wheels chunk their way up the swirling current. Soon enough, one is back on the jolting narrow gauge, making change after change. Our observer motored over the last twenty miles to Purnea to encounter an hospitable welcome. There was no need to stay long, for the arrangements asked for by letter were well under way in the capable hands of Mr. Came, the Executive Engineer of the Public Works Department. It took a day or so to inspect the site of the advanced landing-ground at Forbesganj, to select positions for the canvas hangars and tube wells, and to discuss arrangements with Mr. Sharma, the Deputy Commissioner, and Mr. Bion of the police, each emulating the other in their efforts to help the expedition.

Blacker then returned to Bhagalpur under the hospitable roof of Mr. Dain, the Commissioner, the connecting link between the Government of the Province at Patna and the local officers at Purnea.

The next stage was to Delhi to meet Clydesdale and McIntyre, who had meanwhile arrived in the Moths. Fellowes had decided that it would be wise for the two pilots to obtain personal and preliminary acquaintance with the air route across India, so as to make the subsequent flight with the Westlands as safe as possible. Thus there would be no risk of not knowing the way or of misjudging the distance to the next stage where fuel could be obtained.

The three in two Moths, the Fox and the Gipsy, therefore flew first to Delhi and then on through the air over Cawnpore, Allahabad and Benares to Gaya. They passed by Sasaram, nearly over the wonderful mausoleum tomb of Sher Shah the Mogul emperor, and then over the long railway bridge across the Sone river, to the new landing-ground at Gaya, somewhat difficult to find on the south-west of the city.

"It was on our way here," says Blacker, "that we four, in the two Moths received our first wonderful sight of the mountain. From Gaya we flew towards the great grey sandbanks of the Ganges, athwart our course.

"Beyond, suffused in a dense purple haze, lay the plains of Bihar, Asoka's ancient kingdom.

"Suddenly, up from out of the hard straight line where the haze met the azure basin of the sky, there appeared three wondrous points of white.

"Over our right wings we saw, wreathed in clouds, that which was Kangchenjunga, and ahead there enthralled our gaze, the far distant crests of Everest and Makalu.

"Three immaculate snowy pinnacles swam majestically alone over this wine-dark sea of mist. We could scarcely bear to glide down to land, and so to lose the beauty of this sight, even for an hour.

"At Bhagalpur, the *Boggleywala* of Jos. Sedley and *Vanity*

THE LARGEST BUILDING IN THE WORLD
(Karachi)

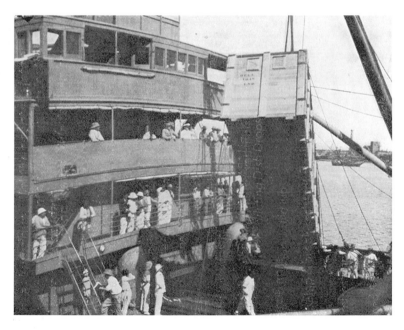

UNLOADING THE HOUSTON-WESTLAND FROM THE P. AND O. S.S. DALGOMA AT KARACHI,
ON 7TH MARCH

Fair, we found not only efficient and energetic preparations in hand for our expedition, but the warmest and most cordial hospitality, from Mr. Dain, the Commissioner, downwards.

"We flew on, the forty miles to Purnea, to find the landing ground already levelled and work well in hand on the hangars.

"The hospitality and kindness of the people of Purnea rivalled that of Bhagalpur, from Rajas and broad-acred planters down to the humblest peasants, who made gay paper triumphal arches, decorated with very creditable aeroplanes of tinsel.

"So good were all arrangements that were being made on our behalf, that we were soon able to fly back to Karachi to bring up the big Westlands for their battle with those elemental forces.

"Allahabad was our first night's stop on the return journey. Here to our misfortune, after we had lashed down our aeroplane for the night, a sudden and terrific storm arose in a few moments. Gusts of wind at over eighty miles an hour tore down hundreds of trees, unroofed buildings, and plunged the city in darkness. We were then in the Police Chief's house, eight miles from the aerodrome, arranging for a guard for the machine, when the sudden tempest came up out of a cloudless evening sky. Hastening back in alarm we found the machine uprooted from the great blocks of concrete, the thick hemp mooring ropes snapped, and the graceful little aeroplane, which had been lifted bodily and high into the air, a pathetic crumpled wreck.

"So we made our way sadly by train to Delhi, where a generous Indian gentleman, Mr. Chawla, who had earned fame by being the first Indian to fly himself out to India, lent us his own Puss Moth, at a moment's notice.

"It is enough to say that this was characteristic of the warm-hearted attitude of India towards our expedition.

"Meanwhile, Etherton had been invited by the Maharaja of Nepal to the fine and seldom visited capital of Khatmandu, to attend the coronation festivities there, the story of which is told elsewhere.

"His Highness was kind enough now to renew to him his

assurance that the necessary second flight would be sanctioned subject to certain conditions.

"It had been recognised at an early stage in the organisation of the expedition that to secure adequate scientific results two flights would probably be necessary.

"Permission for the flight had been given by the Government 'purely for scientific purposes' and it was hardly to be expected that all the mass of complicated and delicate mechanisms would operate without a hitch in those terrific extremes of heat and cold.

"It was a great relief to us to hear that we might expect to receive this essential permission. Without it, there was a serious possibility of some minor hitch in the first flight, compelling us to return in ignominy without achieving the objects which had already been broadcast to the world.

"But before we heard this welcome news, we were back in Karachi where the two Westlands had been assembled, ready for their test flights. We took them up to over 33,000 feet in that pellucid air and found all well. In fact so efficient were Messrs. Siebe Gorman's electrically heated suits, that the observers' knees became uncomfortably hot. Without much difficulty we reduced the heating elements and with excellent results.

"An interesting observation in connection therewith was that the upper air at this altitude was twenty Centigrade degrees warmer than in England in the previous month. This was contrary to expectation, for we had anticipated the same degree of cold almost everywhere at that great height. Hence no doubt the excess of warmth in the suits.

"There followed the now accustomed hurly-burly of departure. A thousand items had to be packed and dispatched, some by train and some by air. Many, such as the oxygen and the signal flares demanded special transportation, whilst at the last moment it was discovered that the spare propellers would go into no ordinary railway wagon. Finally a horse-box was found to fill the bill.

THE FLIGHT TO INDIA

"Thus on the 22nd March, after a fortnight in Karachi, the expedition bade farewell to the officers and men of that efficient Aircraft Depot, and flew in the two Westlands and three Moths across the trackless desert of Rajputana to Jodhpur.

"It was in this way that all our preparations at Karachi had been completed and now we had no less than five aeroplanes.

"The two big Westlands, which had been assembled so efficiently by the Royal Air Force in the Aircraft Depot at Drigh Road, were all ready for the very humdrum task of transporting themselves through Delhi to the advanced landing-ground at Purnea from which they were to fly to the mountain.

"It seemed very unbefitting for their dignity that these two fine machines should be loaded up with miscellaneous suitcases, blankets, sun helmets and the like, not to mention a few copies of the works of Messrs. P. G. Wodehouse and Edgar Wallace, for perusal during the long hours of flight across the deserts and over the sun-baked plains of Hindustan. There were two passengers in each of the big machines for a rating of the Royal Air Force was carried in addition to the observer in each case. Both intended to improve the shining hour, very literally shining, by getting in as much photographic practice as possible on the way from place to place. The fitters were to have an easy time in the air with their heads supported on blankets and their feet tucked away in odd corners and recesses of oxygen cylinder racks, but they had the benefit, on the other hand, of the Edgar Wallaces and the P. G. Wodehouses. The observers found plenty to do when anything was in sight, but it must be confessed that there were a great many hundred miles of simply nothing at all and not the most conscientious photographer could bring himself to expend plates and films upon it. However, what there was there was good and extremely interesting. Not only was it interesting, but it was of real practical utility as a target for the many cameras of different sorts. This was the more so because the quality of the light was essentially different from anything we encountered in England, or even on the flight out across the Middle East. Not only did it differ in quality but, as might be expected, it was very much more intense. It might be thought at the first blush that these two characteristics were one and the same, but a lesson drawn from the work of the expedition taught us to make a difference between the two, and guarded us against the idea that because the whole sky was entirely blue with a sun of brass blazing down from the centre of it, the intensity of light for photographic purposes would necessarily be very high. We found curious paradoxes in this matter which could no doubt be explained by scientists as being due to humidity in the air and also to the presence of dust which was so impalpable as to be indistinguishable to the naked eye, and this dust we found to be present in the air even at amazingly high altitudes. We were destined to receive very great surprises from this source later on.

"However, we resolved not to miss any photographic practice, being convinced in our minds that even the most experienced of us had much to learn.

"As we took off from the Karachi aerodrome in the usual cloud of dust thrown up by the tail skids, 'that agricultural implement that adorns even modern aircraft to the disgust of aerodrome owners,' we came soon upon a marvellous tracery of creeks of which the shore of the Arabian Sea is here composed. A lace-like network which stretches for miles and miles from the Port of Karachi, dividing the featureless, bare, sunburnt yellow of the Plains of Sind from the bright blue of the sea, it was a sight indeed to be remembered. Hardly had our eyes left its amazingly intricate tracery than they were caught by another spectacle which was nothing less than the largest building in the world. This is the vast airship shed or hangar which was built to accommodate the ill-fated ships of the Imperial Service of airships and of which the two sisters met their end, one on the ridge of Beauvais, with many gallant souls on board, and the other at the hands of the breakers who, with steam-roller and oxy-acetylene jet destroyed the hopes of many lives as they tore down its beautiful shape into flattened tangled masses of metal. Whether or not the airships were to be regretted, no one could say, but the pathos of the sight of that tremendous building struck everyone as we all flew over it and its near-by mooring mast, together in formation. The only advantage which it seems to possess at present is that its existence enables the troops to play two games of football at once under shelter from the midday sun. It is reported, also, that indoor polo is contemplated.

"Soon the two aerodromes were behind us, the civil landing-ground which formed then the blank wall which shut off the efficiency and convenience of Imperial Airways well-run liners from the rest of India, and the Service aerodrome, where our machines had spent those busy weeks.

"Below us there now stretched what seemed to be boundless immensity of yellowy brown plains, here and there broken by ravines cut away in tangled patterns by freshets and spates of the infrequent yearly rains. As one looked more closely these apparently featureless wastes became lined and cut-up by great straightnesses stretching unwaveringly mile upon mile through the deserts. These were the new canals and their countless branches which were destined to bring their trickles of life-giving water from the huge river, the Indus, which would turn the waste into a granary. Every now and then, almost by surprise, a single low building, the canal inspector's rest-house, would appear on the bank of some excavation many hundreds of feet below, cut off as it seemed from any other human habitation.

"Away to the westward over our port wing-tips we could see the distant mountains of Afghanistan, their summits tipped with the whitest snow and wreathed round with nestling white cumulus cloud. Beneath these fairy peaks there came the now familiar severely outlined zone of deep purple haze, which cut off all the middle of the hills from our vision. Below this again, forming a junction as it were between this wine-dark belt and the plains themselves, was this hard, rugged and endlessly broken up maze of brown stony foothills, where the Baluchi and the Brahui wander slowly leading their strings of super-cilious camels. More than four hours passed of such scenes, and, as one's mind became accustomed to the monotony, suddenly there loomed on the horizon to the eastward a thin line of dark green, which soon took shape and brought us back, as we felt, from nothingness into an uninhabited world. We flew closer, and slowly, very slowly—because even at 120 miles an hour nothing seems to happen very fast in the air—this shape took upon itself the form of a big city, which was Hyderabad. It lies on the bank of the Indus and is perhaps unique among cities in India insomuch that every one of its many thousands of white cubical flat-roofed houses was adorned with a curious structure which is called in Persian a 'bad-gir' or wind-catcher. This performs a precisely similar function to the bell-mouthed ventilator which must be so dear to the sea-faring mind because every ship seems to have them sprouting out at every possible corner. The 'bad-gir,' however, is made apparently of thin slabs of stone and therefore, for constructional reasons, no doubt, is prism-shaped and not rounded. It differs, too, from its maritime cousin insomuch that it is not rotatable. It would indeed be difficult, one can see, for a stonemason or bricklayer to construct a rotating ventilator in the materials to which he is accustomed. Fortunately, however, in Hyderabad he is not called upon to do so and *tours-de-force* of this sort are obviated by the convenient fact that the wind blows always from precisely the same quarter. It surges, no doubt, down the stone ventilators and freshens up the inhabitants, and anyone who has experience of the lower Indus valley in summer will no doubt appreciate the blessing of even the smallest puff of wind.

"Hyderabad was a very beautiful sight as we saw it in the bright light of an Indian March with these thousands of cream-coloured houses, their right angles throwing myriad shadows and sharp outlines and all bowered by the dark green of the trees. Along one side of this oasis there ran the broad blue Indus and as the pilots crossed this they throttled down their engines and glided on to a good but dusty landing-ground not far from the little rocky ridge which was covered by an ancient fort. As we landed we were greeted by the presence of a whole brigade of mechanised artillery whose officers let their men break off to inspect these interesting new aeroplanes bound for their distant venture, far away to the north-east.

"The brawny gunners produced cameras from nowhere and the outlines of the Westlands are no doubt enshrined on many feet of celluloid.

"Almost from nowhere there appeared the indefatigable personnel of Messrs. Burma Shell, and in scarcely more time than it takes to describe it our tanks were being filled up in the efficient manner of that far-flung organisation, a manner which at first surprised us from its very excellence but to which in due course from many repetitions we became quite accustomed. As if they had been drilled to it like a beauty chorus, one man produced a huge aluminium funnel, its capacious maw meticulously protected with a double layer of chamois carefully fitted on cane hoops, another produced a little hand-pump of the rotary variety, steel barrels were rolled up as if from nowhere, hoses coupled and soon our special fuel was foaming and gurgling into the hundred gallon tanks. We could not dally very long for we had to be on our way and soon the ground engineers were straining the muscles of their arms at the big crank handles of the inertia starters. The sun was well up in the heavens by then and the comparative cool of the early morning was long past, so that it may well be imagined that the work of coaxing into activity these great engines of nearly 600 h.p. gave rise to many a trickle on several honest brows. However, the Pegasus behaved well and so did the starters, the mechanisms that is to say, whilst the human portion felt that they really had not much more than a few minutes' wholesome morning exercise.

"Soon we were off again, to the accompaniment of a cheer from the assembled gunners and the accustomed cloud of dust from our tail skids. The minutes went on into hours, the photographers took their pictures on their plates and ran their ciné-cameras as long as there was a picture to be taken and then settled down to a fresh contemplation of nothingness, or very nearly nothingness, whilst the pilots scanned the dials of their many instruments and watched how the fuel level went as hour passed after hour.

"The level plains, slightly cultivated and seamed with these long miles of dead straight canals, soon gave way to the characteristic landscape of Rajputana and the wastes of the Great Indian Desert. An immense series of little hills, of sometimes sandy dunes, sometimes bare earth and gravel, are covered for tens of thousands of square miles with unending open scrub and scraggy leafless trees. Hour passed after hour where nothing met the eye but this, until suddenly, again, as we had sighted Hyderabad, there came into our vision the almost legendary city of Jodhpur.

"Here is one of the capitals of present-day Rajput rule, whose princes and nobles trace back their ancestry without gap or flaw for two and three thousand years when the Aryan tribes first rode over the passes from the north into India.

"Jodhpur, with its ancient stone castle on the sandstone cliffs of its hills, set in the midst of a vast desert, seems to have endured unchanged since the dawn of history.

"Invasion after invasion has swept over Northern India, white Huns and yellow Huns, Scythians, Ephthalites, Macedonians and Mongols, the followers of Mahmud and the freebooters of Nadir Shah and of Baber have surged across the valleys of the Indus, but have left Rajputana unshaken; unshaken, that is, until the aeroplane has brought the first change to those ancient countries that they have seen almost since the days of Abraham.

"When we arrived, in the early afternoon of March 22nd, Rolls-Royce cars whisked us away to one of His Highness's palaces, specially allotted for the reception of guests. Here, the Maharaja being away, we were entertained by one of the nobles, Thakur Narpat Singh, a nephew of the famous Sir Pertab Singh. So luxurious were our apartments, and so hospitable our welcome, that grave doubts assailed us lest Jodhpur proved to be the Capua of the expedition and we were unable to tear ourselves away.

THE KUTAB MINAR NEAR DELHI

IMPERIAL DELHI. THE VICEROY'S HOUSE FROM THE AIR

"At Jodhpur there is a pleasing mélange of old time Rajput hospitality with that cameraderie which goes with the airmen of all countries.

"Almost under the shadow of the great castle on the cliffs the Maharaja has built a modern airport and one that is probably the best in Southern Asia. The landing-field possesses a level surface well defined and with modern hangars able to shelter the big Fokker liners of the Royal Dutch Air Line and of the French Company on their long flights to Saigon and Java.

"The Jodhpur Flying Club has a spacious club house and each evening finds it full of enthusiastic pupils and instructors, both Rajput and European. Throughout the State a network of regular landing-grounds has been prepared whose white circles greet the eye of the air traveller.

"Adjacent to the airport is a guest house replete with modern comforts.

"The next day saw us early in the air on our way over the desert to Delhi.

"Now in these few hundred miles we were no longer in sight of the frontier hills to the westward. The long straight lines of the Sind canals were behind us and we flew for hour after hour over immense deserts. Here and there we could see the fine, almost imperceptible line marking the course of the narrow-gauge railway, and every now and then a village of huts ringed round with a formidable thorn fence as a protection against wild animals. Occasionally, athwart our course would appear the straight line of a stark rugged range of hills, the highest rocky crag crowned with an ancient castle.

"Round towers speckled with arrow slits flanked the ancient gateways; we could almost imagine cavalcades of Rajput knights in chain mail on plumed horses riding in beneath the two-fold roar of our Pegasus engines.

"As the day wore on the desert gradually softened its austerity. Clumps of greener trees, larger villages appeared then a blur on the northern horizon beneath the immaculate blue of the sky. It became distinct and we then found ourselves flying towards the stone splendours of Imperial Delhi, set amongst the seven cities of the past.

"To the airman's eye New Delhi possesses a real splendour of its own, hidden perhaps from those who only see Luyten's work from the ground-level. Impressed with its majesty we flew around it to enjoy the spectacle of the vast avenue stretching towards the Arch of Victory and the great colonnaded domes of the Viceroy's house. Save for a slight ground haze, the air had the pellucid clarity of springtime in Northern Hindustan. We enjoyed the rare spectacle, at the same time taking in the weird pillar of the Kutab, the castellated red walls of the Mogul forts, the tempered grey of the ancient lichened stones of Purana Kila, the monochrome of the Jumna's sandbanks all forming a setting for the fresh clean lines of the new city. The observers went hard at it with plate and film, nor did they regret their efforts.

"At last it was time to land to be greeted by our friends of the Delhi Flying Club on the aerodrome hard by the domes of Humayun.

"The Viceroy has done much to lead modern India into the air and it is largely due to him and to Lady Willingdon that the cult of flying is spreading so rapidly amongst the princes.

"Next morning we left our kind hosts, in the chilly dawn, on the last section of our long flight from Heston and Croydon. These early morning flights were calm and smooth in the extreme. Not until the day was well advanced did we feel those unpleasantly disconcerting heat 'bumps' which mar the pleasure of long flights in the East. We decided to enjoy the present and to dismiss from our minds the bumps which were to come. The landscape was new and entirely fresh. Gone were the olive-clad heights of South Europe, the yellow deserts of Arabia and Persia, and the brown hills of Rajputana. We were over the real Hindustan—the basin of the Ganges and the Jumna, the prize of innumerable conquerors, from Alexander of Macedon to the Moguls.

"For untold centuries these plains have been the cockpit of Southern Asia, where Scythian, Macedonian, Bactrian, Rajput,

CLYDESDALE BLACKER

H.E. THE VICEROY BLACKER

Afghan, Mongol, Turk, Maratha and Kizilbash have fought to gain the treasure of the East. Napoleon himself said that 'who holds India holds the world.'

"We could only guess at the great distance of the horizon all around us. No hill could be seen; we flew on in the mathematical centre of that huge flat brown disc, whose edge was a vignette border of purple melting into the blue bowl of the sky.

"The brownness of Upper Hindustan has a peculiar quality of its own. It is not the yellow brown or ochre of the deserts nor the sienna of the hills, nor the ruddiness of sandstone ridges, but a sepia or a bistre. This colour does not belong to any particular item of it, neither to the fields, the yellowy grey tracks, nor the green or blue-green leafage of the trees; yet it is the colour of the countryside as the airman sees it. As the sun climbed up from the dusty rim of our circle of vision we came upon circling kites and vultures. We had first met these unpleasant creatures on the flight from Jodhpur and their numbers increased as we flew over the larger towns of Hindustan. They are a real menace to the aviator, but luckily are seldom seen much above 3,000 feet; at 2,000 or so great flocks of them are frequently encountered. The birds themselves are not anxious for a collision with an aeroplane, but are apt to misjudge the speed at which the machine is coming upon them. It is easy for a vigilant pilot to spot single birds and to dodge them, but it is a different matter when the sky is full of these wheeling pests, for to swerve from one means collision with another. The impact is sufficient to break the propellor or any interplane strut or spar. In a light aeroplane the danger is even more acute and the records of Indian flight are punctuated with disasters from such causes. One safeguard is, of course, to fly high, but this we were unable to do on our eastbound journey owing to the necessity of taking as many photographs as possible to ascertain the light values. So we risked the birds and tried not to heed the narrow escapes when a six-foot vulture whizzed past apparently only a yard from our wing-tip.

"We made our breakfast stop at Allahabad, mentally cursing

the ill-equipped landing-field as our eyes met the wreck of our poor Fox Moth. Here at Allahabad the two great rivers, Jumna and Ganges, meet and here on the tongue of land at the confluence stands the huge red battlemented fortress of the Moguls, visible from afar by its wireless masts. For Allahabad, rather than Delhi, was the old centre of Mogul military power. It commanded the junction of the two rivers of Hindustan. In those days rivers were the highways of commerce and even of strategy. To-day the fort with a garrison of British infantry looks out upon the great steel girders which carry the main lines of rail down to Calcutta and the distant sea.

"On we flew through the unwelcome bumps which the heat of the midday sun brought painfully to our notice. This time we passed north of Sasaram, with its imposing palace tomb of Sher Shah, Mogul Emperor, and of Gaya, that old stronghold of the Dutch venturers in the East Indies, over which their descendants now operate their weekly service of Fokker monoplanes.

"Instead we made our way over the big white houses of green and leafy Patna and its pleasant seeming suburbs of Barrackpore and Bankipore. One might assume that Barrackpore is so called from the fact that since the early days of the Honourable Company there have been the barracks of British troops there, and possibly of French Royal troops before them. One would like to think that Bankipore, standing so picturesquely along the tree-bordered Ganges banks, derives its name from that fact. We were disappointed to find it otherwise. In the slang of the sixteenth century Mogul upper ten, the Banki-Log were the 'smart set,' and so Bankipore was their abiding place, the Mayfair or Belgravia of that world.

"Now the country below us had changed again. The open brown spaces of Hindustan had given way to the park-like landscapes of Bengal, full of green trees, square ponds and lakes, with wooden and wattle huts of thatch, occasionally surrounded by palm trees.

"Now the Ganges changed from our left to our right hand;

Clydesdale   Blacker Ismay

        Fellowes   A.D.C.   Shepherd

    H.E. the Viceroy

H.E. THE VICEROY INSPECTS THE EXPEDITION

ALLAHABAD.   THE MOGUL FORT AT THE JUNCTION OF GANGES AND JUMNA

we pored diligently over the maps identifying here a narrow-gauge railway faintly below us, and there the confused tracery of the split-up channels of some minor river which had probably altered its course a dozen times since the map was made. The clear metalled grand trunk road faded away behind us to give place to almost indistinguishable dusty cart tracks. Soon enough we sighted the familiar trees and the turfy spaces of Purnea. A turn or two around it to announce our arrival, then a few minutes on, and our wheels were trundling smoothly over our own landing-ground of Lalbalu where the big canvas hangars were standing ready to house our machines for their voyage into the unknown."

CHAPTER VIII

NEPAL

THE various members of the party were converging on Purnea in readiness for the great adventure, by different routes as we have seen, Blacker, Fellowes, Clydesdale and McIntyre by air, Etherton by the more comfortable method and luxury of the P. & O.

Etherton stayed a few days with the Governor of Bombay (Major-General Sir F. Sykes) before going on to the base at Purnea, situated approximately 300 miles north of Calcutta in the province of Bihar. Sir Frederick Sykes is himself an airman of repute, and consequently took the greatest interest in our plans.

Etherton travelled overland by rail, going first to Patna, the head-quarters of the Government of Bihar and Orissa. Sir James Sifton, the Governor, and the officers and staff of his administration had made excellent arrangements for the welfare of the expedition at Purnea; no efforts had been spared to ensure its success and we shall see how well the plans worked out under the cordial co-operation and ever-ready help that were accorded.

From Patna to Purnea is a rapid journey when made by air, but a long and tedious business by rail, since it necessitates the crossing of the Ganges in paddle-wheelers which probably commenced life on the Thames during the early 'fifties.

The Ganges looks anything but the holy river it is; slow-moving and muddy waters flowing through a flat and desolate land at this particular point do not impress the traveller, yet there is no river in the world to compare with it in sanctity and the reverence with which it is regarded by millions of

146

His Highness the Maharaja Sir Joodha Shum Shere Jung Bahadur Rana, G.C.I.E.,
Prime Minister and Supreme Commander-in-Chief of Nepal

Hindus, whose greatest ambition is to die on its shores and for their ashes to be cast into the arms of Mother Ganga.

From its source at Gaumukh in the Mountains of Garhwal in the north to the delta in the Bay of Bengal, the river and its banks are holy ground. Where it emerges from the hills at Hardwar is amongst the holiest; here takes place, every twelfth year, apart from other festivals, the celebrated Kumbh Mela, when the planet Jupiter is in the sign Aquarius (Kumbh), an occasion regarded by Hindus as one of the utmost sanctity. The main object of attraction to the pilgrims is the bathing-ghat, or stone stairway, some sixty steps, one hundred feet in width. At the moment judged propitious by the Brahmins, it is the ambition of each to be first in the holy river, for not only will it cleanse them from all unrighteousness, but is a passport to Valhalla, or the Hindu paradise.

Apart from the immense concourse of people there are numberless fakirs, or religious beggars, who practise every form of penance and self-torture to attain salvation. There are those who strip and expose themselves to the sun, surrounded by blazing fires, others who for years have held their arms aloft until by prolonged tension they are unable to resume the normal position.

Beyond the Ganges lies the same flat country, and as we approach Purnea the land becomes less desolate; the roads are wider, with trees on either side, and more cultivation. From the railway-station there extends an ample road which leads us to the large and shady bungalow we are to make our home for the next few weeks.

So we come to Purnea, and with its attractions and the part it played in the life and well-being of the expedition, we shall deal in another chapter.

Satisfied that all was in order and ready for the arrival of the main body of the expedition on 22nd March, Etherton set out for Nepal, which he would reach through Raxaul about 200 miles to the north-west of Purnea.

The object and import of this journey will now be apparent.

FIRST OVER EVEREST

Along the north-eastern confines of India lies the mightiest range of mountains in the world—the Himalayas, or Abode of Snow to quote the Sanskrit term. No other mountain range can compare with them in variety, in the loftiness of their heights, in the grandeur by which they are surrounded, and the halo of mystery and romance which overhangs them.

The inhabitants of varying race and descent who live along their western and south-western borders, have as near neighbours, peaks towering more than 20,000 feet into the skies and glaciers covering hundreds of square miles.

Although the area in question has been traversed by explorers and surveyors, there are parts that have not been studied by the methods of modern geographical science, for the distances are great, transportation is slow and uncertain, and so far as Nepal Sikkim and Bhutan are concerned, the railway has not penetrated, and they are lands that still remain very much of a sealed book to the rest of the world.

The main chain of the Himalayas stands like a wall dividing Tibet and western China from India, and even along the Indian side of the range there is still scope for geographical Alexanders.

It is with Nepal that we are singularly concerned in the story of the Everest flight, for lying as this independent kingdom does on the side nearest to India and having within its limits Everest, Goddess Mother of the mountains, the world's loftiest peak, it was imperative to secure the permission of His Highness the Maharaja of Nepal, which he so generously accorded and enabled us to bring the flight to its triumphal conclusion.

The scientific and geographic world owes much to the vision and foresight of this enlightened ruler, who paved the way for a historic flight and advanced the cause of aviation.

We had envisaged the possibility of a second flight over Everest, and without wishing to impose upon the goodwill of the ruler who had so readily granted permission for the initial attempt, we realised that success or failure of the photographic survey might well depend upon the results of the first crossing of the peak. Should those results be negative a second flight could alone avoid the defeat of our aims. It was therefore deemed of vital importance to secure from the governing authority in Nepal, the requisite licence to make a second attempt in the event of the first being a partial, or total failure from the photographic and survey standpoint.

This then was the task allotted to Etherton, who had preceded the rest of the party by sea and was charged with the task of arranging with the Nepalese chief for this second flight, apart from the other administrative duties devolving on him.

It was a two days' journey to Raxaul, for the narrow-gauge railways are slow and halts at stations frequent.

Raxaul is two miles outside the Nepalese frontier of India; from it starts the Nepal Government railway, which runs to Amlekganj, twenty-six miles within the Terai. The railroad has been cut through the jungle and rises steadily to the terminus, a puffing and grunting affair for the tiny locomotive, which putting forth its best effort manages to average six or seven miles an hour. At this season of the year the jungles were dry and parched, and not at all indicative of a floral beauty which is their strong point after the rains in October and following months.

The Terai runs almost the entire length of the Indian border of Nepal. It contains many species of big and small game, and was constituted a waste land after the war with the British, as an obstacle to the advance of a hostile force from India. This area comprises extensive stretches of reeds and bulrushes running up to a height of fifteen feet, with forest and open patches free from bog and morass which are a feature of the Terai.

It is notorious for malarial fever, is full of mosquitoes, and only during the cold weather from October to March, is it safe for Europeans. During and after the Indian Mutiny in 1857, numbers of rebels, flying from justice, took refuge in the Terai, and even the Nana Sahib, the butcher of Bithoor, he who had ordered the tragedy of Cawnpore, is said to have escaped into there and died from fever.

There is no doubt a lack of authentic information relating to the fate of the Nana, and it is strange that the fate of a man whose deeds were so notorious should continue to be wrapped in mystery.

On the other hand, accounts we endeavoured to verify relate that the tyrant passed through the fever-stricken Terai in safety, and lived for many years in disguise in Nepal. Various stories were current as to the life of the Nana in Nepal, which may have been exaggerated as stories always are with the re-telling and lapse of time. However, a forest officer told Etherton some years ago that a survivor of the Nana's party declared that their chieftain had died in the Terai when a fugitive from British justice. Be that as it may, his fate will always be shrouded in a halo of mystery, and whether he died in those malarious swamps, or lived happily ever afterwards, the Nana Sahib will go down to posterity as the chief actor in a tragedy which horrified the world, for those figuring in the drama were women and children, and the stage villain one greater than a tragedy writer has ever had the boldness to conceive.

At Amlekganj, the railway terminus, East meets West again in curious contradiction. The shops of thatched huts with their contents exposed to innumerable flies and dust raised by bullock-carts and motor-lorries, seem strangely out of place with petrol pumps, and other things incidental to the modern way. Civilisation in the form of motor transport has penetrated to Amlekganj and you mount a lorry passenger-car, which takes your luggage and yourself, under the guidance of a Jehu whose one ambition seems to be to take corners and speed along the highway as fast as his engine will allow.

The Nepalese have constructed an excellent road from Amlekganj to Bhimpedi, twenty-eight miles, passing over the range dividing the Terai from the valleys at the foot of the mountains. The Nepalese can certainly lay claim to distinction as road builders; they have bridged various torrents with

A MAIN SQUARE IN KHATMANDU

BUILDINGS ARE ORNATE IN SEQUESTERED KHATMANDU

commendable skill, and so rendered the journey a pleasure
instead of the nightmare it formerly was, when one had perforce to journey by night in a dhooly, looking like a coffin on
poles, to the monotonous chant of dhooly bearers bored with
the task of carrying the traveller.

We will now allow Etherton himself to tell the story of his
journey to Nepal.

"Bhimpedi, the end of the motor road, lies at the foot of the
hills and here I found ponies and servants sent by the Maharaja from Nepal. From here on the road to the capital of the
hermit kingdom, is a long climb to Sisagarhi, a fort perched
2,500 feet up and commanding a view of the surrounding
country. The road up to Sisagarhi is excellent, well graded, and
takes only about an hour and a half on the sturdy ponies of
the royal stables.

"There is a bungalow at Sisagarhi for the use of those travelling on official business, or guests of the Maharaja, and here I
tarried for awhile before carrying on to the summit of the
Chisapani Pass by a steep track, but nothing in comparison
with the descent on the northern side. Over rocks and boulders
one goes, slipping and blundering down until the valley far
below is reached, when there is a comparatively easy going
for some miles before tackling the next range.

"The hills on either side of the river running through the
valley are mostly bare of wood, for the inhabitants have for
centuries been levying toll, until now they must go so far
afield in search of fuel that it often means a day's journey for
a man-load. Through the undulating valley you travel until
the ascent of the Chandragiri Pass, an even more harassing and
strenuous pathway than the one down from the Chisaanip.
But once on the summit the view is superb, and if that is any
compensation for physical discomfort one may be considered
as domiciled in luxury. Ahead lies the valley of Nepal backed
by summits of the Himalayas.

"The first thing, however, that strikes one is this Valley of
Nepal and the numerous towns and villages dotting its surface

far below. There is an impression of density; it looks fresh and green, and after toiling through the otherwise barren hills behind, you feel you have gained the promised land and one to which an air of mystery and seclusion has imparted additional charm.

"The inhabitants themselves call the valley Nepal; they apply the term with special reference to it and the capital, and the old records going back long before the Christian era, show that it was then in common use, so that the stamp of age has given added veneration.

"Looking at the northern side there is an opening in the hills from which emerges a river—the Bhagmati, flowing down into the valley and giving to it some of its extraordinary fertility. Even my guide and official major-domo was impressed and told the story of how the Bhagmati originated.

"Vishnu, the Hindu deity who shares the allegiance of his followers with the other god Siva, is an active god who traverses the heavens in three strides, which represent the rising, the meridian, and the setting of the sun. He also descended in one of his incarnations as a tortoise and proceeded to deliver the world. In the course of his athletic activities he came to the Valley of Nepal, and saw that there should be an outlet for the water, so with a mighty swing of his sword he cut an opening through the mountain for the Bhagmati.

"There is no census in Nepal so an accurate estimate of the population cannot be given, but so far as the capital and its adjacent towns and villages are concerned, it is probably about half a million.

"From the top of the Chandagiri Pass, we went down by another steep and rocky path through the forest to Thankot whence there is a good road to Khatmandu, the capital.

"Nepal is a country of contrasts; age-old conservatism and a dislike of the foreigner and innovation are factors in the life of the people, yet motor-cars and lorries are common in the streets of the capital and outside, and an overhead rope railway for transport of goods is in operation from Bhimpedi to Khatmandu.

"After having struggled up and down the tortuous and rocky paths from the foot of the hills to the capital, and over huge stones and boulders, in many places with a gradient of one in three, we were all the more impressed with the energy and carrying power of the Nepalese coolie in bringing these cars and lorries into the country. They are carried in bodily, only the wheels being removed. Eighty or more coolies shoulder the long stout poles to which the cars are attached, and with a popular chant, much pulling and persistence, they are borne over the hills and down into the comparatively level ground of the Nepal Valley.

"They may do only a mile or two a day, but that matters little in the Orient, where the more leisurely mode of progress is preferred to the hurry and rush of the West.

"So it was I came down to Thankot five miles below the pass, to find an up-to-date motor from the Maharaja's garage awaiting us.

"Nepalese chauffeurs could never be accused of loitering; the instant I was in the car the driver "trod on the gas," gave an impressive hoot and went off like a rocket. Along the road we tore, past slumbering cottages, sundry pedestrians and live-stock in the streets, whom we missed by inches, and in and out of the night traffic and peasants hurrying home to bed with bundles upon their heads. The marvel is that we didn't hit anything. My chauffeur felt the weight of his position, he evidently appraised me far higher than I did myself, and so, having thought of all my past sins, I was resigned.

"During my visit to Khatmandu I stayed at the British Legation, with Colonel C. T. Daukes, C.I.E., who had paved the way for a second flight over Everest and had kept the Maharaja informed of developments, so that the latter was already in a position to appreciate the geographic and scientific standpoint of the expedition.

"The Legation is situated on rising ground to the north of

the city, of a curious but pleasing blend of architecture, a mixture of the Swiss chalet with its overhanging eaves, and the battlemented walls of a medieval fortress. It has large gardens which the talented wife of the British Envoy has done much to improve. Mrs. Daukes appears to specialise in many things as befits the wife of a warden of the marches—amongst them the cultivation of beautiful flowers.

"Soon after arrival I went to call on the Maharaja of Nepal at his palace. Maharaja Sir Joodha Shum Shere Jung Bahadur Rana, G.C.I.E., Prime Minister and Supreme Commander-in-Chief of Nepal, succeeded to his high office in September, 1932, on the death of his brother, the laws of succession directing that the nearest male relative of the ruling chief shall follow him. The government and administration of Nepal present a curious anomaly. The Maharaja is the virtual ruler of the country, his word is law, and he controls the machinery of government, whether it be military, political, or commercial. Above him, and yet without executive and administrative powers, is the King, who is rarely seen or heard, and enjoys a mythical sort of existence, a kingship devoid of worry and work, in strange contrast to the usual lot of monarchs.

"I had met other rulers in various parts of the world, but not a Nepalese one, so there was a distinct spice of romance about the visit. I suppose the world largely imagines that Nepal is a land of fierce warriors who swoop down from their mountain fastnesses armed with their kukris, headed by their ruler as the champion warrior, just the sort of people we read of in the story-books. Actually they are not aggressive but staunch and loyal friends.

"Daukes and I motored to the Maharaja's palace, where we were received by a guard of honour at the entrance, the Maharaja being there to greet us. He welcomed me without formality of any kind and with an easy courtesy betokening pride of birth and place. Following the introduction he led the way with a simplicity which is sometimes more alarming than the pomp of a European court.

THE ENTRANCE TO A TEMPLE IN NEPAL

DISC WHEELS ARE MORE IN EVIDENCE THAN MOTOR-CARS IN NEPAL

"There were no gorgeously dressed flunkeys to waft me hither and thither, no inquisitive chamberlains to look me up and down and pass me on through innumerable corridors and state rooms. We ascended the grand stairway, the Maharaja conversing in English and pointing out the ornaments that graced it, drawing attention to the painting of the King George's shoot in Nepal when His Majesty visited India for the Coronation Durbar in 1911.

"We spoke of this shoot in the Terai arranged by the then Maharaja. Two camps were pitched, the King's shooting-quarters being almost a perfect example of a royal residence in London, with lawns and rose-beds as garden decoration. For more than a year prior to the King's arrival, preparations had been going on. A special road was cut through the railway through the dense forests, a distance of thirty miles, to the camp, while over six hundred elephants were employed for ringing the game.

"When the King arrived in the camp he went out shooting almost at once, and the elephant ring had only just closed when a large tiger burst out, with a roar taking a flying leap over a wide stream. As it was in mid-air the royal shikari hit it with a beautiful shot through the neck, killing it instantly.

"In the afternoon of the same date the King was out again, and as the line of elephants advanced through the jungle, two rhinoceroses suddenly appeared just ahead of his elephant. Although they can move with great speed the King dropped the first with his right barrel, a clean dead hit, and brought the other down with the left, despatching it with a second shot.

"The Nepalese speak with enthusiasm of the King's prowess, and relate how another day he took a right and left at a tiger and a bear as they burst out of the long grass, killing both, each with a single shot. Small wonder that the natives regarded him in the light of a wizard whose eye and aim nothing could escape.

"We then went into one of the large drawing-rooms and

talked about things in general and the Everest flight in particular, the Maharaja expressing agreement with our plans
and giving his approval to a second flight if required.

"To facilitate local government the country is divided into
sections each under its own governor or district official, whose
duty is to apply the law and rule the area committed to his
charge as the local representative.

"The revenue of Nepal is derived mainly from the land, the
taxation being based on its area and productivity, that in the
Terai from its greater fertility being valued at a much higher
rate than ground in the hills. Revenue collection is simplified
for the tax-gatherer for all he has to do is to go on his rounds
armed with a rent roll and a cheerful face. From the proceeds
of his collection he is granted five per cent., in addition to
being allowed a call on the services of each man in his area
for one day per annum. The servant problem is thus solved
by this patriarchal system of free service.

"The rise of Nepal forms a fascinating chapter in Eastern
history, and an object lesson in the art of conquest, with its
collective gain. About the time when the star of the Moghul
dynasty in India was beginning to set and the American colonists
were throwing the taxed tea forced upon them by George III
into Boston Harbour, a small but warlike band of adventurers
came into Nepal from Central India. They claimed descent
from the Rajputs, the military and fighting sect of the Hindus,
and had inherited their martial qualities from a long line of
free-booters and soldiers of fortune, to whom war was a
passion.

"They settled at Gurkha, a town some thirty-eight miles west
of Khatmandu, and there inter-married with the Mongol stock
of the country. India was in the melting-pot, ancient dynasties
were breaking up, and many of the native states of Hindustan
were in transition. The English and French were striving for
mastery in southern India and Bengal, with the determined
and resourceful English gradually gaining the upper hand and
carving out a new empire.

NEPAL

"It was a great opportunity for the Gurkhas, as they had styled themselves after their head-quarters capital, and so they, too, determined to set up a new kingdom. Reinforcing their ranks from the martial tribes around them, and by the grant of a liberal share in the spoils of war they set out on their conquering career, engaging in the most colourful fights in history. They marched over a thousand miles through the Himalayas laying waste the land and bringing the beaten tribes under their rule. They even penetrated to Tibet, invading that country in 1792, besides overrunning Sikkim and Bhutan.

"The cradle of Gurkha history lies in that little-known town of Gurkha, now deserted by the ruling race for a more imposing capital. From there the swashbuckling campaigns continued unchecked until they fell foul of the British in the opening of the nineteenth century. Their warlike raids and forays had given them a false idea of their own power and resources, and when the Honourable East India Company, the old John Company, tried negotiations with no effect, war was declared in 1814.

"The Gurkha War, in so far as the generalship is concerned, was not an inspiring effort, although here and there are bright individual patches. Three or four generals in succession proved their incompetence, until General Ochterlony appeared upon the scene and by his skilful moves brought the campaign to a close. But if we had won the victory we had not won the peace, for the Nepalese refused to come to terms and the war had to be renewed. Ochterlony once more took the field, outwitted the enemy in sundry turning movements, and occupied ground of strategic and political importance with a minimum of loss. The Gurkhas had reckoned without their man and seeing the futility of further resistance, capitulated in March 1816. So ended the Anglo-Gurkha War and from it dates a friendship and mutual admiration that has increased with the passing years.

"The treaty concluded between the old John Company and Nepal, is of remarkable interest for under its terms the Gurkhas lost much of what they had gained by right of conquest.

Sikkim and Bhutan, as well as Garhwal and Kumaon to the north and north-west, were lost to them besides a large part of the Terai, but less than a year later part of the latter was restored, a friendly and magnanimous gesture which had a good effect.

"The agreement between the two sides is of further interest in that it allowed for the creation of three Gurkha regiments for service under the Indian Government. They acquitted themselves so well that gradually other regiments were raised up to the existing number of ten. The military service thus open provided an outlet for the martial aspirations of these people, and kept alive the old fighting spirit which has been shown in our interests on more than one occasion.

"Prior to the war with the British, Nepal had, as already related, engaged in one with the Tibetans. This excited the anger of the Chinese, of whose kingdom Tibet was a dependency, and they despatched an army of seventy thousand men to deal with the ubiquitous Gurkhas. The march of this Chinese army across 4,000 miles of plains and forest, and over the highest inhabited portion of the globe, was an astounding performance and probably one of the greatest of its kind in military annals.

"The story goes that the Chinese general received his orders from the Son of Heaven in Peking, as the emperor was called, for, theoretically at any rate, he ruled over all beneath the sun, and the nations on the earth were his vassals. The commander-in-chief was given a nondescript army, some vague instructions as to the direction of the enemy and what it was all about, and told to get on with his task.

"His march across Asia without supply, transport, or medical services, is an example of Chinese tenacity and patience. As long as they were in a more or less inhabited area the army lived on the country, but once beyond them it was no longer possible. The general was, hoewver, equal to the occasion. He collected and halted his roving force, marked out the area round their camps into plots, the sword, the musket, and the

WOMEN CARRY LOADS AS WELL AS MEN IN NEPAL

AN ABORIGINE OF PURNEA

lance were laid aside, and in their place were taken up the shovel and the plough. Cereals and vegetables were sown, and in the fulness of time the crops were garnered; with renewed supplies the army continued its march until the goal was reached.

"So well did the celestial general carry out his orders that he advanced to within a few miles of Khatmandu and forced Nepal to submit to his terms.

"In 1854 the Gurkhas again came up against the Tibetans and after a war lasting two years, fought under extraordinary conditions of intense cold and hardship, for operations were carried on at altitudes of fourteen and fifteen thousand feet, the Gurkhas triumphed.

"China this time left the Tibetans to fend for themselves, being pre-occupied with internal troubles at home and the menace of flood and famine which have ever been a nightmare to the Chinese. The Gurkhas' terms, imposed and accepted, were the secession of certain territory and the annual payment of 10,000 rupees. We were told a story relative to the question of supplies in this campaign. The Gurkhas being orthodox Hindus could not use oxen as food, since the cow is sacred, but their ruler was a man of resource. Yaks, the oxen of high altitudes, could certainly not be so treated as long as it remained an ox, so the raj guru, or chief priest, officially declared it to be a deer, so that its eating could be legalised, and the food problem was thereby minimised.

"But on the other hand it looked like a cow and doubtless there was a certain tradition in favour of regarding it as such, and consequently a sacred animal. But in the end, as we have seen, it was ruled that it was not a cow but a deer, and perhaps for a consideration should ever the necessity again arise, it might be ruled that although not a cow, it is as it were a cow.

"The government of this mountain kingdom of nearly six million people is military; indeed, the Gurkhas are one of the most martial peoples in the world, their major occupation is military service both in their own country and in India. The Maharaja rules and controls the army which is formed on the British model and drilled with English words of command, the armament being modern rifles and a light artillery of a highly serviceable character.

"Officers and men are dressed similarly to those in the British Army in India, and to see the officers riding up and down the ranks of their battalions, and the Maharaja taking the salute, equipped and clothed as a British general would be, made me wonder if I were not back on the parade ground at Lucknow, or at a march past in Rawalpindi.

"Whilst staying in Khatmandu I was present with the Maharaja at a review of the Nepalese army, held in connection with the coronation festivities, and attended by the leading officials throughout the country. It was a remarkable and practical demonstration of what Nepal can produce in a military sense. The march past took place in the afternoon, the Maharaja at the saluting base accompanied by his staff and ministers. The parade ground lies to the east of the city, an extensive grassy plain that, but for the Oriental buildings beyond its edges, might be at Aldershot.

"Thirty thousand men marched past, the regiments comprising all the fighting classes of Nepal, mostly infantry, with some brigades of light mountain artillery, the whole forming a force of which the Nepalese may well be proud.

"During my stay in Khatmandu I visited most of the famous places, and those intimately associated with the history and life of Nepal. Generally speaking, the buildings in sequestered Khatmandu are ornate and the main squares, such as those into which the principal streets lead, filled with a bewildering array of palaces, temples and houses, fancifully decorated with wood-carvings and multiple roofs.

"Market, or bazaar days, are the time when the people can be studied to advantage, for then the main and subsidiary streets are crowded with town and country folk, who come in from the surrounding districts laden with the produce of the field

AT THE GATEWAY OF A TEMPLE IN NEPAL
Those entering touch the door with their foreheads

AS IT WAS IN THE BEGINNING.   GRINDING CORN IN NEPAL

and loom and every kind of indigenous manufacture. All roads lead to the Khatmandu bazaars, and they are thronged from early dawn with a motley collection of men, women and children, making for the area allotted to the sale of particular articles. It is a bright and animated crowd that greets you, all classes from the rich and affluent merchant to the beggar who clamours for alms amid the din of buying and selling.

"In the schools realism can be studied with effect. They, in common with most of the buildings, conform to the prevailing essential idea of house construction; the same architectural plan is followed that gives it the appearance of a moral law revealed from heaven, and handed down through all the ages for the architectural guidance of the people.

"The children sing whatever is set them for study, for the Oriental treasures the theory that knowledge comes through the ears rather than by the eyes, so that progress towards classical honours is in direct proportion to the vocal capacity of the student.

"Of the trades and professions that one sees in the streets, perhaps the most lucrative are fortune-telling and letter-writing. The fortune-teller is in constant evidence in the bazaar while the professional letter-writer is quite an institution. He sits cross-legged with pen and paper spread out upon his knees, clients gather round him and narrate the text of documents, petitions, and letters, and the scribe commits it all to writing. Education being still at a low ebb the professional amanuensis comes into his own on bazaar days, when the terms of a bargain have to be recorded and deeds of sale drawn up.

"Sometimes you may see what corresponds to a tea-shop, in England where the patrons sit on a floor of beaten mud. The vendor of cakes and sweetmeats is there to supplement the liquids, and he takes the coin in payment, using his mouth as a purse. It is all very inspiring and gives an idea of how the other half lives.

"There is a distinct air of cheeriness and goodwill in a Nepalese bazaar crowd; the majority of them toil hard, raising scanty crops in the hills, or tending cattle, but they are cheery and hospitable to the few strangers who visit their isolated kingdom.

"Much of the merchandise and various articles that are seen coming into Khatmandu are carried on human backs. Women as well as men carry surprisingly heavy loads, usually suspended from a strap across the forehead. A story is current that one woman carried a piano for more than a hundred miles up hill and down dale into the capital, an amazing feat, but yet not to be wondered at when one has seen some of the coolies with their burdens.

"The roads into Nepal are purposely kept in poor repair, for the Nepalese prefer to discourage visitors and live a life apart. It is said that with the foreigner comes trouble, and with the Bible comes the bayonet. There are, as already indicated, a few excellent roads and probably later on these will be increased as the Nepalese become more accustomed to the modern way.

"Leaving Nepal, a three days' journey through the hills and the Terai, on foot and pony, by motor and rail, brought me to Delhi, the sacred Moslem city of India, the Rome of the East, and the seat of government in the cold weather months from October to April. Legend tells us that Delhi has from time immemorial been the site of a capital city, and there are few places that one approaches with greater curiosity and anticipation.

"A few days prior to my arrival, His Excellency the Viceroy had honoured us by inspecting both the Westlands and their complicated installations with the greatest interest. Lord Willingdon is to a high degree air-minded, and travels by air whenever possible, recognising the great future that lies before aviation, especially in India the land of vast distances which the aeroplane can encompass with rapidity and comfort.

"Lady Willingdon, a personality of abounding energy and perspicacity, is likewise a protagonist of aviation, and realizes that India, no less than Britain, stands to gain immensely by the development of air services. This acute and eminently responsible observer of events and tendencies in India, has availed

A HOLY MAN OF KHATMANDU TELLS HIS BEADS

herself of the opportunity to gauge the needs and potentialities of aviation there. She has thus enlarged the wide circle of personal contacts with the princes and ruling chiefs, and has been of service to India in dispelling misapprehensions with regard to aviation, and inculcating the spirit of the air with which the future of the country is bound up.

"The Viceroy's house is the outstanding feature of New Delhi, and from it emanates the governing influence, where difficulties are transformed into gains, where prejudices and rivalries are adjusted to the common good, and strong and reliable bricks are made from uninviting straw.

"During my stay in this attractive place a reception and dinner were given typical of Eastern splendour and a sidelight on the magic Orient.

"There were enough princes at this banquet to fill a book of fairy tales. Among them was the Maharaja of Bikanir and an example of how English an Indian ruler can be. This polished and cultured gentleman with his perfect command of English, lives much like our own royal family. He is in personal touch with his state, treats his subjects of every grade justly, and has hobbies that read like a page of *Who's Who*. A fleet of cars, an arsenal of sporting guns, and an English table with a squad of Goanese waiters are numbered among them.

"There was the Maharana of Udaipur, who claims descent from the mythical king of Ajodhya and is recognised as the premier Rajput prince. Even in the days long before the Christian era Ajodhya was the court of the great King Dasaratha, the fifty-sixth monarch of the solar line in descent from Raja Manu, so that Udaipur can certainly lay claim to pre-eminence in pedigree.

*　　*　　*　　*　　*　　*

"Back once more in Purnea I found the place a hive of activity, and preparations in full swing for tackling the objective. One of the light scouting aircraft had just descended on the landing-ground by Darbhanga House; from a height of fifteen thousand feet the óbserver had seen the awe-inspiring array of peaks culminating in Mount Everest, and the course they must follow when cruising over the roof of the world.

"They would follow the great gorges of the Arun River which cut like a furrow through the Himalayas; with powerful binoculars the gorges were distinguishable, showing countless cliffs of black rock and ice slopes. No Cæsar of India could ever cross these super-Alps, but they act as one of Nature's greatest irrigation reservoirs, storing masses of ice and snow that ultimately become the streams that provide the water and carry the silt which give life to millions of people in the northern plains of India."

CHAPTER IX

LIFE AT PURNEA

EVERYONE in India from the Viceroy downwards, extended towards the Everest Flight the greatest kindness and help. In Purnea the Maharaja of Darbhanga, generously offered the loan of his house, refurnishing and fitting it out to our requirements, which he and his managerial staff had anticipated with singular success.

The bungalow was a long, single-storied building, one room wide, girded with a spacious verandah extending down its length and round both ends. It stood in its own grounds in which was laid out the local golf course; a hundred yards in front was a pear-shaped open space used at first as an aerodrome for the Moths, after some trees had been cut down that rendered landings a little too hazardous to be popular, once the first excitement had lost its novelty. Across the park lay the local club-house with attendant tennis courts, and about a mile away, alone in its glory, the Raja of Banaili's private race-course smiled an invitation. The surroundings, in fact, had the surface aspect of a well-equipped country club that for strictly Asiatic reasons preferred brown clothes to green ones.

The Raja of Banaili, a cheery personality, who had shot over a hundred tigers, offered us his fleet of motor-cars, remarking that, if possible, he would like to retain one or two for his own use. He had seventeen. He seemed astonished, as if at an unusual display of moderation, when only three cars and a lorry were required.

The hospitality of all these friends, truly Eastern in its charm, left everyone very much in their debt.

At first the whole party inhabited the bungalow, or adjoining tents, but after a few days it became evident that for the sake of efficiency, the men would have to live on the spot, at the main aerodrome at Lalbalu, with its excellent landing surface, ten miles away. Accordingly, the three hangars for the small and large aircraft, lent by the Royal Air Force, were erected there, and tasks allotted.

The daily routine at head-quarters began with chota hazri or early tea at 5.15 a.m. Mr. S. N. Gupta, the meteorologist, arrived about six, with the full weather report in his pocket, a forecast of which had been submitted the previous night. If the advance reading was favourable, Fellowes had, on most occasions, already left to carry out an aerial reconnaissance in the Puss Moth. On the actual morning of the first flight over Everest, Gupta sent up a balloon in an endeavour to secure a definite indication of the wind at the working height required, and succeeded in confirming the report of the previous night. This, and the result of Fellowes' reconnaissance, decided that memorable day.

Breakfast followed the morning meteorological discussion. Those going to the aerodrome would leave at 7.30, and most mornings would be spent preparing in different ways for the star flight, foremost in the minds of everyone, or in fitting up and employing various cameras, and scientific instruments. Despite delays and postponements, due to variable weather conditions, life at the aerodrome seldom had its idle moments and hardly ever a dull one. The road from the bungalow to the aerodrome, making leisurely in the general direction of Darjeeling, treed and dusty, proved a most popular highway abounding in human, animal and vegetable interest. Jute, sugar-cane, and grass-fields cover the tracts of surrounding country, punctuated by little straying villages, gleaming pools like hollow eyes and trickling water-courses. Owing to the abundant supply of water, no falling off in the numbers of birds or animals occurs, except during the extreme midday heat when one and all seek out the shade of thickets and the denser fastnesses of prickly scrub and jungle.

Every day we motored out to the aerodrome, passing over

this same road that the British soldiers had used a hundred years ago. We wondered what they thought of it in those days of long ago, when they tramped through the dust and the heat; were they enthralled by the brilliant sunsets, by the foliage which only a tropical environment can show, or did the dust in their throats and the pinch of their boots, no less than the stifling heat, claim all their attention and their curses?

During the cool hours there streamed along the highway a variegated procession of bullock carts, donkeys, cows, dogs, brown and bony human beings, many of them carrying elderly and almost ancestral black umbrellas with which to ward off the rays of the sun, while occasionally across the road's hot dusty surface would dart an enquiring mongoose or handsome scurrying tree rat. Monkeys jumped in the tree-tops, chattering like schoolchildren. Solemn birds clutched branches. Sitting back in a car the novelty and interest of such surroundings soothed the mind and charmed the eye: a state of satisfying nirvana, often rudely shattered by a grotesquely-hopping, squabbling, group of vultures and carrion crows, hideous sounds of strife receding into the distance, only to be succeeded by the sight of a beggar afflicted with sores, or, more fortunately by a vision of supple, brown figures, swaying rather than walking, each swathed in a single-coloured garment flung back from the shoulders, and carrying smoothly and efficiently their luggage on their heads. Their conversation centres on their own small circle of life and death, the crops, and the prospects of the next rainy season.

Conservatism and age-old custom are met with on every hand in India, and among the tribes and races on and adjacent to the border line. The Asiatic as a general rule, does not like rapidity in anything. He prefers his progress to be on slow and dignified lines, and any attempt to force the pace is fatal to success.

A few years ago when Etherton and Blacker were journeying up to Turkistan on a special mission, they took with them a motor-cycle, as the nearest approach to mechanical transport that could be carried across the mountains along the Indian frontier.

The appearance in the bazaars of Central Asia of this incarnation of the devil, set the whole population on edge; ponies and donkeys were the orthodox methods of transport. They had carried the people and their goods and chattels since the dawn of history, and the Mullahs were determined they should go on doing so until the end of all things.

Nearly every pool had its group of half-clad human beings, bathing, fishing in attitudes of resignation, or washing clothes; the latter operation being best described as a practical demonstration of how to break stones by slapping them hard enough with cotton cloth.

Near the aerodrome at Lalbalu, was a large shallow pool, lying in the hollow of a dried-up river bed. This piece of water was afterwards turned into a bathing-pool for the party, with results which if they did not exactly make history, produced some dramatic and most uncomfortable moments for all concerned.

A great deal of mud and reed was cleared away to make the pool fit for bathers, under the supervision of the local executive engineer, Mr. Came, who dived in and swam round when all was completed, both by way of declaring the baths open and to show his contempt for the whispered word "crocodile," that had begun to circulate stealthily from ear to ear, though no one apparently was listening. But a few days later the rumour took upon itself the shape of reality when one of the airmen reported that a crocodile head looked at him while bathing. Nobody believed him. Fellowes, however, knowing something of the strength of an Indian fable when it happens to possess two powerful jaws, a sinking feeling, and a tail like a battering-ram, forbade all bathing except in parties of six. The idea, of course, was not that six people should be consumed instead of one, but that there was safety in noise and numbers.

The next day the crocodile was seen again. His existence was now no longer doubted, and it only became a question of time

THE ORCHESTRA AT THE SANTAL DANCE

THE BEAUTY CHORUS AT THE SANTAL DANCE

before one of the ground staff shot him with a Rigby rifle. After that morning it was arranged that whenever anyone entered the pool, two Indians should swim in first, stick long bamboo poles into the bottom of the pond, watch beside them, and allow no one to bathe except from the safe and shallow end. This duty, the natives were quite willing to undertake for eight annas a day. They also kept on the watch for any wandering crocodiles that might be about, tough leather-skinned customers, traversing the countryside at night and often taking a fancy to midnight bathing. An extra thrill was added to the daily plunge into cool waters, by the thought that there was always the chance they might be harbouring an unwelcome visitor. One more representative of the tribe of scaly ones tried to become a member of the aerodrome bathing-club, and was shot for the sins of gate-crashing.

Crocodiles are the bogey-men of India. They are the real footpads of the plains. Snakes, where booted Europeans are concerned, are not one quarter the peril they are generally supposed to be by people who have never visited the tropics; insects do not assume the same sinister importance as in Equatorial Africa or the wilds of Southern America; meetings with tigers, and man-eating panthers, can be left nowadays to the hunter and the lonely forest officer, but always, wherever there is the presence of water and the sweep of rivers across parched and thirsty plains, the menace of the crocodile remains. There are travellers' tales of these ubiquitous saurians that match the long-bow stories of any fisherman. To many of the crowding millions of Hindustan they have become almost legendary figures, guardians of temple secrets, and of the spirits of the dead. It is said of them that a certain species burrow deep into sandy banks and river mud, remaining there happily for months and sometimes years, waiting for torrential rains that bring them out by thousands to terrorise the local villages, while they make up for their long period of fasting.

Whatever fancy may concede to these lurking monsters, the facts themselves are strange enough. A crocodile has five fingers and four toes and can bellow like a bull. His stomach is small, but his digestion so powerful that every bone of his victim is dissolved while still being stowed away in his gullet. By means of a fold in his tongue, pressing against the roof of his mouth, he can breathe comfortably through his nose while the whole of his mouth gapes open under water; birds act as his obliging dentist, free of charge, and a buffet from the tail of one of these fully-grown reptiles can knock an unsuspecting man into the water.

Altogether, a crocodile is a most unpleasant sort of neighbour in a swimming-pool. Englishmen in India, particularly army subalterns, sometimes indulge in the sport of crocodile-fishing. A large bait, the more putrid the better, is thrown into the river on an anchor attached to a steel hawser, or strong rope, and when the beast is hooked there ensues a tremendous tug-of-war. Two strong sticks tied crossways will often serve the purpose of steel hook, since the jaws of a crocodile, like those of a bulldog, never willingly release their prey.

This sport was first referred to in one of the oldest writings of man, the Book of Job:

> "Canst thou draw out leviathan with an hook? or his tongue with a cord which thou lettest down?
> Canst thou fill his skin with barbed irons? or his head with fish spears?
> Lay thine hand upon him, remembering the battle, do no more."

Only those who have tried their hands at this form of sport in India, know the truth of the old chronicler's graphic remarks.

Besides bathing, the other great form of recreation at Purnea and Lalbalu aerodrome, was polo. This was played on sturdy Bhutiya ponies with a sprinkling of walers and country-breds. Polo is part and parcel of Indian life, and one of the great attractions of a country that has mothered and fathered the sport for centuries, sending in the course of time the challenge of her supremacy across the seas to the Argentine and the United

States. It is said that Baber, poet warrior, and first Mogul emperor, brought the game with him out of Central Asia to temper his many stern activities with a little recreation. The Moguls, who had need of resolute quick-witted men, of men of resource, found that polo revealed the character of the players, tried their courage, and control, and proved their fitness, or otherwise, for the strenuous life of those times. Hence skill at polo became a passport to imperial favour and advancement at Court.

The true inwardness and waywardness of this noble game, its origins and scope, and its influence on the different nations of horsemen, after the manner of fox-hunting as applied to Britain, makes a fascinating theme for discussion. Polo holds pride of place as the oldest stick-and-ball game in the world. Beside it, golf and cricket are mere children. Long before Hurlingham was anything except a meeting-ground for painted savages, and Meadowbrook the haunt of roaming bison, polo flourished in the East. Probably the earliest records came from Persia where it was played as a highly organised four-a-side affair, corresponding to Gilgit polo in India at the present time. The Tibetan word "pulu" means a ball. China had its own special blend, 600 years B.C., with a wooden ball and a suspended bag for goal. The Turks of Stamboul used racquets instead of sticks. In Japan, ancient feudal custom still survives in a game played with a paper ball covered with bamboo fibre and directed into round goals with sticks shaped like a racquet. The sport as played in olden times, with no limits to the numbers of riders engaged on each side, must have developed sometimes into little short of a pitched battle.

At Purnea, one of the mightiest exponents of the game was Tom Smith, an indigo planter. Tom was big and hearty, with a voice that could be heard all over the country. To see him riding his tiny Bhutiya pony, his legs almost trailing on the ground, his face wreathed in smiles, was one of the most cheerful sights imaginable.

Tom Smith was the kind of man who should have a book

written about him by an attendant Indian Boswell. His words were worth keeping. The years pass quietly over the printed places of English literature and Dr. Johnson is left undisturbed with the character stage all to himself.

Most mornings Tom came over to Darbhanga House at daybreak, his voice awakening all sleeping figures in the bungalow. He was the John Peel of Purnea, and a human alarum clock.

His wife, too, was one of those people without whose help the expedition would have missed a great deal. A model of efficiency, she took the whole party under her wing and superintended the entire commissariat for her knowledge extended everywhere from how to stalk a tiger to the making of a chocolate soufflé. The two mess-men, subordinate to her orders, were Parsees, Framjee and Golwalla, both exceedingly proud of their ancestry and the ancient sect of fire worshippers. According to Framjee there are a quarter of a million Parsees in the world, and their religion aims nowadays more at physical and material than spiritual welfare; he cited their rules as to bathing, physical exercise, and mature age for marriage, as proof of this. Parsees attach special importance to benevolence. The last ten days of each year are supposed to be devoted to acts of charity and philanthropic deeds.

It is not uncommon on the fighting frontiers of India to have murderers for servants. Blood feuds are numerous and knife hands quick. In some Pathan villages a man is not thought much of until he has taken life. A cynical critic once asked how many murders went to make a trans-border Moslem of the north-west frontier, but he was hardly being fair to a conservative, and, on the whole, law-abiding race of fighting men.

In places like Purnea the most important people are the money-lender and the barber. The one is the local Lloyds; the other, who caters for marriages, the Lyons of the district.

Villages are full of kite-flying enthusiasts; broken glass and bottles often adorn the strings, to cut the opponent's line when

ANCIENT TRANSPORT MINGLES WITH THE MODERN

possible; pie dogs slink by day; plump little children trace fingers of fate in the dust.

One day at the bungalow, a dog sneaked in and ran off with a joint of meat. Some silver knives and forks were unaccountably missing at the same time, members of the staff maintaining that the dog was responsible; but Etherton, who was once an examiner in Hindustani and knew the language intimately, soon disabused them of this idea. Magically, in their appointed places, the lost cutlery returned to the table; the servants, grave as the Sphinx, declared that the dog had produced them again.

Another time a native witness was suborned in a case of petty theft. Etherton ordered the man to take his shoes off and stand on the verandah when answering questions. Then was seen the wisdom of the initiated, for Etherton has a theory, the truth of which he has often proved, that few natives can keep their toes still if they are telling a lie. This is an idea that, provided the secret judgment remained well-kept, might be extended with success to police courts.

A classic story is told in the East of how a thief once stole a house. Hearing that a newcomer had recently come to live in a certain town house that he coveted, the thief took careful stock of the place, both inside and out, and then went before the magistrate declaring that the house was really his, and the newcomer the father of lies and an interloper. He produced various false documents, in support of his claim. The judge, tiring of the lengthy proceedings, decided, as he thought quite justly, to make the two claimants describe the interior of the house in detail, so that the true owner might at once be apparent. But the unjust thief was so much more correct and accurate in his answers than the rightful occupant, that he obtained the verdict.

The bungalow soon became a centre for all kinds of comings and goings. The food problem, especially the feeding of the aerodrome eight miles away, developed into an intricate business; Ellison, one of the reserve pilots, was appointed transport officer, fulfilling his duties with a cheerfulness that soon supplied the oil for the wheels of communication to run smoothly.

Then there was Sayid Ali, whom Etherton put in charge of stores and expeditionary gear.

Sayid Ali came from Blacker's regiment, the Guides, one of the few corps in India that has a permanent home. There they keep all the family heirlooms from trophies of the chase and the loot of war down to Buddhist statuary. There is a swimming-bath in the garden of the officer's mess and a huge wire and muslin contraption that looks like a gigantic meat safe in which breakfast is taken in the hot weather free from the flies.

They say that the Guides are recruited from the pick of the fighting races in India, and you can see them strolling about the lines in enormous baggy trousers with the light of battle in their eyes. It is their home as it was that of their fathers, for the militant clanman puts his son's name down for the Guides as we should put ours down for the "Senior."

There is something distinctly alluring about these North Indian and frontier Moslems. They are so jovial and devil-may-care, so independent and so hospitable and courteous on occasion. With them fighting is a passion, and those beyond the frontier are always challenging the authority and strength of the British forces, and when not engaged in fighting a common enemy they quarrel among themselves. The battle and plunder-loving tribes of these rugged mountain areas are continually on the look out for an opportunity to descend from their rocky fastnesses into the plains to plunder and kill. It appeals to them, for war is both a business and a pastime.

When they are not defying the suzerain power, there is the blood feud, an ancient and honourable institution to which all else is subservient. Any insult or injury must be wiped out by gun or knife, according to a code of rules.

Up in the mountainous tracts of the north-west frontier where the eye looks over naught but peaks, ravines and canyons, cold and gaunt and ghostly too, with memories of dead men who walk when the moon is high. It is a savage land, and on seeing it you realise why its people hold life cheap. Nature has shown them how to be pitiless. With them murder is not a crime but a creed, and to be a successful robber is a social honour. Might alone is right, and weakness is held in withering contempt.

All along the north-west frontier from the Indian Ocean to Peshawar, a distance of 1,400 miles, lies what is characterised as the most turbulent area in the world, the happy hunting-ground of Pathans and Baluchis, who both have strong tribal organisations.

The Baluchi is feudal and follows his chief, but the Pathan is intensely democratic and he only bows to the decision of the tribal council when he knows it will be enforced by the dagger or the rifle.

This long frontier may be compared to a wall over which the eager Pathan and Baluchi are looking, while beyond lies Afghanistan with its semi-regular army of 120,000, and a further 200,000 irregulars. All these fighting races of northern and central India, with the Afghans beyond them, the Gurkhas of Nepal to the east, and the tribes of the Hindu Kush mountains to the north, not to mention those from Central Asia, all fanatical and plunder-loving, would make a bid for supremacy if the British left India to-morrow.

Broadly speaking, Hindus and Moslems are two distinct communities or peoples, but their respective attitude towards life, their social habits, traditions and beliefs, divide them so completely that the fact that they have lived in the same land for centuries has contributed nothing to their fusion into a nation.

There is no sense whatever of real nationalism in India; races and tribes are too many, religions so dominant, and caste so exacting that nothing could make a nation from this cosmopolitan mass of three hundred and nineteen millions.

The Government of India is a mighty thing to contemplate; it demands much that is not dreamed of in the philosophy of most people, curious manners and customs to adjust to modern ways, difficulties of religion and creed to be overcome, tribal and caste relations to be preserved. Through all the generations since we first came to India, successive administrations working on the same lines of justice and equity, have had the cause of the social victims ever before them, but it is a matter of extreme delicacy and one in which every move must be made with the utmost caution.

So much for India and its many complex problems.

Native pedlars and mendicants paid their calls and tried to sell their goods, squatting upon the verandah. At first they were all smiles and self-sacrifice, but the moment anyone picked up one of their wares the sound of bargaining would fill the air and go on until sunset if not stopped. Where trade is concerned in the East the sun stands still. Time is the vulture who never alights save on the dead. A clock tower in the bazaar is like the hyena who raises his voice in the night when no one bothers to listen. Naturally, when a native says he is going to the bazaar, he does not mean he is going to buy anything, but merely to lounge, dose, bargain, and above all to gossip. "Tell me a story, and then let me tell it better," is ageless in the East as anywhere else.

Once, on the way from the bungalow to the aerodrome, a monkey passed riding on a bullock! Everyone made way for the monkey and his mount, and motor-cars braked reverently, for Hanuman, the monkey god, is a sacred person to Hindus. When he crossed from India to Ceylon he did it in one stride, and where his foot touched earth in India a temple marks the holy spot.

Various visitors and friends turned up from time to time at Purnea. Richardson, of the Climbing Expedition, came down to tell of the large wireless station he had set up at Darjeeling, by which he hoped to establish communication with the climbers at their base camp and relay the news. The Rev. Dr. Graham, formerly Moderator of the Church of Scotland, a friend of Clydesdale's, arrived one day and arranged that

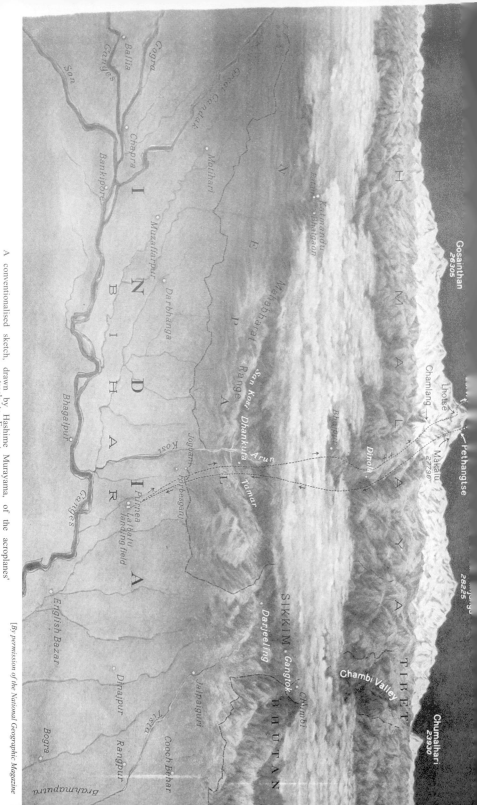

A conventionalised sketch, drawn by Hashime Murayama, of the aeroplanes' track to Everest

[By permission of the National Geographic Magazine]

the latter should drop notices on the natives at Kalimpong so as to let them see an aeroplane for the first time. The effects of the flying visit were much greater than could have been anticipated for most of the people remained under the impression that they had seen a god.

We took part in races; we numbered ourselves amongst the "also ran," and we did it on Bhutiya ponies, who, like Nicholas Nickleby, are notorious for their straight legs. When off the race-course they have an ambling pace quite foreign to the trot as we understand it. You just sit still in the saddle and shiver along, like the monks of medieval England must have done when they left their abbeys to ride to London.

Apart from our hours of ease and recreation, a peep behind the official scenes at the bungalow would have revealed much the same routine work going on every day, for each one of the expedition had his own special place in the general scheme of operations.

The team spirit was highly developed; it was inspiring to note the unison and harmony in which all worked, how difficulties were moulded into gains, how prejudices were turned to good account, and the dominant spirit of self-sacrifice and subordination to the common good. Bennett, our doctor, and Ellison would be consulting about the food question and the camp at the aerodrome. At the next table would be sitting Clydesdale and McIntyre working out some navigation problem, with Blacker tearing himself away from preoccupations over photography to interject fresh suggestions. McIntyre was the navigation expert and Clydesdale constituted himself general critic of all navigational and photographic schemes, prior to their adoption. Barkas was the filming expert, and Fraser, an R.A.F. man, superintended the dark-room. Inside the bungalow, Shepherd would be preparing his next dispatch for *The Times*; while Etherton held a palaver with local residents whose assistance had been invoked upon some vital matter. Fellowes had his office in his dressing-room, where Gearing held sway, and from there the former emerged when not at the aerodrome, to play his part in the shaping of events. Preparations thus proceeded apace, working up by definite stages towards their climax.

In the heat of the afternoon either sleep or bathing generally claimed the energies of the party. Tea came at 4.30, and then the conference on the next day's film activities, with Barkas in the chair. The difficulty, always uppermost in these screen discussions, was that if the weather became suitable, the film programme had inevitably and instantly to be cancelled in favour of flying, the primary aim of the expedition; in fact members of the party who had no leanings towards becoming film stars, could never be made to realise how lightly they were let off in the matter of repetition and rehearsal of scenes. Naturally they were reluctant, as good pilots, to leave their machines in the sun for long periods, or to start up the powerful engines of the big aircraft unnecessarily. Geoffrey Barkas, too, had his work affected by limitations in the field of insurance and petrol; but he made the best possible use of the available material and afterwards reaped the harvest of his reward.

A full stop and usually a finish was put to these excursions and discussions by the arrival of Gupta bringing the evening meteorological report. As a general rule this was a disappointing one, dealing with boisterous winds or cloudy conditions in the upper stratas of the air.

We dined once or twice with a local raja and his wife in the privacy of their home; the ranee runs her house like an English woman, and is probably regarded by her own people as almost a foreigner. This cultured lady is an exception amongst the women of India, for they have no official position in either the Hindu or Moslem religions. But many a strong-minded wife or mother-in-law governs the family from behind the purdah curtains. In the world outside the home, the age-long devices of harem intrigue have failed the Indian woman and she has not found a new technique.

Several women are members of the legislative assemblies, and in the larger cities some have been elected to the local

MEMBERS OF THE EXPEDITION PREPARING FOR A FLIGHT
Etherton, Clydesdale, Fellowes, Blacker, McIntyre, Bonnett

Clydesdale   McIntyre
THE TWO PILOTS

councils. But caste-bound men are afraid to take a woman's advice in public, whatever they may do in private.

Even if they are allowed to go to school and mix in the world for a few years, Hindu and Moslem girls retire into purdah at a very early age, seeing no man except near relations, and only going out in a heavy veil or a closed carriage. Purdah presses very hardly upon the poorer women, who are often shut up in small windowless rooms with only an opening high up in the wall for ventilation. In parts of Rajputana a woman may not leave the house to fetch water, even if the well is close by and surrounded by bushes and trees.

As a result of this rigid life many Indian girls are stunted in growth and suffer from tubercular disease. As with the enclosed nuns of Europe, the system comes before the individual, and just as a nun may not leave her convent, even if it is essential for her health, so a woman in purdah may not see a doctor whatever her suffering. All she can do is to thrust a tiny model figure through the curtains and explain by its aid where the pain is.

This purdah system leads to some amusing scenes. When one of our party was a magistrate in India, a woman had to give evidence in a family land dispute. First of all a palanquin, completely veiled, was placed in the hall of her home. Into this she popped when the coast was clear. Then the bearers came in, took her up and bore her into court. There the Brahmin barristers and disputants were asked if they were satisfied that she was the woman required and not some other person. At this they advanced to the litter, muttered a few words through the curtains, and then assured the judge that the case might proceed.

Women in harems are as carefully protected from light and gaze as though they were so many photographic films. They live in their special quarters under charge of senior ladies, one of whom attends the wife whenever she goes out in the screened car or carriage.

In discussing that strange mixture of contradictions, the

Indian woman, it must be admitted that education has never been denied her. It is a sacred tradition that Hindu women should, as far as practicable, receive an education on a level with that of their men-folk, and one of the most notable of ancient Indian poets was a woman. Most Indian women are content with their life; deeply conservative, they prefer to exercise their influence on public affairs through their husbands rather than through the ballot box.

These and other topics we discussed when the long Indian day had blazed itself out, and evening came with a soft breeze stirring the creepers in the trellis-work. The pale moon rose streaming through the trees, in the stillness of a tropical night, broken occasionally by the drumming of distant tomtoms or the barking of a village dog; the members of the flying house-party would often turn their eyes, in the words of the psalmist, towards the hills, and to the beckoning white mountains that lay beyond.

CHAPTER X

THE FLIGHT TO EVEREST

A SENSE of the great prize at hand dominated our efforts; we were all so ardent, our leader so confident, the need of securing good results so clamant, and a decisive victory over Everest seemingly so near, that only doubts as to the weather conditions clouded our thoughts. The work and preparation of more than a year which had continued at their utmost tensity, seemed likely to be crowned with success.

But always the wind and the weather governed our deliberations, every sacrifice had been made; was the toil to be achieved?

Whenever the clearness of the sky allowed the theodolite observers to see the balloon up to 25,000 feet and above, the wind velocities became alarming, and seldom under seventy miles an hour.

Previous official estimates showed that a thirty or possibly forty-mile wind to be the highest in which it would be safe to make the attempt.

It will be understood that a strong wind from the west, its usual quarter, would tend to make the machines, travelling from south to north, drift sideways out of their course. Steering into the wind to counteract this, would be equivalent to flying a longer course, and hence burning more fuel. Thus the stronger the wind "at height," the more fuel burnt.

It was a question, therefore, if we made the attempt in a stronger wind than that specified as permissible by the experts, whether there would be sufficient for the return journey.

As a precaution, we had prepared an advanced landing-ground near Forbesganj, forty-six miles north of Purnea.

So we waited anxiously day by day for the wind at 30,000 feet to drop to a reasonable figure.

Sometimes, when the wind speed seemed promising the mountains would be covered in cloud, a matter fatal to photography. We could not even afford to have the valleys on the southern slopes of Everest cloud-filled, as this would cause a gap in the continuity of the all-important strip of air survey photographs.

In April the weather at Purnea seems to go in ten or twelve-day cycles. It starts with a "disturbance," which might be a storm of rain. Then there are several clear days with little wind, but characterised by cloud-caps on the mountains. As these cloud-caps melt away and the peaks stand out clear, so the wind speed appears to rise. Every morning one of our scouting Moths went up to a few thousand feet, at which height, the three great mountains were always clearly visible and it could be seen to what extent they were free from clouds. We waited anxiously for the evening telegram from Calcutta, with its weather forecast, and then for the early morning reports from the scout pilot, and the balloon observers. Should we ever get a moderate wind, without a mass of cloud? All seemed to depend on this. The weather factor had become a much greater one than we had anticipated.

Anxiously we all discussed the matter, always with the able advice of the meteorologists.

The Friday of that memorable week came, then the Saturday. The wind reports showed great, but diminishing velocities. On Sunday the speeds had lessened. We could scarcely sleep for anxiety. The evening telegram foretold a still further drop. Would it be borne out in the morning? Would the clouds have gathered, or the pendulum swing again back to greater winds? We decided that the risk must be taken of flying in a much higher wind and watching the fuel consumption carefully.

Then came Monday, an auspicious day, so said the astrologers. The scouting Moth reported the mountain crystal-clear, the

COLONEL ETHERTON HANDING UP THE EVEREST MAIL

meteorologists gave a wind of fifty-seven miles an hour at the altitude, not so great as to stand in the way of an attempt on Everest.

The die was cast; we drove breathlessly the ten miles to the landing-ground and fretted and fumed at the manifold last minute preparations, which had to be made by our splendid skilled aircraftmen.

There were a hundred tasks to complete before the big machines were ready for the flight. Everything possible had been done the night before, but necessity compelled us to leave a number of details to the last minute.

Chief among the preparations was that of the cameras. The fine, impalpable, all-pervading dust was everywhere. For this reason the cameras could not be left on the aerodrome, still less in the machines themselves. In fact, it was found necessary thoroughly to clean every one of the numerous delicate items of camera equipment each night, and to wrap them up in a double layer of newspaper before putting them back each in its appropriate chest. Even these precautions were not excessive, but the result was that nearly an hour's hard work devolved on the aircraftmen every morning in installing all the many items; work which had to be done with great care and with the accuracy of the scientific instrument maker.

In addition to the fitting of the photographic equipment, there are many other minor tasks which could not be done overnight. Even the actual man-handling of the machines out of their tents took something like twenty minutes, so that it was not till after eight o'clock that the two aircraft were lined up in the aerodrome ready to take off.

We lowered ourselves clumsily into our machines, sweltering already in the heavy suits. The engines were ticking over and running as smoothly as could be; then a few final words with the leader and Etherton, who handed up the Everest mail containing letters to be carried over the mountain, the pilots opened the throttles, the huge engines roared, and with a cheer and a wave they were off on the great adventure.

Let Blacker, chief observer in the Houston-Westland, tell the story in his own words.

"A few minutes after we left the ground I had to busy myself with my routine duties. At the start of all high-altitude flights, a number of vital checks must be made, and to avoid the chance of omitting any I had compiled a list.[1] No less than forty-six separate jobs were included, and though each one was trifling in itself none could be omitted without risk to the eventual success of the work. It was the more necessary to prepare such a list since we were inhaling oxygen the whole time, and one of its effects on the human mind seems to be to create a tendency to concentrate on the idea or task that is uppermost to the exclusion of everything else. As most of the forty-six tasks were small details, it was all the more necessary to have them down in writing so that each observer could consult his list at any particular time during the flight, and thus ensure that every piece of work had been done by the appropriate time. The flight might be ruined, for instance, by omission to remove the caps from the lenses of all the cameras, and in this dusty climate they had to be left on till the last moment.

"The leading aircraftman photographer was responsible in the programme for removing all these caps, counting them and reporting to the observer the moment before the chocks were removed from the wheels.

"Everything passed off without incident as the two great machines soared up through the haze over the brown plains, except that just for a moment the dynamo refused, as electricians put it, to build up. This is a temperamentalism to which all dynamos are liable. So, almost in a panic, I had to take off the cover of the cut-out of the electrical system, undo the screws with my thumbnail, pressing the platinum contacts together by hand. All was well, the generator behaved perfectly throughout the flight, and a supply of current kept us warm from first to last.

"By the time the initial batch of these tests was completed

appendix 1.

L/AC. Fraser, Clark, Cpl. Bradley
Read, Flt.-Sgt. Greenwood, Gupta, Hughes, Shepherd, Bennett, Hensley, Burnard, Pitt, Connachie, Sweeny, Young
Barkas, Etherton, Clydesdale, Fellows, Blacker, McIntyre, Bonnett, Ellison, Fisher
THE MEMBERS OF THE EXPEDITION

we had been flying for some ten minutes, and for the next half-hour I had nothing to do but to sit conning over and recapitulating in my mind my duties. This part of the journey was the more humdrum because the plains and foothills below were almost lost to view owing to the thick dust-haze which had, unfortunately, on that day, chosen to rise to a phenomenal height. Gradually the dull monochrome of the brown chequer-boards of the ploughed fields of Bihar fused together into a uniform carpet, and every now and then the cluster of tiny rectangular roofs of a village stood out from the scene.

"This haze almost invariably ceases at about a 5,000 or 6,000 foot level; the present case its continuance above that height was infuriating in the last degree.

"We did not rise clear of it until actually about 19,000 feet, and so the southern ground control, which was the river confluence near Komaltar, was practically invisible to the pilot. He could not find it with sufficient accuracy, a decided mis-fortune, since it was the point from which the photographic survey was started.

"Nevertheless, I was just able to see an infinite tangle of the brown mountains of Nepal, seamed with black forests, and caught occasional glimpses of the swift Arun river in its gradually steepening valley as now and then I opened the hatchway of the floor and looked down through thousands of feet of purple space. We crossed the frontier of this forbidden kingdom at 13,000 feet. Then, suddenly, a little after our craft sprang clear of the haze into the wonderful translucent air of the upper heights, and away to our right an amazing view of Kangchenjunga in all its gleaming whiteness opened out against the blue.

"For a few minutes nothing else could be seen against the sky but this.

"Fumbling with the catches in my thick gloves, I threw up the cockpit roof, put my head out into the icy slip-stream and there over the pulsating rocker arms of the Pegasus, showing level with us, was the naked majesty of Everest itself. Just a tiny triangle of whiteness, so white as to appear incandescent, and on its right, a hand's breadth, another tiny peak which was Makalu. For some time nothing could be seen above this purple haze but these three incredible white peaks—Everest and Makalu just to the right of the engine, and Kangchenjunga behind the right wing. It was fortunate that the wind from the westward caused the machine to lie with a drift of eighteen degrees, obliquely to our track to the mountain, and thus we had a clear view of our goal straight beneath a point on the under-surface of the upper wing, eighteen degrees from the centre line.

"Gyachungkang was masked by the engine, but soon Gaurisankar showed over the port wing.

"I was not long able to remain watching these wonderful sights, for soon the machine soared upwards, unfolding in-numerable peaks to right and left and in front, all in their amazing white mantles, but scored and seared with black precipices.

"The light on the snow was a wonderful thing in itself. A quality of whiteness, as much more brilliant than the snow to which ordinary human eyes are accustomed, as that snow is more vivid than the unclothed landscape.

"Somewhat to our dismay, there streamed from the crest of Everest away towards its sister peak, Makalu, eastwards, that immense ice-plume which is the manifestation of a mighty wind raging across the summit. Lifting from the prodigious cliff face, countless particles of ice are driven over the summit with blizzard force.

"Soon, very slowly it seemed, we approached closer and closer to the big white mountains, and all my time became occupied with work on the cameras.

"Now I crouched down over the drift-sight, peering through the great concave lens and adjusted the wires across it. I rotated them carefully and this gave me the angle of drift of eighteen degrees. I passed this to the pilot, who needed it for navigation, and then I adjusted the big automatic survey camera, turning it through the same angle in its mounting.

FLYING TO EVEREST, 3RD APRIL, 1933
The Mountains of Nepal below

THE FLIGHT TO EVEREST

"I had to look to the spirit-levels, longitudinal and transverse, and to adjust the tilt of the camera in both senses, until the bubbles rested in the middle of their travel. This required delicacy and judgment as the machine swayed every now and then. The adjustment had to be made in each case just at the moment when the machine happened to be level, neither one wing-tip up nor down in either direction nor pitching. I glanced at the big aluminium actuating-knob, and saw that after twenty seconds or so it turned by itself as the pilot had switched on the current into its motor. The camera was warm, the current was running through it, and all seemed well.

"Now, without getting up from a prone position, I could move myself back a little on my elbows, open the hatchway in the floor, and look vertically down on the amazing mountainscape, bare of trees, seamed with great glaciers, and interspersed with streaks of scree and shale. This was the beginning of the range, insignificant enough to our eyes at the height we were, which rises up to the culminating 24,000 feet peak of Chamlang. Then shutting the hatchway and, laboriously taking great care to keep the oxygen pipe unentangled, and myself clear of all the various electrical wires, I could stand up and look again through the top of the cockpit. I caught a glimpse over the pilot's shoulder of the brilliant red light on his dashboard, which flashed for a moment as the camera shutter operated itself.

"Up went our machine into a sky of indescribable blue, until we came to a level with the great culminating peak itself.

"Then, to my astonished eyes, northwards over the shoulder of the mountain, across the vast bare plateau of Tibet, a group of snow-clad peaks uplifted itself. I hesitated to conjecture the distance at which they lay in the heart of that almost trackless country, for by some trick of vision the summits seemed even higher than that of Mount Everest. The astonishing picture of this great mountain itself, whose plume for a moment seemed to diminish in length, and with its tremendous sullen cliffs, set off the whiteness of Makalu, was a sight which must for ever remain in one's mind.

187

"I had been hard at work with the cameras first exposing plates, uncapping dark slides, winding and setting the shutters to seize a series of splendid views. The scene was superb and beyond description. The visibility was extraordinary and permitted the whole range to be seen on the western horizon. It seemed that the only limit to the view along the mountain was that due to the curvature of the earth's surface. The size of the mountains stunned the senses; the stupendous scale of the scenery and the clear air confounded all estimates of size and distance. So I went on, now exposing plates, now lifting the heavy cinema camera to run off fifty feet or so of film. I crouched down again, struggling to open the hatchway, to take a photograph through the floor. Everything by now, all the metal parts of the machine, was chilled with the cold, the cold of almost interstellar space. The fastenings were stiff and the metal slides had almost seized. I struggled with them, the effort making me pant for breath, and I squeezed my mask on to my face to get all the oxygen possible. I had to pause and, suddenly, with the door half-open I became aware, almost perceptibly, of a sensation of dropping through space. The floor of the machine was falling away below us. I grasped a fuselage strut and peered through my goggles at the altimeter needle. It crept, almost swung, visibly as I looked at it in astonishment, down through a couple of thousand feet. Now I had the hatchway open and the aeroplane swooped downwards over a mighty peak of jagged triangular buttresses, which was the South Peak.

"Below us loomed an almost incomprehensible medley of ridges, ranges and spurs of black rocks, with here and there the characteristic yellowy-red of Everest showing through. We had suddenly lost two thousand feet in this great down-draught of the winds, and it seemed as though we should never clear the crags of the South Peak on the way to Everest now towering in front of us. However, the alarm was short-lived, for our splendid engine took us up through the great overfall. Again we climbed; slowly, yet too quickly for one who wants to make

The Houston-Westland about two-and-a-half minutes' flight from the summit of Everest. Taken a moment before coming into the big down current

use of every moment, our aeroplane came to the curved chisel-like summit of Everest, crossing it, so it seemed to me, just a hair's breadth over its menacing summit. The crest came up to meet me as I crouched peering through the floor, and I almost wondered whether the tail skid would strike the summit. I laboured incessantly, panting again for breath to expose plates and films, each lift of the camera being a real exertion. Every now and then my eyes swam a little and I looked at the oxygen flow-meter to find it reading its maximum. So I bethought myself of the little cork plugs I had whittled down to fit the eye apertures of the mask. Tearing off the heavy gloves and fumbling with cold fingers, I managed to stuff them in.

"Now I had worked my way up again to a standing position, with the cockpit roof fully open and its flaps fastened back. I had my head and shoulders out into the slip-stream, which had become strangely bereft of its accustomed force. I was astonished for a moment till I suddenly remembered that the wind here only weighed a quarter as much as at sea-level. Now I could take photographs over the top of the machine much aided by these fortunate cork plugs. Without them, if the aviator has his head sideways in the slip-stream the oxygen tends to be blown from his mask and the flow stopped before it can reach his mouth, in much the same way that a trout may be drowned by pulling him upstream against the lie of his gills.

"Thus almost, and indeed before I expected it, we swooped over the summit and a savage period of toil began. The pilot swung the machine skilfully again towards the westward into the huge wind force sweeping downwards over the crest; so great was its strength that, as the machine battled with it and struggled to climb upwards against the downfall, we seemed scarcely to make headway in spite of our 120 mile an hour air speed. I crammed plate-holder after plate-holder into the camera, releasing the shutter as fast as I could, to line it on one wonderful scene after another. We were now for a few moments in the very plume itself, and as we swung round fragments of ice rattled violently into the cockpit.

"We made another circuit and then another as I exposed dozens of plates and ran off my spools of film. We could not wait long over the mountain-top for the oxygen pressure gauge needle in my cockpit was moving downwards, an ominous sign. We had no very exact idea of the length of time our return journey would take with that violent wind blowing, and fuel was needed for emergencies. After a quarter of an hour or so, which seemed perhaps on the one hand like a lifetime from its amazing experiences, and yet was all too short, we turned back. Soon we saw this wonderful view with serried peaks, row upon row, in fairy beauty, surmounted by Everest and Makalu almost grotesquely outlined by the aluminium-coloured fabric of our rudder. We came back towards the terrific Arun gorges over a bewildering medley of peaks, ranges and spurs, interspersed with broad grimy glaciers littered with moraine, scree and shale. These peaks must be a great height and yet they seemed insignificant enough to our eyes.

"160 miles home passed surprisingly quickly, the journey, marred by the discovery that the second film in the ciné-camera had become frozen despite its warm jacket, and was so brittle that I could not reload. My oxygen mask, too, plugged as it was with cork stoppers, had become a solid mass of ice. Steadily we came down, gradually losing height with the throttle of the engine fairly well open to guard against the carburettor freezing. It was in another struggle that I managed to change the magazine of the survey camera and adjust it to the drift now coming from the opposite side of the aeroplane.

"Soon the semi-circle of gleaming peaks faded from our sight as the straight line of purple dust-haze rose to overwhelm it."

So much for the chief observer's record. Clydesdale and he had no communication during the flight, their positions were several feet apart, there was a bulkhead between them and their telephone had not been in an accommodating mood. The pilot was therefore in a position to form his own impressions independently and we cannot do better than quote the report made:

Looking down on to the summit of Everest for the first time, 3rd April, 1933. On the right, over the black rock faces, is the route of the climbing expedition

THE FLIGHT TO EVEREST

"This morning the Indian Meteorological Officer at Purnea, Mr. S. N. Gupta, whose information and advice have been of great value to the expedition, reported from balloon observations, that the wind, whose velocity previously had been unsuitable, had dropped to fifty-seven miles per hour at 33,000 feet, which altitude we had decided would be the most suitable working height for photographic survey.

"Our two machines took off from Lalbalu aerodrome, near Purnea, in still air, the Houston-Westland crewed by Col. L. V. S. Blacker and myself, and the Westland-Wallace piloted by Flight-Lieutenant D. F. McIntyre with Mr. S. R. Bonnett, who is aerial photographer of the Gaumont-British Film Corporation, as observer. Our direct route to the summit meant flying on a track of 342 degrees. This necessitated changing the compass course at intervals more to the west, on account of the increase of wind velocity with height, according to our weather report.

"We had relied to some extent on overcoming the difficulty of accurate compass navigation caused by this frequent change of wind speed, by the good landmarks near and along the track.

"A heavy dust-haze, rising to a considerable height, almost completely obscured the ground from Forbesganj towards the higher mountain ranges. This (as it proved later) made aerial survey work impossible. We climbed slowly at low engine revolutions to a height of 10,000 feet. By this height, the crews of both machines had tested their respective electrical heating sets, and McIntyre and I signalled to each other that everything was satisfactory.

"After thirty minutes' flying we passed over Forbesganj, our forward emergency landing-ground, forty miles from Purnea and at a height of 19,000 feet. Everest first became visible above the haze. We flew lower than our intended working height in _____ ndeavour to pass over Komaltar, close to _____ ontrol from which we were to begin our _____ possible to identify any landmarks at all _____ within twenty miles of the summit.

"At nine o'clock we passed over Chamlang at an altitude of 31,000 feet. On approaching Lhotse, the South Peak of the Everest group, the ground rises at a steep gradient, and both machines experienced a steady down current due to deflection of the west wind over the mountain, causing a loss of altitude of 1,500 feet, despite all our efforts to climb. Both aeroplanes flew over the summit of Everest at 10.5, clearing it by 100 feet.

"The wind velocity was noticeably high near the summit, but no bumps were felt by either aircraft. Fifteen minutes were spent flying in the neighbourhood of the summit, and on account of the smooth flying conditions the taking of close-range photographs was rendered possible.

"The visibility of distant high peaks was very good. The great Himalaya range could be seen extending to great distances and provided a magnificent spectacle.

"The return journey was carried out at a slightly lower altitude, so as to secure better conditions for oblique photography. The machines landed at Lalbalu at 11.25. Both pilots pay the highest tribute to the splendid performance of the engines and aircraft. So we landed, full of happiness, with the realisation that we had been where no man had been before.

"But soon our jubilation was marred by the discovery that the survey photographs were not a success. That phenomenally amazing haze of dust had obscured the lower mountains to such a degree that the strips of photographs would neither overlap nor show the ground controls near the Komaltar ridge.

"The actual flyers were tired and entranced by their experiences and by what they had seen to the point of exaltation, so it took some time for the situation to be accurately appraised. In fact it was not until the next day that we were able to pin together the hundred prints from each film. Meanwhile the letters we had carried over the mountain were despatched to H.M. the King, the Prince of Wales and Lady Houston.

"We were thrilled beyond description by what we had seen; but of all we had been through, our passage into the heart that plume or jet of ice particles was the most intriguing.

THE WESTERN END OF THE CHAMLANG RANGE TAKEN FROM ALMOST OVER EVEREST

"Before the start of this flight, we had seen the mountain on several occasions from the Moths, from 5,000 feet up, which had taken us above the ground-haze, usually only 5,000 feet from the ground level, but enough to entirely obscure the mountains from the plains.

"From the Moths we had seen what previous explorers had called 'the plume' of Everest and had somewhat readily taken it for granted that it was merely a cloud, of which the component particles would naturally be frozen, and similar to that one usually sees in the vicinity of high mountains.

"Kangchenjunga for instance, was seldom without such a cloud wreath, throughout April.

"When, however, the machines went actually into it, we realised that it was something quite different to what we had conceived. Here was no drifting cloud wisp, but a prodigious jet of rushing winds flinging a veritable barrage of ice fragments for several miles to leeward of the peak.

"The force of the *rafale* was indeed so great as to crack the celastroid windows of the Houston-Westland's rear cockpit.

"We soon realised too, that this 'plume' could not be composed of frozen matter carried over by the blizzard from the windward face, for the reason that the windward faces, that is the south-eastern sides, were practically bare, as may be seen from the photographs.

"Perhaps some day science will find a solution for this riddle, the enigma of the great mountain.

"We ourselves are inclined to the opinion that this phenomenon is due to the immense overfall of the winds over the crest, giving rise to what aerodynamical experts call a 'burble' on the leeward side, that is, a zone of reduced pressure, which tends to draw up the air from the Tibetan side and with it great masses of old snow and fragments of ice. Perhaps, too, drops of moisture are drawn up from lower levels, frozen in the process, and projected back down wind when they come into the grip of this vast maelstrom.

"This is merely a tentative theory, and we can but hope that scientists will take up the mystery of this singular 'plume.'

"We realised that our passage through it, and through the complementary 'downfall' on the windward side, hard by the South Peak ('Lhotse') had been the great adventure of our flight.

"Still, it was not our business to have adventures, for adventures are eschewed by all well-organised expeditions."

ONE OF THE GREAT DECLIVITIES OF EVEREST

CHAPTER XI

THE FLIGHT OVER KANGCHENJUNGA AND THE SECOND FLIGHT TO EVEREST

THE first flight over Everest on April 3rd had encountered difficulties in the matter of the vertical cameras and telephone gear, while certain inconveniences in the heating suits were manifest. The results obtained by the oblique cameras appeared to be very good, but those of the vertical had been spoilt by the dust-haze, and we were therefore not certain whether the right exposure for the conditions had been given for them. All this gear had been satisfactorily operated over Karachi at the same height—35,000 feet. But it was deemed advisable to try again at the maximum height, and over snow, to make sure that all was correct. As snow scarcely exists at this season south of Kangchenjunga, we decided to fly over the summit, the height being approximately 28,200 feet, and secure aerial photographs of what was unknown country. The meteorologists considered that the fine weather experienced on April 3rd, the day of the first flight over Everest, was unlikely to last much beyond the 4th, and so the attempt upon, or rather over Kangchenjunga, was planned for that day. It meant hastening preparations, as the flight was scheduled to start from Purnea at 8 a.m. Even so, owing to the numerous adjustments necessitated before the flight, the take-off was delayed, owing to the vital necessity of having everything in order before leaving the ground.

There were two main objects to attain; perfection in the apparatus for the next attempt over Everest, and good cinema photographs of mountain scenery. The crews consisted of Fellowes and Fisher in the Houston-Westland, and Ellison and Bonnett in the Westland Wallace.

The consequences of the delay were unfortunate, for when the aircraft rose through the haze, encountered at a height of 19,000 feet, Kangchenjunga appeared tantalisingly close on the port bow, perfectly clear and free from clouds; but by the time the mountain was reached, 1,500 feet of cloud completely enveloped the top. This piece of bad luck definitely prevented us from going vertically over the summit or obtaining a clear picture of the upper part of the mountain. From the photograph it will be seen that the summit only shows dimly through the clouds; when it was taken the aeroplane was almost vertically over the summit.

The 'planes took off separately at ten o'clock, it being the first occasion on which either Fellowes or Ellison had flown this type of aircraft. They climbed slowly at first though the haze to gain familiarity with the controls, and by the time 12,000 feet was reached, both pilots felt thoroughly at home with their machines. At that height Fellowes pulled his oxygen mask up to his face; he had carefully adjusted this when on the ground, but found that the system of straps which had appeared so satisfactory on the aerodrome, now failed completely to hold the mask in position on his face, if he moved his head at all. This meant that every time he looked at the instruments, or over the side or tail, he had to readjust his mask, and eventually to hold it on with his hand. Ellison was experiencing the same difficulty. To quote Fellowes' own description of ensuing events:

"Finding that I could hold my mask on with my left hand, without unduly interfering with control of the machine, I decided to go on mainly because the expedition's supply of fuel and oxygen had been finely cut, and it would have been difficult to justify another experimental flight over Kangchenjunga, supplied as we were with a limited quantity of petrol and oxygen to make this attempt. So we proceeded, and at 19,000 feet obtained our first sight of the mountain over the haze, although still some distance from the hills which rise steeply from the plains on which our aerodrome was situated. They are only a few hundred feet above sea-level and extend

An infra-red photograph showing the summit of Everest over the clouds, and Chamlang outlined against them. Taken from a hundred miles away

KANGCHENJUNGA
Taken on infra-red plate from a hundred miles away, from 21,000 feet

for hundreds of miles north-west and south-east. These hills, which appear insignificant from the air, are most imposing when viewed from the ground, rising to a height of 5,000 or 6,000 feet within a few miles of the plain.

"Our first sight of Kangchenjunga standing out in all its white majesty against a clear hard sky, was truly magnificent, and enthralling, since it was quite free of clouds. We now set our course for the confluence of the great Rangit at Tassading, whence we proposed to take a straight photographic strip to include this confluence and the mountain-peak. I wondered if I would be able to recognise it, hampered as I was by goggles and oxygen mask. Disappointment was in store, as it soon became apparent that a mass of clouds lay between the foothills and Kangchenjunga, completely blotting out the area we had proposed to photograph. This did not affect the test, the important point being to secure vertical photographs of the snow regions, and to ensure that the automatic vertical cameras, when set in motion by the pilot continued to work, allowing timing intervals to be changed, and the cameras to be stopped and started. The cameras were operated and tested in every possible way, responding satisfactorily, this being done by the pilot. During the flight over clouds the mountain was drawing nearer and nearer, and was now no more than some thirty miles away, but the summit was becoming blurred. It seemed as though the photographs of the top we had set our hearts on getting, might not after all be obtained. After examining the instruments, in turn, it was comforting to see they all registered the correct readings.

"Then a look round revealed a wonderful scene. I was amazed. Behind lay the plains of India, cut in all directions by the broad and winding sand-courses of the many river beds flowing from the Himalayas and constantly forming new channels for themselves. Nearer still lay the green hills of Sikkim with their mane of trees and vegetation, their heights varying from 4,000 to 7,000 feet. Irregular in formation, being deeply cut up by deep valleys, gorges and river beds, it was strange at this moment to ponder how these hard and knobly-looking hills grew the plant that provides the homely cup of tea. . . . Directly beneath the aircraft was a sea of clouds, and looking forward as the mountain came nearer and nearer, great peaks of over 20,000 feet upreared themselves from the clouds which lapped the upper slopes of Kangchenjunga and its main range. We were now looking down on scenes never before viewed by the eye of bird or man.

"Kangchenjunga is not a mountain in the ordinary sense; it is a mass of mountains reaching out southwards from the main Himalayan range stretching in a north-westerly, south-westerly, and south-easterly direction, mighty beyond imagining, bounded on all sides by such awe-inspiring scenery as human eye can rarely gaze upon. To attempt to describe it by saying that in these directions lay a stretch of snow peaks, glaciers and tumbled valleys, giving the appearance of a terrific sea, imparts little idea of the unspeakable reality of what lay beneath us. Still less can the camera convey the wonderful impression of the illimitable magnificence and immensity of the scene. Away to the north-west Everest and its companion towered up into the sky, and far beyond them, stretching into the blue distance appeared an array of lesser mountains. All this time the great mass of Kangchenjunga was drawing nearer, and now it became certain that the cloud formation at the top was rapidly growing denser and higher. Forty minutes after having seen the mountain-top completely clear of all cloud, there had formed a huge cloud cap 1,500 feet thick, and many miles in area, completely obliterating the summit. Looking away from this disappointing coverlet the cold mountains were putting over their heads, I saw Ellison quite close, with Bonnett busily operating his camera. Fisher, who had been quietly preparing for this moment, now asked if he could open his cockpit. I agreed, as we had by then attained the desired height of 34,000 feet. Again I looked over the side and saw Ellison coming up almost wing-tip to wing-tip. Incidentally, I had to be careful about moving my head because of my

FLYING TOWARDS KANGCHENJUNGA, 4TH APRIL, 1933

SNOW SLOPES OF KANGCHENJUNGA

oxygen mask; and yet move I must to see my instruments, to look over the side, and to manipulate the camera. We were now approaching the great cloud over Kangchenjunga itself. Eventually we were so close to its edge that we could look down almost vertically over the top, and so we proceeded to fly round it, but, owing either to slightly inaccurate flying or to a down draught, we gradually lost height as we circled the mighty peak. Eventually, we must have dropped to approximately the same height, although it was difficult to be certain of this. We were now very close to the mountain, and gaining the north-east or easterly side, ran into a prolonged and severe disturbance, as a result of which my accelerometer registered 2.8 g. It was so sudden that for a time I seemed to lose all control of the ailerons and rudder, and did not know what was going to happen. The machine rocked, twisted and shook in a way I had never experienced before in eighteen years continuous flying. Once it seemed certain we must drop into a spin. However, after what seemed an eternity, but was probably not more than half a minute, we ran into still air with only a trifling loss of height, and renewed our efforts to go over the top. The accelerometer, it is true, only registered 2.8 g, but the sensations that *we* registered, had it been possible to do so as a measure of nervous disturbance, would have vastly exceeded any such scientific relativity. In such critical circumstances there is no time for fear. There is too much to do. At that great height even in quiet air some nervous tension was natural, and certainly for several minutes I experienced that blurred feeling one gets after a bad shaking.

"Soon after this the two machines became separated, due to a turn which I made without realising that Ellison had again come up close to me on the north side, and causing him suddenly to lose height. I had not sighted him for some few minutes and imagined he had gone back. After cruising another quarter of an hour in the vicinity of the mountain, I gave up all hope of being able to cross the summit, and turned back, flying first to the north, and then heading south for home.

But I could not recall which of the various courses I had written down on my map was the correct one, to avoid the Nepalese border. This lapse of memory I put down to want of oxygen caused by my ill-fitting mask. My brain was definitely too tired to enable me to reason out the correct course which, in normal conditions, I could easily have done. There are no signposts in the sky. The mountains now on my port quarter were of no avail in assisting me to determine the southerly course. The whole country was completely covered by clouds as far as the hills extended, and so I flew due south, being now able at last to think clearly enough to be certain that this would take me in the right direction and away from Nepal. Once beyond the hilly country, I descended through the haze and looked round for any familiar objects, but Indian maps are on a small scale and it is difficult to recognise rivers or railways unless distinct in their formation. However, I seemed to recognise one place and made out a course on which I flew for nearly half an hour. Still unable definitely to identify the country below me, the idea came to me that I was too far west, whereas in reality I was much too far east. Having circled round for some time and still finding it impossible to locate any suitable landing-ground, I determined to alight in the first suitable area near the railway line along which I was then flying. I chose a fairly large field in an apparently uninhabited area, apart from a few huts. But I very soon realised my limitations as a censor, for a couple of minutes after landing I was surrounded by thousands of wildly gesticulating Beharis, those nearest the aeroplane endeavouring to touch or finger it; so much so, that like Gulliver on his travels, I was despairing of being able to get away again, especially as all the children and young people seemed seized by an irresistible desire to sit on the tailplane. Meanwhile, I kept the engine running slowly as I had no means of starting it. The starting-handle had been left at Lalbalu to reduce weight; in any case it could only be operated by two people who knew all about its use, a third man being required in the cockpit at the controls. Every few

SLOPES OF KANGCHENJUNGA

minutes I had to draw on that precious supply of petrol by opening up my engine to drive the people away and frighten them off the wings. Fisher and I shouted to ascertain if anyone in the crowd could speak English. Eventually, an individual came to the side of the cockpit who appeared to understand what we were saying, so Fisher produced the map. Although he could not speak English, he understood what was said to him, could write the language, and more wonderful still, read a map. Singularly intelligent, he pointed out without hesitation our position—at Shampur. So we pushed the people away like policemen at a cup final, and climbed in.

"I had then to take off as best I could, ringed in on all sides by a brown, struggling mass of men, women and children, inextricably mixed up with dogs, cows and donkeys. I had already used the engine to frighten the people away from the aeroplane; now I fell back on the threat of the throttle. Rumbling the engine, I gradually turned the 'plane round in the direction for taking off. Fortunately the crowd, including the live-stock, seemed to understand the danger and fell away to either side, with the exception of the children and sundry odd brown babies who continued to run across our path, as well as cows and innumerable dogs. Impatiently we waited until all but the dogs were clear of the track, then opening the throttle, made our 'get-away,' hoping for the best. All went well, and I was once more in the air, but only ten gallons of petrol were left. With this Purnea could not be reached, but I could get nearer home, so followed the railway line until reaching Dinajpur, with its large Maidan. Unfortunately, the plain is punctuated with trees, and a crowd of people filled what appeared to be the only possible landing-place. There was no petrol left, so land I must somewhere. Selecting the best available area, due to providence rather than my own good piloting, I alighted safely, managing only by inches to clear a schoolhouse surrounded by railings and a couple of large trees. It being the first time I had flown this aeroplane, with two forced landings, the second an extraordinarily difficult one, I felt that the inscrutable influence some call luck, and others providence, was with me, notwithstanding that I had been unfortunate enough to lose myself. We were most hospitably received by the local magistrate and an Indian gentleman whose first form of welcome was to provide us with cooling drinks. Then the Superintendent of Police, and later the Collector, put in an appearance.

"Our first action on landing was, of course, to get into touch by telegram with the head-quarters at Purnea, which we had not been able to do at Shampur, there being no telegraphic or other facilities to be found there. The helpfulness and courtesy of all concerned was really delightful. I was very much impressed with the Indian magistrate and the Indian police officer and the way he handled his men. I gathered the latter was a bit of a hero, and that attempts had been made on his life in revenge for his efficiency.

"In the evening, just before dusk, Clydesdale arrived in his own Moth, with various items necessary to picket and cover in the machine during the night. Characteristically, he had thought all this out and got it ready as soon as he knew I was missing. He had also flown my wife over from the main aerodrome at Lalbalu to the head-quarters at Purnea, so as to be in touch with the telegraph office. Petrol he was unable to bring, since his Moth could not have carried enough to refuel the larger machine.

"The Collector kindly arranged to put us up for the night at the rest-house, and later on we were entertained by the members of the Methodist Mission on their lawn. Dining under a full moon on a calm and scented evening proved a restful and peaceful way of ending a rather hectic day.

"Very early the next morning Ellison appeared in the Puss Moth with Pitt as passenger and twenty gallons of petrol. How welcome they were! The speed and efficiency with which Pitt refuelled the Westland and started it up, was typical of his work for us. I then took off before an enormous crowd, with whom early rising, normally regarded as a virtue, appeared to

Approaching the Chamlang range, Everest
and Makalu looming larger

Closer, but still fifty miles or so away

The first view of Everest and Makalu from
about 20,000 ft. and eighty miles away

About three minutes' flight from the
summit, and a moment before coming
into the big downfall

Still twenty-odd miles to go which will
take only ten minutes

me on this occasion to be a vice, and returned to Purnea, leaving the two Moths to follow on and their occupants to be entertained at breakfast by our hosts of the night before.

"It was interesting to note the state of mind of the natives at their first sight of these aircraft. It was their first view of an aeroplane. Fortunately they did not see me when I arrived, as I kept very low, but at the sight of the aircraft a surging mass instantly surrounded us. It was due entirely to the Indian police, who waded in with sticks and staves and cleared a space round us, that no damage was done by these people, impelled to touch and finger more by curiosity than by any wish to do harm. Within ten minutes of landing we were in the midst of a shouting and gesticulating mob of at least ten thousand people. The Collector told me that his entire court immediately emptied itself despite all his protests.

"When Clydesdale landed we had the greatest difficulty in clearing the ground to give him space, but eventually by strenuous use of the voices of all those willing to act as human broadcasters, we managed to get them into line, by which time their numbers had increased to 18,000 or 20,000. The next morning when the Puss Moth arrived, there was no difficulty; they seemed to understand all about it and lined up with little trouble or shouting, the same condition of affairs prevailing when I took off.

"As a result of this flight it was possible to put all the apparatus into thoroughly good order for the second attempt on Everest, thus fulfilling the main object we had set out to accomplish. We also obtained some excellent cinema photographs.

"It is never any good crying over spilt milk, but were we so disposed we should undoubtedly have been very mournful over our bad luck in finding such desperately bad weather conditions over and near Kangchenjunga. These completely ruined our chance of getting any photographs of value from a geographical point of view. It was a remarkable thing on looking back to realise how quickly the clouds covered Kangchenjunga after we had first sighted it. Then it was as clear from clouds as was possible for a mountain to be. Again, it was astonishing how quickly the weather in the whole area altered; we must have arrived at the very moment when it was on the change. Bad luck with the various little things delayed us at the start, otherwise the trip, instead of being only partially successful from the photographic point of view, would have successfully compared with either of the Everest flights. It was unfortunate, to say the least of it, that we were unable to repeat this flight over Kangchenjunga.

"Ellison and Bonnett, who had found their way back to Purnea after leaving Kangchenjunga, had been vividly impressed with the area covered by the series of peaks surrounding the summit, and were equally disappointed that it had not been possible to secure satisfactory photographs of Kangchenjunga itself—one of the world's most massive and spectacular mountains, and still a virgin peak."

*   *   *   *   *   *

It had been brought home harshly to us that our labour on the first flight had been in vain. The main object of the expedition was still unattained. There were no recriminations; the personality of our leader had welded the whole expedition into a band of brothers, and into a structure based upon our deep-seated confidence in him and each other.

In any case recrimination would have been of no avail. None could have foreseen that the dust-haze would extend to the amazing height, as it did, of 19,000 feet. There are no scientific processes for measuring the upper limits of such a haze, other than going up to see for oneself in a balloon or aeroplane. Certainly there were no previous observations on record. It was this unprecedented dust-haze which prevented us, more than any other cause, from obtaining any useful vertical photographs on April 3rd. The dust made not only the southern ground control, but also the details of the country up to the mountain, invisible.

Even in the earliest phase of our plans, we had foreseen the

Makalu, 27790

The Summit

Looking steeply down on to the actual summit of Everest. Taken by Blacker from the Houston-Westland at close range

possibility that a second flight would be necessary. There was such a mass of sensitive and delicate devices and gadgets, any one of which might well go wrong in those exceptional variations of heat and cold, and invariably required to work without any lubrication, for oil would freeze.

But a more probable source of trouble lay in the presence of clouds in the higher country. A mass of cumulus lurking in one of the big valleys close up to the mountain, would probably have been invisible from the air until too late, when the machines had already been committed to crossing the Nepal frontier. Such a belt of cloud would have broken the continuity of the strip of vertical photographs, and thus rendered it valueless for plotting onto the map or, in fact, for any scientific purpose.

Even had the verticals of the first flight been entirely satisfactory, we recognised long before the expedition left England that we owed it to science to obtain an adequate result from those splendid aeroplanes, and enough to show our appreciation of Lady Houston's generosity.

It would, in any case, have been incumbent on us from a sheer sense of duty, to have made a second flight to increase the area photographed on the first.

There was such an immense extent of unknown country that a dozen flights would not have been adequate to map it.

In any case we could not have refrained from making a second flight for the cogent reason that the Government of Nepal, who had treated us with so much consideration and courtesy, had imposed the condition that permission for the flights was given solely for scientific purposes. Scientific purposes could be nothing else than the making of a continuous strip of vertical photographs, which we had not yet succeeded in doing.

We felt that it would have been failing in our duty had we accepted the facilities so cordially granted by the Nepal Government, and the hospitality and assistance accorded by all branches of the Government of India, and not justified their confidence.

Perhaps the greatest factor actuating us was the realisation that, had we abandoned our objective without attaining it, we should have brought discredit, not only upon ourselves, but indirectly upon Lady Houston as a protagonist of British aviation.

We felt it more especially a bounden duty to her because we had called the expedition by her name, and were determined to do her credit.

Not unexpectedly, we soon received a cablegram from Lady Houston herself, addressed to Clydesdale advising him, in sympathetic words, not to run the risk of further flights over the mountains. This message we ascribed to the promptings of a warm and generous heart, which could not quietly contemplate men going to face risks which are the proper lot of youth.

However, the cablegram did not contain any categorical prohibition, but when it became known that the Government of Nepal had actually sanctioned the essential second flight, we were assailed by a barrage of telegraphic messages.

No doubt these were sent with good intent, but they could not see our point of view, and adjured us in varying phraseology and for assorted reasons, to abandon the flight. We were too occupied at the time to examine these missives critically, being preoccupied with the sole aim of achieving success and justifying the confidence of our splendid backer, and we felt it the more imperative since full powers in the control of the expedition were already delegated to the leader and the executive committee, who were in Purnea.

We recalled to mind the fate of an airman, General Nobile; as luck would have it one of our party had been well acquainted with him and his story. He scouted the idea that it was out of regard for his personal safety that General Nobile acted as he did in the Arctic, and for which he was broken.

The cynic would remark that before he was broken by his own government he had already been judged and condemned

MAKALU (27,790 FEET)
From the direction of Everest

unheard by ignorant outsiders, by the howls of an uninformed public opinion.

So we remembered Nobile and fully realised that had we abandoned our efforts to make the expedition a success, the cause of British aviation must inevitably suffer.

Of our troubles the principal was that due to the weather which behaved in a manner infuriating and worrying to the last degree.

As already remarked, there seemed to be a ten- or twelve-day cycle in its vagaries at this time of the year. At its commencement we would receive a telegram from "Weather" Calcutta announcing a disturbance on the north-west frontier. These reports from the Indian Meteorological Bureau were almost uncanny in their accuracy. We soon appreciated that the disturbances to which they referred were neither political nor brigandly, but meteorological, and that they travelled westwards, taking four or five days to cross India and reach Purnea.

The disturbances brought with them downpours of rain and dust storms, accompanied by high winds at the upper levels.

Then the lofty mountains, which had been smothered in thick clouds would gradually clear, and at the same time each day's report of the wind velocities, taken from the balloons, would show a lessened force.

We were between two dangers. If, on the one hand, we played for safety and waited for the wind to abate to its lowest, as recorded in the afternoon, there was every possibility that by next morning it would have increased again. If, on the other hand, we were to risk going to Everest in a high wind, we courted trouble from running short of fuel and so being unable to complete the return journey. As related in another chapter, to fly from one point to another and back in a high wind, is equivalent to flying by a curved, i.e., an indirect or longer route.

The ingenuity and resource of our scientifically-minded second pilot, McIntyre, came to the rescue.

We knew that the winds at low altitudes usually blew from

the east and were seldom very strong. Conversely, the upper winds were from the west and correspondingly powerful.

McIntyre worked out a plan by which the two Westlands would fly in company for approximately one hundred miles to the westward, or slightly north of west, at a height of about 3,000 feet. This would bring them to a point roughly over the frontier of Nepal well to the westward of Mount Everest in under an hour, since the wind would be favourable. They would then climb to 18,000 feet to attain adequate height over the minor mountains, at the same time turning towards Mount Everest, or north-east. As they climbed and flying in this direction, the powerful winds at that height would be behind them, at any rate sufficiently in rear to give appreciable aid.

This stratagem promised to go far towards solving one of our main difficulties, and we all applauded the skill and ingenuity of its creator.

Apart from the weather and the question of personal risk, there was no obstacle to a second flight.

*　　*　　*　　*　　*　　*

So, after waiting for a spell of cloudy weather to clear away, the two 'planes took off from Lalbalu early on the morning of April 19th.

At dawn we had hurried to the observatory roof to see the wind reports. They were disquieting. The wind strength at 24,000 feet, taken from the theodolite readings, was eighty-eight miles an hour, and at greater heights even stronger than that formidable figure.

The early reconnaissance by our light scouting Moth gave a result both tantalising and disquieting. All had been clear as regards clouds just after daybreak, so went the report, but they were showing ominous signs of coming up from the west, at least into the lower valley of Nepal.

Now Blacker, the observer in the Houston-Westland tells his story.

"I was determined that nothing should prevent my making

208

Approaching Everest on 19th April, 1933. Everest is between the struts, Makalu behind the rear strut. Makalu is 12 miles from Everest. The clouds are at 18,000 feet. Note the very great angle of drift and the long "plume," due to the high

the camera work, so, crouched over it, and as soon as the pilot switched on for exposure and I saw the flexible drive give its preliminary writhe, I seized the knob of the hand-working gear and turned it gently to help the electric drive over. All was well, and this process was repeated every twenty seconds. For something like an hour I must have been huddled over the vertical camera feeling its pulse, as it were, and coaxing it along. Everest lay straight before us and great cliff-bound valleys streaked with snowfields were clear beneath us. The all-important camera was working.

"Suddenly a message came from the front of the cockpit. The electric plug was vibrating out of the pilot's oxygen heater and refused to stay in place. It was a critical matter for the pilot to have to hold this in one hand and yet fly the exceptionally steady, level course demanded by the air survey with the other. Fortunately our telephones were working and so we could consult. Previous misfortunes with the gear had led me to take up a screw-driver, which I passed forward with the suggestion that Clydesdale should prize open the split-pins of the plug with it. This he did and his troubles in that respect were over. Next I had a fresh struggle because the drift clamping screw of the survey camera had seized with cold, and the screw-driver was used in an effort to release it. This was not entirely successful because I was afraid of wrecking the whole camera.

"On we went up to 31,000 feet, the mountain getting ever closer, and now I started busily taking oblique photographs of those unexplored declivities, ridges, and ranges which run south-west from Everest. This was indeed to be the main prize of our flight, because it is precisely these aspects of the massif that are unknown to science. All went well. I alternated between diving down to the survey camera to help it to do its appointed task, and leaning over the side of the open cockpit to take obliques and train the cinema camera on magnificent spectacles. I had besides the still camera a Kodak baby ciné-camera, and a hectic time dividing my attention between them in the twenty seconds' interval between the exposures of the survey camera.

" Our previous experience had shown where we might expect the great horizontal eddy on the windward side of the South Peak, and our common sense led us to avoid entering it as only harm would ensue from the tilt which must necessarily be imparted to the vertical photographs.

"Meanwhile my own busy task kept me hard at work indeed, panting for breath and racking my lungs to fill them with oxygen. Every few seconds I was forced to get down to the cockpit floor to supervise the fixed camera. Between this I had to spring up, reload the trusty Williamson P.14, uncap the slide, set the shutter, select an object, steady the camera solicitously against engine vibration, and release the lever. Then quickly the slide had to be covered again, and placed carefully in the cunningly devised slide box, with its spring lid. We had been forced to make these because of the intensive powers of penetration which light seems to possess at these altitudes.

"In our early trial flights I had found it creeping in around the edges of dark slides and fogging the margins of the plates in the most exasperating manner.

"The pilot handled the machine with that hardihood and surpassing accuracy which filled me now, as ever, with complete confidence.

Soon we flew once again over the cliffs of the South Peak, scarred with its huge triangular crags. We came close once more to Everest, which had lost none of its entrancing beauty.

"The machine circled serenely, unmindful of the hurricane blast to which the six-mile long 'plume' from Everest summit bore witness. I photographed incessantly, striving always to remember the gaps of the first flight and to make them good for science.

"Now we were over the spurs of Everest, and now over the peak of Makalu and the yet untrodden tangled ranges to the south-east.

The Houston- Westland with its wheels almost over the South Peak ("Lhotse")
on 19th April, 1933, about 3 minutes' flight from Everest

THE EVEREST GROUP FROM THE E.S.E.

"Meanwhile the mountain came ever closer, bare and clear in the wonderful atmosphere and free from cloud, except for its great plume, now bigger than ever. In the crystal-clear weather I was delighted at the view over great Khumbu glacier and the terrific ridges which bound it. Again to the west, for an immense distance, stretched a chain of countless peaks, while in front to the east the great range continued, broken slightly by the Arun Gorge, then sweeping round to the huge mass of Kangchenjunga, Kabru, and Sinilochun. On we swept, veering a little more to the north-east to skirt the southern declivities and shape a course practically on Makalu.

"Having come to the apex of our course, practically over Makalu, Clydesdale now steered south for the homeward journey, giving me wonderful views as we flew parallel to and on the west side of the great Arun Gorge. On our right now was the lofty snowy Chamlang range, behind us great snowfields, while below was the unbroken tumble of side valleys that run down to the Arun. The air beneath was still and clear and the survey camera, helped every now and then, continued its scientific work. Presently my screw-driver again came into use in reloading my cinema camera with a new film. When the job was done I was congratulating myself, though slightly breathless from winding the clockwork, when the priceless screw-driver fell from my hand, and in a moment I saw it flashing through the open floor hatch with a glint of sun on its shaft as it sped on its way to Nepal.

"All my plates had been used, and we were steadily losing height, though we had not been able to regain touch with the other machine. Most of our work had been carried out at an aneroid height of 31,000 feet.

"Soon enough our time was finished. We could not linger, so regretfully had to turn southward once more. Our rudder was silhouetted against the snowy pyramid of Makalu, the great gorges of the Arun opened out to the east, and the sombre pine forests of that valley appeared with the swift-flowing river, occasionally passing grey sandbanks. We crossed, transversely, the Mahabharat range, almost indistinguishable in comparison with the mountains we had come from. Soon we were back over the familiar chequer-board of Bihar, and descended gracefully to our landing-field.

"Now came the greatest anxiety of all. We had risked everything to make the survey photographs a success, and any one of a hundred mischances might have nullified our efforts. No cameras had ever before been asked to operate in those torrid heats and depths of cold, running unlubricated, and never free from the impalpable all-pervading dust of the plains.

"I tore off my mask in the air, then gloves and helmet, and unfastened the innumerable wires of my electric harness before the wheels touched the familiar green turf of Lalbalu. An anxious hour followed as the skilled fingers of Aircraftman Fraser worked in complete darkness.

"The excitement and anxiety were intense, while we waited later on outside the dark-room to learn the results. Fortunately for me the suspense was mitigated by having to go up on another flight during the afternoon to take infra-red photographs, necessitating a climb to 21,000 feet without oxygen. On landing I was overjoyed to find the spools had come out, the quality of the photographs admirable, and that both aeroplanes had secured an absolutely unbroken survey strip. These must assuredly be unique, because never before have such tremendous glacial mountains been photographed from above.

"Hasty examination showed the overlaps to be complete, and all exposures astonishingly free from distortion. This is partly attributable to the skill and good flying of the pilots, also to the remarkable calmness and freedom from bumps, even when the wind velocity was, as it proved to be at times, of the order of 120 miles. In fact in the second leg of our course, it was necessary to change direction somewhat in order to make any headway at all. Everything worked excellently, except that the trouble I had on the first flight with the accumulator cut-out repeated itself, but this time there was a screw-

THE HOUSTON-WESTLAND FLYING TOWARDS EVEREST ON APRIL 19TH, 1933, AT ABOUT
29,000 FEET

THE SUMMIT
From E.N.E. and slightly above

driver instead of my thumb-nail for dealing with it. Although without oxygen till 18,000 feet, neither of us felt any ill-effects. The consumption of oxygen during the flight was surprisingly small. It is a testimonial to the care with which the oxygen was prepared in England that there was no vestige of trouble due to moisture in the valves. No doubt we shall derive valuable lessons in the mechanical design of cameras for use in extremes of temperature.

"We feel that we have accomplished our task—to demonstrate that inaccessible country may be photographed from the air even at extreme heights."

* * * * * *

"After this flight we found that of the potential sources of trouble only two had eventuated. Fortunately neither was of primary importance.

"One was due to the thick blanket of cloud which stretched up to within about fifteen miles of the foot of Everest and prevented the observer using his drift sight to measure the drift. Consequently, during the approach flight from the south-east both machines were carried further to the westward than we actually intended. Thus they did not actually fly over Dingboche but came up and over the South Peak from a direction slightly west of south.

"No great harm resulted; it meant that when plotted the photographs would give strips running up a valley with less explored ground in it than the one containing Dingboche. A southern 'ground control' would therefore be more difficult to find; indeed, it might be necessary for a ground party to triangulate one specially to serve as an anchorage for the strip. In the circumstances this was only to be expected. If we approached the mountain from the south-east we could not expect that fortune would provide us with a ready-made 'ground control.'

"The second minor hitch was that the azimuth clamping screw of the Eagle camera mounting, had been set a shade tighter than was advisable. It then passed through a drop in temperature of 150 degrees, so not unnaturally it seized. The observer was unable to rotate the camera to allow for the drift, even by exerting physical efforts which completely winded him.

"He had refrained from further exerting his lungs, now full of oxygen, fearing that the added strength imparted to his hands and arms might tear the camera loose from the machine, so he desisted and hoped for the best. When the film was developed we found no serious loss had been sustained. We had not made allowance for the very considerable drift, but on the other hand, the overlap was so great that it more than compensated for any shortcomings in the amount of ground covered.

"On both flights we had been fortunate with our oblique photographs. The first venture of April 3rd produced thirty-five, the majority from the excellent P.14 on the 5 ins. by 4 ins. size, and the balance from the pistol camera. On the second flight we secured as many as fifty, practically all of good quality. It was, however, the verticals on the second flight which disclosed to our anxious gaze the mysterious heart-shaped black patch, high up on the frozen white flanks of the great range, which is doubtless a hot lake, and one no man had ever gazed upon before."

CHAPTER XII

DARJEELING AND THE HOMEWARD FLIGHT

MOUNT EVEREST had fallen to the assaults of aerial science, our task had been achieved, and all too soon we must turn homewards, to leave the joys of Purnea and its cheery hospitable people who had looked so kindly on the strangers within their gates.

Before moving westwards again Fellowes, Blacker and Etherton, went up to Darjeeling with the film party to secure certain "shots" of the snows beyond that famous hill-station.

We will let Etherton be the historian of this tour to the tiny city in the clouds, and the subsequent aerial progress across India.

"We motored from Purnea to Siliguri, about eighty miles, at the foot of the Himalayas below Darjeeling. The General Manager of this famous little hill railway, Mr. R. N. Nichols, had issued orders for our entertainment at the railway dining-rooms before continuing the onward journey to Darjeeling. We motored up, following the road which practically runs the entire way parallel with the railway. This railway is remarkable for several things; it has a two-foot gauge, and for fifty-two miles climbs at the rate of four feet to the hundred through the foothills and lower slopes of the mightiest range of mountains in the world.

"We came part of the way by this toy line, a fascinating experience through a wealth of plants, of bamboo and tea gardens. It is a world of its own; the sort of world one has conjured up in books, a world that is expressed in vegetation, and always when going up to Darjeeling, you mount higher and higher, passing round curves so that you can almost touch the carriages running parallel to your own. It goes on over slopes that look as though they might topple down at any moment from the vibration of the train; then it passes over a bridge spanning a mountain torrent above the place it passed five minutes ago and below another which it will pass in five minutes' time.

"Twisting and turning, the little railway carries you up into the clouds and Darjeeling. It is perched on a long ridge with other ridges round it, some running down into the valleys below which are a blend of woodlands and green fields. Beyond are the Himalayas, or the Abode of Snow, range upon range of them; they look so close that it almost seems as if you could throw a biscuit on them. But they are over forty miles away, with Kanchenjunga towering above the rest like a king in silver armour enthroned among his barons.

"We were hospitably entertained by Sir John Anderson at Government House which commands a magnificent view of the snows. The Governor of Bengal spends part of the hot weather at Darjeeling, but his tenure of office does not overburden him with leisure, the administration of so large a presidency calling for continued attention.

"We spent most of our time in Darjeeling filming the snowy range from Tiger Hill, the popular point of vantage about seven miles out, where the clouds gather soon after sunrise, so those who would see them in all their glory must needs rise early. Both the early rising and the journey up the hill on a rough country pony are well worth the doing, for when you gain the summit of Tiger Hill the view unfolded is an immense snowy battlement lining the horizon.

"Darjeeling was the final parting of the ways for us. Blacker was going home by air from Calcutta, Fellowes and his wife and I with McIntyre, across India in the Moths, Clydesdale and Ellison were flying the big Westlands to Karachi, and others of the expeditionary party were dispersing to their various destinations.

"On our way down from Darjeeling we visited the Goomti tea estate belonging to Mr. O'Brien whose gardens are justly

MAKALU

[By courtesy of Messrs. Oford

with Everest behind a bank of cumulus
[Taken on 19th April, 1933, from a distance of over a hundred miles, with infra-red
plates]

famous. We saw how tea is produced, from the planting of the tree, the gathering of the leaves, the drying and all the many processes until it appears on the tea-table. O'Brien cuts and prunes and generally interferes with the course of nature, to the benefit of those who are fortunate enough to be numbered among his clients.

"We motored from this model tea estate to Purnea, arriving late at night and next morning after final farewells took the air for Darbhanga to bid good-bye to our genial host the Maharaja. We lunched there that day, leaving afterwards for Hathwa, about two hundred miles to the west, to be the guests of the Raja of Hathwa, who met us at the landing-ground surrounded by a vast concourse of his people, to whom aeroplanes were unfamiliar and who doubtless preferred the mode of progress in vogue in the days of their forefathers.

"At Lucknow we were met on the aerodrome by the genial Commissioner, Mr. Darling, who took us in hand for a tour of the places made famous for all time by their association with the immortal Lawrence and Havelock. It was a burning-hot day, eleven o'clock had come and the sun had climbed into a hard blue sky, making movement an effort, even though there was Darling's luxurious car to whisk us hither and thither. Darling has a sense of humour, and as we looked at our comfortable car, and heard of the luncheon that Mrs. Commissioner had prepared for us in their cool and lofty bungalow, we thought of those war-worn heroes of long ago on these same ramparts waiting, watching, and fighting, in the stifling heat, with little but muddy water to drink and scarcely anything to eat, hearing at long last the skirl of the bagpipes that told of the coming of the Highlanders. We looked at Darling, we looked at the car, we looked at each other—and blushed.

"To give a general and comprehensive account of our progress across India, would fill a volume. Events, receptions, and hospitable gestures at every stage of the journey like débutantes at a Court, trod so closely on each other's heels that many must pass unnoticed and most can only claim slight attention. But I will take from the passing show a few, notable for the fact that they impressed us at the time, and from them the reader may appraise the quality of the rest.

"Amongst our hosts was the Maharaja Rana of Dholpur. Lieut.-Colonel Sir Udai Bhan Singh Lokindra Bahadur, to give him only a quarter of his names and honours, is a personality of unusual charm who lives in Central India thirty-five miles south of Agra. Without the walls of his palace at Dholpur stretches the immense scrub-covered plain dotted with the ruin and wreckage of cities and settlements, for all this part of India has been swept by a score of armies of Mongol and Mogul and other conquerors. There are roads leading out to another palace and a shooting-box of the Maharaja Rana, across the wilderness through a land of stones and dust.

"As far as the eye can reach you see only the stunted bush and scanty trees, a land that is half desert, with a scanty rainfall and a sandy soil, intersected by small ravines. Dholpur is a crop-producing country, and has wonderful quarries of fine-grained red sandstone.

"The ruler of Dholpur is air-minded and has his own landing-ground, which he intends to improve in the interests of aviation. He is a first-rate motor-driver and should handle an aeroplane as adroitly as he does a Vauxhall car.

"On leaving Dholpur we headed north for Agra, passing over a desert of ruin and the traces of former cities. The entire country is one of stones, of crumbling forts where Mogul and Rajput fought for mastery, a vista of desolation that must be the modern prototype of the plains of Sodom and Gomorrah.

"When the Normans were invading England Moslem armies were over-running Northern and Central India, principalities large and small were cropping up, each concentrating on its own preservation and maintained by constant fighting. Finally there appeared Baber, the Lion, first of the Moguls, who invaded India in 1526, and did so well on his conquering quest that when he died four years later he left an empire which

24,240 ft

×

×

×

The cross shows the pe
is considered to be

SOUTH PEAK
LHOTSE II

These photographs are a portion of the vertical strips taken on April 19th and are shown compiled in the form of a rough mosaic. The "plume" of Everest is visible in the bottom left-hand corner and obscures the ridge leading from the South Peak ("Lhotse II") to the summit of Everest. The point Lhotse II and 24,240 ft., as marked, were fixed from the north side by Major Wheeler in 1921 and serve here as control. From these photographs a map can be contoured in a simple stereoscope with a fairly high degree of accuracy, and further form lines of sourrounding features will be sketched in from the obliques.

stretched from the delta of the Ganges at Calcutta, to the Amu river in Central Asia.

"In our northward flight we passed over and circled several times round Fatehpur Sikri, the city built by Baber's grandson, Akbar, a soldier and diplomat, who succeeded to the throne in 1556, and under whom the Mogul dynasty rose to the zenith of its power and fame.

"Fatehpur Sikri stands without an equal in the world; its origin is unknown, and its desertion after being occupied for only a few years is likewise wrapped in mystery. We only know that it was quietly abandoned and for nearly four hundred years its palaces and walls, its terraces and streets have been empty, save for the jackal and the porcupine that haunt its numberless passages and make their home beneath the shadow of its frowning walls.

"Fatehpur Sikri lies twenty-three miles south of Agra, the road to it being marked by quaint milestones, each twenty feet in height and placed at intervals of two miles. From our aeroplanes we could trace the road in almost a straight line to Agra.

"Various reasons have been assigned for the building of the city, but the generally accepted and certainly most romantic, is that connected with the hermit saint, Salim Chisti, whose descendants still live within the city. Akbar was returning from the conquest of Southern India, he and his army encamping by the village of Fatehpur. Till then Akbar was without an heir, and the great heritage that he had created seemed in danger of becoming a bone of contention between rival aspirants for the throne, after the manner of the Orient when there is no direct descendant to take up the sceptre.

"The legend tells us that the emperor visited the hermit, who counselled him to build a city at Fatehpur Sikri and that his desire would then be gratified. So Akbar, characteristic of the Mogul dynasty, took the work in hand, and shortly after the foundations were laid, a son was born to him who in time became the emperor Jehangir, known as the Conqueror of the World, but whose reign was chiefly noted for the time spent in drunken revelry. An ambassador from the English court visited Agra, and was received in audience by Jehangir, whose leading questions turned on the amount the envoy could drink in a day, the relative qualities of beer and Indian toddy, and the feasibility of brewing beer in Agra. No more weighty business was discussed, and the ambassador returned to Europe to report to his sovereign that beer alone could cement the friendship between the two monarchs.

"Chapters might be written on the innumerable buildings in the city, and the quaint legends and tradition surrounding them. There are halls of audience, the royal baths with floors and ceilings of marble, and the palaces of various sultanas.

"The great Gate of Victory dominates the land for many a league around; it is the loftiest gateway in the world and stands one hundred and fifty feet in height. If the emperor could pass through it to-day, he would find that the hand of time has touched it so lightly that it might have been built but yesterday.

"Visible from the air is a gigantic draughts-board of marble laid out in black and white squares, where the game of 'pachisi,' a form of chess, was played. Akbar did things on a royal scale; he occupied a revolving chair in the centre of the board, and the pawns were lovely slave girls appropriately dressed and bejewelled, who moved as the game progressed.

"Akbar the Great, was a man of broad views whose ambition it was to weld together the many conflicting creeds of his time. To this end he founded a religion of his own, based on the leading faiths, but his followers were few, for not even the genius and power of a Mogul emperor could graft a new religion upon a people whose watchword is conservatism. Akbar's reign was contemporary with that of Queen Elizabeth and, singularly enough, while Sir Walter Raleigh was introducing tobacco to the English court, Akbar initiated the pipe at Fatehpur Sikri, whither it was brought by Portuguese adventurers, who showed the emperor how to fill and light it, and soon pipe and tobacco were used throughout the Mogul empire.

THE HOMEWARD FLIGHT

"From Agra, with its book of kings, we flew to Jodhpur; a terrific storm on the way nearly proving our undoing. We had risen high above the Agra plain and were some seventy miles on our way when in the far distance a mighty brown wall seemed to rise sheer out of the earth, a barrier that mounted higher and higher and became ever more black and menacing, as though it would say, 'thou shalt not pass.' We pressed on to meet the challenge, rising still higher until the altimeter registered 12,000 feet; but we might as well have risen to the stratosphere in the effort to get clear of the enemy, for the dark brown wall rose higher than we did, its vanguard was already in touch with us, whistling and howling around our tiny aircraft like a legion of devils.

"It was getting black as night, nothing was visible but the rampart of dark brown dust, sweeping onward in an attack which was evidently going to be of a desperately determined nature. It was plain that before many minutes we should be fighting for our lives in the air.

"A terrific gust struck the 'plane which shivered as a boxer might from a savage upper-cut to the jaw. There was no time to be lost. We must either turn about and seek safety in flight, or crash through the storm and trust to luck.

"McIntyre never hesitated; he knew that the sane thing to do was to turn and, flying before the storm, make for the landing-ground at Agra. No other course was open to us. under the circumstances; once there we might effect a safe descent and let the fury of the tempest pass on and beyond us It was a wise decision; and so making a wide circuit to the left in the darkness we tried conclusions with the hurricane. Those who have only battled with a dust storm on the ground, should see one in the air when seated in a tiny Moth!

"We swirled along, slap-dash we burst into the very thick of the pursuing storm; gusts of the typhoon seemed to leap over us like harlequins in a pantomime. We were going all out; such a skedaddle was never witnessed. On we went, gaining on our pursuers and getting into a clearer atmosphere, but always with the storm close behind us, its force mobilised and trying once for all if it could not, by a tremendous effort, drive us from the air and sweep us off the face of creation. It very nearly succeeded; only the skill of the pilot saved us.

"I peered over the side of the cockpit; it was clear enough to make out the Agra aerodrome, and then I found myself touching earth and the 'plane gliding towards a walled enclosure. It pulled up; Mac and I leapt out and by a tremendous effort pushed it into safety under the lee of the protecting wall. Not a moment too soon; the storm was at our heels, it had now reached the wildest pitch of intensity and we felt as though both the 'plane and ourselves might be worsted if the struggle went on much longer.

"It galvanised us into even greater activity; we carried huge stones as though they were so many apples, anchoring them to the machine with rope that the resourceful Mac produced from apparently nowhere. We held on to the wings, for by now the fury of wind and dust had closed in upon us, we clung to the 'plane resisting all attempts to force it from our hands and deliver it over to this devil's guild.

"Gradually the cyclone passed, the deafening notes that sounded to us like the voice of Gehenna gave way to the hissing and bubbling that marks the rearguard of such an encounter, until all became comparatively quiet and resumed its normal composure.

"We stayed the night in Agra, leaving again the next morning in a glowing light, an atmosphere of calm beatitude, without the faintest indication of the scenes that had been enacted the previous day.

"A glorious run ensued to Jodhpur, and it was good to land on the magnificent aerodrome constructed by the Maharaja of Jodhpur, who is himself a pilot of distinction and the greatest of India's air protagonists. We found Fellowes and his wife there, he having circumvented the storm on the previous day.

"We were amongst the Rathors, the ruling clan of Jodhpur, a house of ancient lineage even for Rajputana, for their pedigree

AN ANAGLYPH MADE FROM VERTICAL PHOTOGRAPHS
TAKEN ON THE FLIGHT APPROACHING EVEREST FROM
THE SOUTH AND ABOUT 7 OR 8 MILES FROM THE SUMMIT

dates back from the dawn of history, and their conquering kings crossed swords with Afghans and Moguls, until the British came to give them not only peace but prosperity.

"It is strange to think that the ruler of Jodhpur, the sturdy and athletic young Maharaja, the social structure of whose family is the oldest in India, and whose ancestors made the closest acquaintance with battle, murder, and sudden death, should be so accomplished an airman and display so intimate a knowledge of the aerial way. He and his staff are equally at home in the air as they are on the ground; few ride so boldly and so well as the horsemen of Jodhpur, whether it be in a cavalry charge or on the polo field. It is fitting that aviation in India should have such champions.

"Jodhpur is famous for its polo players; many epic games have figured in Indian annuals, but one of the greatest ever played on a polo field was that between Jodhpur and Patiala, in the final for the Rutlam Cup, which took place at Delhi in 1922. The Patiala team was renowned the world over, all that money and assiduous practice could accomplish had been done. Jodhpur was in equally good fettle.

"The outstanding figure that day was the Maharaja Sir Pertab Singh, regent of Jodhpur, whose state was the Mecca of polo players, pigstickers, and sportsmen of every kind. Descended from an ancient and noble line he was both an excellent horseman and an astute personality. He devoted himself to the interests of his state and once sent a telegram in reply to friends who urged him to come and join them in a pigsticking camp:'I first catching revenue then catching pig.'

"He had a wonderful way with him, and was loved by British and Indians alike. He wisely never adopted European dress and looked magnificent in his richly-coloured Indian costume with the famous Rajput turban. He was devoted to the memory of Queen Victoria, and always wore on the front of his turban a miniature of her, set in the finest pearls. When he went to France in 1914 with the dashing Jodhpur Lancers, it was his chief ambition to meet death at their head in a cavalry charge. To his bitter regret he came through the War and died in his state in September, 1922.

"Sir Pertab lived in a fortress on the top of a rock that reminded me of the Acropolis at Athens or the famous Castle at Edinburgh. It is the age-old stronghold of his race. Out in the plain are other gigantic buildings, one of them housing the Maharaja's confidential priest, the other kept up for the ghost of the priest's predecessor, so important a person that he has a bed with silken sheets and coverlets, and a gorgeous canopy above it. The building is open for all to wander in, but no person may sleep there.

"Sir Pertab, despite his noble birth and the influence of the Brahmins, once resolutely defied the priesthood. At one of his sporting camps a young British officer contracted typhoid fever; Sir Pertab was terribly distressed and watched beside him, day and night until the end came. Then he helped to carry the poor lad to his burial; the Brahmins were aghast and went in a body to protest. The Maharaja would be outcast, irretrievably ruined. 'Sixty thousand years in hell' would be his fate. 'Caste and hell; he is a soldier, I am a soldier. I am soldier caste and great raja caste,' thundered Sir Pertab. The Brahmins fled in dismay.

"From the opening lead in the great game which Sir Pertab watched Patiala play Jodhpur for the Rutlam Cup, Patiala did well. At the third chukker the score was three nil; Jodhpur was seemingly unnerved at the yells of triumph from the vast crowd of Patiala supporters. Then the Jodhpur side scored a goal; it was the turning point in their fortunes that day and new life came to them. They realized that all India, in a sense, was looking on, since there were at least four score chiefs and princes from all parts of the country. The Viceroy and the Prince of Wales were present. Obviously Jodhpur had much to live up to.

"Close by sat the majestic Maharaja of Patiala resplendent in jewelled turban and priceless silks. Once he shifted uneasily when a terrific struggle was going on in dangerous proximity to the Patiala goal. The score was five all and only three minutes to go. Another minute went by and then another.

"Only one left now . . . one last minute. The immense crowd was wild with excitement. Dignified officials, generals, stately Indian princes stood on tiptoe, waving headgear and shouting, cheering themselves hoarse. Women screamed; only one figure sat immovable, old Sir Pertab who might have been carved in stone.

"In the second half of that last thrilling minute, Jodhpur scored its goal and won, amid such a scene as the eye of man has seldom looked upon. Sir Pertab stood up to find the Prince of Wales shaking him vigorously by the hand; the tears poured down the old man's cheeks. The second of his great ambitions in life had been achieved.

"After Jodhpur came Udaipur, one of the loveliest places in India, situated off the beaten track, for it is seventy miles from the junction of its small gauge branch line with that of the main railroad to Delhi and the north.

"Apparently no one had ever arrived in Udaipur by aeroplane, so the whole place was agog with the new excitement. The city lies within a cluster of hills forming an encircling rampart and this beautiful amphitheatre when viewed from the air is an amazing panorama of fields, green and prosperous, of lakes and islands covered with marble palaces, of clumps of trees and the domes of temples shimmering in the sunlight, just such a picture as gives the impression of being over the Italian lakes.

"We were the guests of the Maharana, who housed us in a building complete, as advertisements would say, with all modern improvements, and commanding a fine view over the city.

"We visited the ruler of this garden of Eden and were shown the palaces and lakes, the temples and fortresses which are a pocket history in themselves. We went out forty miles to the largest artificial sheet of water in the world, made by a capricious ruler of medieval times, to this Italy on the edge of the tropics, where palm and coco-nut trees displace the oleander and the olive, where miniature palaces of the purest white marble take the place of the gaudy villa and resplendent hotel, and where a cloudless sunlight shines over all and the waters of the lake have the blue of the Dalmatian coast.

"Extremes meet in Udaipur. A few miles out is a wild and lonely spot with a battlemented structure that looks out over the jungle. Here at eventide comes scores of wild pigs to be fed by custodians of the fort, a grunting, scrambling, squealing mass of piggery, that fight and charge for the largest share in the scattered grain, and having eaten their fill return to their lair in the jungle.

"Time was getting on, the hot weather was upon us, and we reluctantly had to make up our minds to quit this lotus-eating existence amongst the principalities and peoples of India and turn resolutely homewards. Fellowes and McIntyre were going by air, and so at Udaipur we separated, they making for Karachi to follow the aerial route to England, I to Bombay and the sea.

"It was a glorious May morning when they took off, circling over the city and giving the inhabitants an object lesson in the latest form of transport; they zoomed above the marble palaces and the placid waters of the lakes, dipped in salute to the Maharana, and then headed for the far West, whilst I turned southward by rail to the gateway of India.

"Time did not permit us to take advantage of the many offers of hospitality and invitations to visit other states and ruling chiefs who so good-naturedly wished to do us honour, but we had seen and experienced enough to form many impressions, and none more vivid and convincing than those governing aerial science in Hindustan.

"The moment is therefore opportune to give those impressions for our aerial activities in India, and the surmounting of the world's highest mountain from the air by all-British aircraft and engines, had enabled us to form a definite opinion on the future of aviation in India. Air is the universal element; fire

Everest

Makalu

FLYING SOUTH FROM EVEREST ON 19TH APRIL, 1933 (I)

FLYING SOUTH FROM EVEREST ON 19TH APRIL

The gorge of the Arun where
it breaks through from Tibet

The Arun valley in
Nepal

and water are to some extent restricted, but the air is everywhere and is free.

"In viewing the coming years from the point of view of aviation, one paramount fact stands out in bold relief. Transport in the future is going to be largely by air. The whole spirit of the world is changing and its problems are new. Speed is the dominant keynote of life—speed and energy. A new calling has come into being, which is really the spirit of the old pioneers aflame in a new form—transport by air, the uninterrupted navigable ocean that comes to the threshold of every man's door.

"Civil and commercial aviation is the modern way that opens up a vast field of enterprise, a new field for the rising generation, and one with unlimited scope. Nations and individuals are acquiring an air sense, and soon the entire globe will be covered with an organised network of air lines.

"This problem of the air and transport has an immediate bearing on our own daily lives. To the initiated, the expert and the visionary, our present-moment systems of transport are already archaic. Those who know and have travelled the airways of the world can feel not a little amused at the elaborate efforts to dissipate the traffic congestion of our streets, for the simple reason that aerial science is solving that vexed problem, and in no uncertain manner. The time when the transport of to-day will be largely superseded is well within view; it is no more the dream of a Jules Verne, but a definite certainty.

"Just as we no longer see the hackney carriage, the horse omnibus or the cable tram, so in the near future we shall largely be bereft of the stately motor-car, the motor-'bus de luxe, and that already effete method of transportation—the tramway-car.

"Mr. Smith, who works hard in the city, but lives at Surbiton, will not think it at all unnatural to step into his mass-production aeroplane and hop home minus the discomforts of crowded railway carriages. Indeed, should it be a nice, summer evening, Mr. Smith will not hurry straight home to

Surbiton, but will probably go for a little joy-ride via the Yorkshire dales and the Lakes, in an aeroplane that will travel smoothly, safely, and rapidly, at the not too extravagant speed of four hundred miles an hour. His altitude may be anything up to 20,000 feet, the height depending upon climatic conditions, above or below storms, as the case may be, but the expert Smith will avoid them in very much the same way as we now avoid people in the street.

"It is patently evident that soon there will be a linked air service round the globe. With every day that passes the efforts towards perfecting aerial transport make their forward way. Those who gaze with tremulous wonder at a big aeroplane and thank their stars that they are on terra firma, will find that it will pay them to dismiss that fear.

"Already the air as a means of transport is safer than the comparatively peaceful transit of a busy London street. Whether you are travelling to Bombay or Sydney, to Leeds or Edinburgh, you will be in an air liner with sleeping-rooms, restaurant, and promenade decks. You will look down upon other liners passing, rushing through space and over the world's continents, each, according to its category, whether passenger or cargo, being allotted a definite flying level to obviate the risk of collision.

"In the days now fast approaching there will be landing-stages at your door, distance will not be the threat that it was, and travel will be deprived of its tedium.

"We shall be journeying to India in two days and less, leaving London, for example, on Monday morning, and arriving at Bombay in time for dinner on Tuesday evening. Within a few years the time to Bombay will be anything from twelve to twenty hours, for aerial science is concentrating on revolutionary forms of propulsion.

"The flights over Everest and Kangchenjunga drew attention to the rapid strides it is making. With every day that passes the efforts towards perfecting aerial transport and developing civil and commercial aviation make their forward way. With them comes the task of providing a thoroughly efficient ground staff for the operation of commercial air services, who shall be conversant with air organisation, aerodrome management, control of staff, air line operations, navigation and meteorology, use of wireless, lights and signals, control-tower operations, stores procedure, commercial practice, and aviation law; in fact, every phase and branch of civil and commercial aviation.

"With the spread of imperial and international co-operation rapid communication with all parts of the world becomes vital, and air transport offers speedier service than any other means of conveyance.

"India is the land of vast distances, it has in its different provinces so many important cities and centres of commercial influence, that the rapid maintenance and necessity of getting from one place to another in the shortest possible space of time, with the maximum of efficiency and comfort, are the dominating factors.

"India, therefore, provides ample scope for development and extension of air services. Its commercial connections with all parts of the world, and its commanding position at the cross roads of East and West, make it essential for India to develop commercial aviation as the normal utility service.

"Let us now see some of the new wonders of the air that will give an idea of the immense future lying before civil and commercial aviation in India. As already remarked, the time is close at hand when the main line of progress will be in the air, and it will centre on swift-carrying passenger and freight machines, rather than on single-seaters and similar small 'planes.

"It is the day for multi-engined air liners with Schneider trophy performance, cities and towns throughout India will be joined up; they will be in constant touch with Europe and Asia, and centres which are at the present time to all intents and purposes, poles apart will be linked together, tending towards closer friendships.

"Aviation will make progress along commercial lines, for therein lies one of its greatest potentialities. That is why it is essential to go on developing commercial aircraft. In the past it has been quite easy to develop a fast 'plane carrying one or two passengers a short distance, at racing speed, but we want the super air liner with the luxury and refinement one gets on the ground, coupled with the speed of a Schneider trophy winner.

"Aeroplanes conforming to the above conditions are in the making, with up-to-date ideas as to comfort, and arriving at a given destination with complete baggage, or, as Henry Ford expressed it, 'with top hat and gloves.'

"In the fitting out of the aeroplane of the immediate future, television is contemplated.

"Television has made great strides; at the present time when we set out on a long voyage all visual touch with the land is lost, but soon those who take to the air or the sea will keep in visual touch with their friends ashore. Moreover, colour television is coming in, thereby greatly improving the natural effect of the image as depicted upon the televisor screen. The opening of this new field in television research will be another milestone on the road of scientific discovery.

"It will soon be possible to transmit images in stereoscopic relief; these developments will bring to us not only the sounds but also the view of the lands, all correctly reproduced in natural colours as well as in stereoscopic relief. We shall see all that lies ahead; indeed, we shall be able to imagine ourselves transported into the middle of the scenes displayed on the screen of our stereoscopic colour televisor, the sounds of which will be faithfully reproduced by means of the loud-speaker.

"The latest news, the play at the theatre, and noteworthy events all over the world, will be obtained by merely varying the wavelength, and you will see and hear the Grand National and watch and listen to 'Faust' at the opera while on the flight from England to India.

"Greater speed will also result from high flying to forty and fifty thousand feet, in the tenuous and comparatively frictionless upper air, thus avoiding the resistance met with in the lower and heavier layers of atmosphere, and travelling without difficulty at maximum speed. To resist the low temperature and rarefied atmosphere, oxygen will be provided, and the enclosed passenger 'planes will be fitted with it so that they may soar to a height of six or seven miles, well above all ordinary directional traffic.

"With this rapid advance in aircraft industry, the demand will naturally arise for ground engineers, aerodrome, managerial and executive staff, supply services, and technical grades of every kind. It is impossible to over-estimate the importance of the ground staff, reliability, safety, and economy—three foundation stones on which the goodwill of aviation must be erected—depend upon their efficiency. It is true to say that the man on the ground keeps the machines in the air.

"To meet this demand for trained and competent personnel which will be required in numbers in the immediate future, is the *raison d'être* of the College of Aeronautical Engineering, in conjunction with which, as we have seen, the Everest flight was initiated. The College, the first of its kind in the world, is located at Brooklands and Chelsea in London, and has been rather aptly termed the 'University of the Air.' It has an international character, for the students are not only British and Indian, but Continental as well, and the diploma granted to successful graduates at the close of the two and a half years' training will be a degree in aerial engineering, and all that pertains to civil and commercial aviation.

"It is clear that India is not only becoming air-minded, but there is a pronounced desire on the part of Indians to acquire a sound grasp of civil and commercial aviation, and to see it developed on lines commensurate with the status and needs of India."

CHAPTER XIII

FILMING THE FLIGHT—BY GEOFFREY BARKAS

THE scientific value of this chapter can best be gauged
by the fact that the writer was at no time during the
operations nearer to Everest than eighty miles from the
summit, and that he is, to this day, uncertain which of the
peaks that rocked to and fro in the field of his binoculars was
actually the Goddess Mother of the mountains.

However, an impression from the viewpoint of the film
party, to whom the scientific objects of the flight meant little
and the opportunities of making pictures much, will have a
degree of interest.

When the Gaumont-British Picture Corporation had secured
the rights to produce "Wings over Everest," the first point to
be decided was whether the Indian scenes should be "talkie"
or "silent." The difficulty was one of practice—not policy.
the box-offices of the world demand talk, or at any rate noise,
with their pictures. Could we successfully employ sound
cameras on such a task?

Nothing was to be gained by attempting to record sound
on "shots" of the Westland machines in the air. Engine noise
could be put on at any time. There remained the scenes of
preparation and the ground work prior to the take-off. These
could be handled by sending a couple of camera-men to India
with silent cameras, and reconstructing all dialogue scenes in the
studios at home after the flight.

But two factors weighed heavily against this method.
Firstly, it was strongly felt that complete authenticity could
only be obtained by recording events as they actually happened—filming each incident from the "angle" that would
give it the correct dramatic perspective. Secondly, owing to

232

the hazardous nature of the expedition's objective it was by no means certain that the pilots and observers who were to be our "stars" would still be available!

So it was decided that, if it were humanly possible to transport and maintain on location the diverse and delicate equipment of sound-film production "Wings over Everest" should be a talkie.

Enquiries through the India Office as to the state of the roads round Purnea and other scenes of operation, and the climatic conditions, warranted the attempt. We could now get down to detail.

The immediate necessity was selection of the production unit. Seven was the smallest number that could handle talkie production in the field. A director, three camera-men, two sound experts, and an assistant. S. R. Bonnett was an obvious choice for one of the men to film the flight over the world's highest mountain. He had great experience in the air, having filmed, *inter alia*, Cobham's flight to the Cape. A. L. Fisher, another camera-man, also possessed the rare qualifications needed; on these two rested a heavy responsibility. The work of weeks and the expenditure of thousands of pounds would be focused on a period of perhaps twenty minutes over and around the summit of Everest, in conditions that none could foretell. If either of them failed to take full advantage of those brief, hectic minutes, our film would be a "flop." In V. Veevers we had yet another whose experience of filming in India was to prove invaluable in ground work and still photography.

The selection of the sound recordists also needed care. We knew that we should be working almost always under rush and tear conditions, beset by the difficulties inseparable from removing the capricious microphone from the shelter of the sound-proof studio. Accordingly we chose R. L. Read from the staff of the Sound News, and in due course presented him and his assistant, W. H. O. Sweeny, with a series of technical problems guaranteed to tax even the ingenuity of a star news reel man.

I had already been appointed director, perhaps because of a certain experience in the production of documented films and an aptitude for presenting actualities in picture form.

All the technical posts were now filled and there remained to discover one man with the energy, philosophy and fool-hardiness to shoulder the duties of business manager, field cashier, secretary, storekeeper and "continuity" writer. We found him in T. D. Connochie.

A period of furious activity ensued.

The Westland machines, then nearing completion at Yeovil, were visited so that special camera positions might be prepared to ensure getting pictures of the summit from any conceivable angle, and from one or two inconceivable ones, to be on the safe side. From conversations with the constructional experts it was soon found that to meet all our requests for mountings, fields of vision and trap doors, would entail such sweeping alterations that they might as well start again and build an aeroplane round our camera. Moreover, it was certain that to take the 'planes off the ground encumbered with all the gadgets we desired would be a hazardous operation, and to climb to the stipulated 33,000 feet or more, a sheer impossibility.

In the end, owing to our sagacity in having asked for five times as much as we had any hope of obtaining, we secured such modifications as would enable the camera-man to "shoot" effective pictures at all heights.

Now came the preparation of special cameras and equipment of all kinds, which had to be designed and tested under the conditions to be expected over Everest. Bonnett and Fisher spent chilly hours in a freeze box at the R.A.F. Experimental Station, Farnborough, to ensure cameras working efficiently at a temperature of minus sixty degrees centigrade. Read and Sweeny went to the other extreme and roasted themselves demonstrating that the sound recording equipment would function under the tropical conditions anticipated at the aero-drome. Special telephoto lenses had to be designed and tested with different types of panchromatic or infra-red film and light filters to cope with the exceptional atmospheric problems.

My principal duty had been to amass all possible information and to give the facts dramatic significance—in short, to prepare a working scenario. Here lay the great difference between this and the ordinary story film. In a play one builds up to a known climax. I was faced with the unknown. Everest herself must write the climax and dénouement; so the script was worked out in detail up to the morning of the famous flight. The machines would leave the ground—and then a blank.

Two days before sailing the last of our equipment was finished and tested to our satisfaction. The extent of it was a surprise even to us. Whereas all the equipment that could actually be flown over Everest for the crucial high spot of the film could have been comfortably stowed in an ordinary suit-case, the total shipment necessary for the entire production could have been crammed with difficulty into a two-ton motor-lorry.

There was the complete combined sound and picture camera with its film boxes, tripods, microphones and stands, the amplifier, spools of cable, and four or five accumulators the size of car batteries. Then the motor-driven "silent" camera with all its attendant gear and more motor-car batteries. Three complete clockwork camera equipments of the type to be used on the high flight. In addition, a gigantic crate containing a petrol motor and electric generator for use in charging the batteries where ordinary facilities were unobtainable; several large trunks packed with spare parts, valves, high-tension batteries, boxes of office materials, and thirty wooden cases containing 80,000 feet of negative film allocated to the Everest picture and to the short subjects we intended to take as opportunity offered. The whole equipment represented a value of nearly ten thousand pounds.

The voyage out was uneventful. Each camera in turn was brought on deck and thoroughly tested. Designed to get close-up scenes of peaks and clouds from enormous distances, the telephoto lens presented some difficulty, for there was nothing far enough away to give an adequate test. Ultimately we found that by mounting the camera on the extreme stern of the ship we could just manage to get a head and shoulder portrait of the captain on the bridge.

Our first view of India was an ideal introduction to the country. Just before midnight on the 2nd March the P. & O. *Mooltan* slowed down to pick up the pilot. Ahead, reflected in the muddy water in a myriad spangles were the lights of Bombay, row upon row, like strings of pearls, while the moon hung like a Chinese lantern over the dark shore line. Quite definitely we could smell India—the romantic scent of the East which we diagnosed as being curry and burning cow-dung, in equal proportions.

Next morning our eighty pieces of baggage were transferred to the smaller steamer which sailed at ten o'clock for Karachi.

At Karachi we filmed the arrival and unloading of the huge crates containing the Westland machines—and the scenes of their assembly at the R.A.F. depot there. Here also we took full advantage of the splendid workshops at the aerodrome and the helpfulness of the Royal Air Force in making adjustments to the cameras. Bonnett and Fisher also had their first flights in the Westland Wallace and a chance for camera practice from the cockpit.

We made immediate acquaintance with the servant problem.

The report soon spread of the arrival in the city of seven new Sahibs, and as we came down to breakfast on the morning after our arrival, we were waylaid by some forty perfect servants, if one might judge by their tattered recommendations. Veevers, with a fine flow of language, reduced them to something like order and we looked them over one by one, picking the seven that looked the least dirty and rapacious. They represented a wide range of religions. Two Hindus, two Mohammedans, two alleged Christians, and one whose beliefs still remain a mystery. My boy was one of the Christians; a scholarly-rimmed looking man of indeterminate age with a fierce moustache, steel glasses, and eyes painted round with blue. His name was "Charly," and we decided that his air of melancholy must be due to prolonged and unsuccessful study for a degree. He had probably been ploughed for spelling, for the laundry bills presented from time to time were one of my minor problems. Here is one of them, with translations.

"Wasing"

2 Baid sitt (bed sheets)
1 Pilo kais
3 Towol
2 sili pin sutt (sleeping suits)
6 kalair (collars)
2 And baist. (This puzzled me a lot. It turned out to be "undervests.")
2 Daraj (drawers)
6 Hingi Chip (handkerchiefs)

However, he was a good servant and robbed me with discretion and moderation. One cannot expect more than that.

At length the machines were declared ready for the flight across India to Purnea. Bonnett went in the Houston Westland as far as Delhi—filming on the way whatever might look interesting from the air, to "cut in" as part of the story. At Delhi, Fisher was to take Bonnett's place and handle the second half of the journey. The rest of us went by train.

Neither of them was able to get much material—it was curious that right across India the visibility was appalling : over everything lay a thick haze which our cameras could not penetrate even with special light filters, and air conditions were rough, much more bumpy than anything experienced over the mountains on the Everest flights.

As for the rest of us, we rolled for what seemed an eternity across India, through the Sind Desert, to Lahore, Delhi, Lucknow, on to a narrow-gauge railway with a sinister reputation, but which proved to be quite tolerable.

On the way I re-read and revised the working script of the

Purnea sequences, and evolved a number of beautiful ways of filming the morning of the great flight. Grand shots of the 'planes being wheeled out in the dawn light on the tiny landing ground while the mighty rampart of the Himalayas reared up into the sky. It was a masterly effort.

Now and again I looked out of the window, feeling that the country should be getting hilly, but it remained stubbornly flat, and I was still looking for the mountains when the train reached Purnea. Never have I seen so long a stretch of country so flat. I looked for the Indian atmosphere, and remember thinking, "They'll never believe any of this Purnea stuff was taken further away than Heston." I asked where the mountains lay, imagining we were just unlucky in arriving on a day when visibility was bad. But no. It transpired that you may sometimes see the snows from Purnea—but not in March—only in November or December.

A few days later, however, I did see Everest and Kangchenjunga—thanks to Fellowes who took me up in the Puss Moth. At a height of 10,000 feet, we broke through what was humorously called the ground-haze, and saw the huge mass of Kangchenjunga and then the mighty wedge of Everest. That trip, and a later one over Darjeeling and towards Kangchenjunga at a height of 18,000 feet, is what enables me to write with such authority on the subject of Mount Everest!

There followed days of work around the aerodrome, during which we filmed all the necessary scenes of final preparation—reconnaissance flights, testing of heated suits, oxygen cylinders, and survey cameras.

Then we settled down to wait for the great day; but not in idleness. From my notes of actual conferences held by the pilots, observers, and the leader, I wrote condensed sequences which we produced as and when the fliers could be spared from their duties.

On these occasions we experienced all the difficulties of recording in the open air. The conference table would be placed on the verandah or under a tree in the garden. Rehearsal of the scene would be smoothly carried out, but the moment we began to take a gentle breeze would stir the branches and by some trick of "frequency" the sighing of the wind would come through the microphone like a barrage on the Western Front, or a bird in a distant tree-top would begin a soliloquy and by virtue of its superior recording quality drown the voices of the entire staff.

Then the conditions would become perfect; but by this time the heat of the sun had penetrated the walls of the camera and the "blimp," with the result that the perforation holes of the film were no longer in absolute register with the mechanism of the gate. So that when the motors were started all went well for about ten seconds, after which the film would jump the sprockets and tie itself in an inconceivable tangle, to leap out like a jack-in-the-box when the door was opened to adjust matters.

After a few more days we had filmed all the incidental scenes it was possible to arrange at the aerodrome and round the head-quarters. I remember that as a remorseless maker of films I worried Fellowes and Etherton, and indeed every one in turn, for special flights and for hours of special take-offs and landings, but they were not to be drawn from their policy of keeping the engines carefully tuned ready for the big flight, and the 'planes in the hangars sheltered from the burning sun that would have impaired their efficiency.

The 'planes were ready, pilots and observers were ready, and so were we. But the weather was not and a period of high winds and poor visibility set in, a time of suspense that was a trial to all of us. We were in a constant state of "stand-to," for none could say more than a few hours ahead whether a flight would be possible or not. One thing seemed conclusive —that if a flight were possible it would be an early morning dash—out before dawn and off the ground by first daylight. Accordingly the standing orders for my party were, up at 4.45 a.m., breakfast at 5.15 a.m., and all equipment loaded on cars and trucks at 5.45 ready to "shoot," with the Everest cameras tucked away in their special heating-jackets.

Each morning at six o'clock, in the delicious and all too short coolness, Gupta, director of the weather station, came crunching up the gravel drive with his chart of wind velocities . . . and after a few noncommittal remarks would deliver himself of some disappointing forecasts. He would promise us strong winds at 10,000 feet, gales at 15,000, and "winds of hurricane force" (impressive phrase) at 20,000 feet. Often he would decline to tell us what it would be like at 30,000—either because he had exhausted the possibilities of scientific nomenclature, or his balloon had been blown inside out by some stratospheric disturbance beyond his power to record.

Without waiting to hear more, I and my party would creep away to breakfast and prepare the cameras for work-a-day use. This meant stripping the Everest cameras again of all their high-flight gear—an hour's work. Then we would toil through the day, sometimes on fresh scenes for the big film, sometimes on subjects such as a pagan harvest dance in one of the aboriginal villages near Purnea.

After dinner we would work again, the camera-men unloading and despatching the exposed film, for it had to be sent away at the earliest possible moment from the heat of the plains, and patiently reconditioning the cameras for the morrow, the sound experts busying themselves on adjustments and tests of the recording system, and Connochie and I writing reports, making plans and attending to correspondence. Then we would turn in, after reading yet another wired forecast from Calcutta that was bad, but not bad enough to remove all hope for the next day.

One of my clearest recollections is of lying in bed on the verandah of Darbhanga House, looking up at the night sky through the roof of my mosquito net and hearing Bonnett, who was detailed for the first flight and occupied the next bed to me, saying in a tone of suppressed bitterness: "Well . . . well . . . well . . . well, well, well!"

FILMING THE FLIGHT

After being asleep for what seemed a couple of minutes, we would be wakened by a noise like someone hammering on a copper saucepan. It was a family of birds known locally as the "coppersmiths," who occupied a tree at our corner of the verandah, and considered four-thirty an appropriate time for choir practice. Again I would look at the sky and wonder whether it was cloud or just night that made the sky so black. My doubts would be settled by seeing a faint wisp of cloud go by between the house-top and the tree at alarming speed, although there was not a breath of wind at ground-level. Then "Charly" would be heard shuffling along the verandah with morning tea.

"Chota hazri, master," he would say, "Not clouding to-day. I say, God bless my master."

This would wake Bonnett who greeted the dawn with another: "Well . . . well . . . well . . . well!"

So began a new day, and another disastrous prediction from Gupta would send us off into the bush to look for filmable subjects that we had not already "shot to ribbons." On a few days, baulked by circumstances of my desire to use the aeroplanes for purely film purposes, I managed to dragoon the members of the flight into playing scenes in which they appeared in the full regalia of heated suits, helmets and goggles. As these manœuvres were carried out on the burning plains of India, instead of the rare and refreshing altitudes for which these feather-bed boiler-suits were designed, I was surprised at the docility with which they consented to play after the first occasion. From a later experience of my own, I am astonished that they did not collapse with apoplexy.

But even this activity was presently denied to us, for, by what I then regarded as a Machiavellian stratagem, it was decided that the heated suits could not be further worn for practice purposes, since constant donning and doffing might damage the electrical circuits that carried the heating currents.

At length there came a day when the Calcutta weather forecast was less gloomy than usual and the word went round

241

that if only Gupta could moderate the antics of his observation balloon in the upper air, and persuade it to bounce about in a less eccentric fashion, the flight would be on.

Once more overnight preparations were made; once more Bonnett said, "Well . . . well . . . well, well, well!"

Next morning the attentions of the coppersmith bird were unnecessary. We were all awake before him, and at 6 a.m. Gupta came beaming up the drive to say that a mere seventy mile per hour breeze could be expected over the top of Everest and that visibility would be good, at any rate during the early part of the day.

The departure of the unit went like clockwork. Bonnett and myself in a fast car dashed off to the aerodrome with the flight cameras, leaving the motor-truck to bring up the rear. It was a perfect morning as the aeroplanes were wheeled out of the hangars, and it promised to be hot. By the time they were ready to take the air the sun was high and the day becoming uncomfortably warm.

Then it occurred to me that our sound equipment and the rest of the party were taking an unusually long time to reach the flying-ground. The engines of the Westlands began to tick over. Still no sound truck.

Almost giving up hope of photographing the actual take-off, for which we had waited so long, I went to the main gateway for one last look along the road. Far away a cloud of dust was rapidly approaching. It tore past me on to the landing-ground and pulled up with a violent jerk and squeaking of brakes. It was not our lorry!

It was one of the smallest omnibuses I have ever seen and full from floor to roof with sound cameras, amplifiers, boxes of film and coolies. Outside and on the roof, hanging precariously at every possible resting-place, were spools of cable and tripods, and squeezed in beside the driver and on the back step were the balance of my party, including the all-important sound recordists.

Our truck had chosen this vital day to break down completely a quarter of a mile from the house, and it was here that Connochie had shown his resourcefulness. After half an hour's struggle to bring the engine to life, a native motor-'bus appeared, packed with native passengers, rolling along the road to Purnea. He had stopped it and, by sheer determination, and in spite of a complete ignorance of Hindustani, had induced the driver to eject his paying passengers on the side of the road, turn the 'bus around, and pile into this rickety conveyance twice as much baggage as it could properly hold, and so reached the aerodrome in the nick of time to film the start of the historic flight.

I well remember the moment of departure, the pilots giving the signal for the chocks to be removed, the engines roaring up, the shimmering heat-haze making the air quiver as we looked across the aerodrome, the blast of hot air in the slip-stream of the propellers, and the last view of Bonnett in one machine and Blacker in the other, goggled and masked, as they closed down the covers of the cockpits for the early part of the climb.

Then the three hours' wait, the mental calculations as to how many flying hours the machines could manage before we need feel any anxiety for their return, the frequent glances at wrist-watches when the time came to expect the first distant sound of their return, and the listening look in people's eyes as they talked of other things. At last the quiet voice of one of the mechanics, saying, "That's them!"

The two machines appeared over the aerodrome wing-tip to wing-tip, performed a perfect "break formation" above the hangars, and came down to a perfect landing.

The great flight was over. Everest had been conquered from the air.

Two other things I remember vividly.

I ran up to Bonnett, who was standing in the cockpit, his mask and goggles thrown up, and asked him how he had fared. "Everything," he said, "went splendidly, except that he had had 'a little trouble with his oxygen.'" He showed me the feed tube from the cylinder with a fracture so large that at the peak of the climb, 33,000 feet, he had been deprived of his supply. It was astonishing that he had not passed out completely, but when I asked how he had managed to survive, he remarked that, "it had been a bit awkward—yes, he'd felt a bit queer—sick in fact—but had managed to tie a handkerchief round the tube and carry on." He had been over the top of Mount Everest and could claim to be the first person to be sick on that lofty summit!

My other recollection is that when I handed up to Bonnett the last two metal magazines of film just before the take-off, they had been burning-hot to the touch, after a few minutes' exposure to the sun. When he handed them down to me from the cockpit of the Westland Wallace they were icy-cold.

CHAPTER XIV

THE AUTHORS' APPRECIATION OF THOSE WHO CONTRIBUTED TO
THE SUCCESS OF THE EXPEDITION

AS experienced travellers who had encircled the globe and travelled far and wide, we devoted much time and attention to what we were to take, the things we were to use, and what would contribute most to the success of our enterprise. When we contemplated the result we decided that whatever happened from volcanic eruptions to glacier slides, avalanches, and forced landings, we would be suitably equipped and prepared for the occasion. Our principal anxiety was that everything should be in good fettle and tuned to a hair. It never does to leave anything to chance—or to run the risk of discovering when you are in the Himalayas that some vital necessity has been neglected.

We thought, too, of our Honorary Secretary and the responsibilities that rested upon him. In expeditions, as with Governments and States, when great preparations are in hand, the organisers, whoever they may be, are held accountable for failure and reap the corresponding reward of success, so we had at any rate a door whereat we might lay the blame or credit for the result.

Further, the issue depends also upon the co-operation and skilled assistance, as well as the material, of those associated with the venture, so that everything may go according to plan. We were fortunate in our choice of both the material and the assistance, without which we could not have achieved such gratifying results.

First and foremost we would cite the Peninsular and Oriental Steam Navigation Company who transported the big machines and material to and from Karachi free of charge, besides granting such members of the expedition who went by sea passages at preferential rates. For generations the P. & O. have been the high criterion of comfort and satisfaction on the high seas, and the new liners mark yet another era in sea travel. We were glad to feel that this famous company was associated with us in a venture of such geographical and scientific interest, and are sensible of their practical support and ever ready help.

We have dealt with aircraft and all that goes with them, with oxygen and cameras, while electrical suits and aircraft instruments have been given the praise which is their due, and we would here complete the tale of successful endeavour.

The practicability of the flight from the fuelling point of view was thoroughly discussed with the Shell Company's technical staff, who considered that, although the problem of providing a fuel capable of giving the necessary performance at extreme altitudes was a difficult one, it could be solved if their chemists worked in close collaboration with the manufacturers of the engine.

The problem had two aspects: the fuel must give maximum performance without physical or chemical alteration, at an outside temperature of 60 degrees below zero Fahrenheit; it must continue to develop full power in an atmosphere so attenuated that, apart from the comparative lack of oxygen, the pressure was but one-seventh of that at sea-level.

As a result a fuel largely on the lines of Shell Aviation spirit, but blended rather differently, proved the most suitable and was used without giving the slightest trouble; indeed, it was one of the main factors in the success of the flight.

The organisation necessary to provide adequate supplies of spirit where needed, was in the hands of the Burma Shell Company, and the assistance they gave is worthy of the highest tribute.

As regards oil we put our trust in Wakefield's Castrol Aero Coil, and if there had been a better oil we should have used it.

The new way of proceeding to India and the East is by Imperial Airways, travelling with a maximum of speed, comfort and scenic enjoyment. These mighty air liners, where you may sit at ease as you might in your arm-chair at home, sail gracefully through tumbled clouds or tropics, giving you peeps of wonderful lands, and have reduced air travel to a fine art.

In planning an expedition there are legal questions to be considered and there may be something for the lawyers to wrangle over. We entrusted our legal fortunes to Messrs. Baddeleys and right well they justified the selection.

Messrs. Thomas Cook & Son were the honorary agents of the expedition and their ways and means relieved us of many details and ensured the maximum of efficiency in delivery of the mass of material we had; indeed, it was inspiring to note what could be accomplished under their arrangements.

In the matter of finance we were accorded the knowledge and experience of Messrs. Deloitte Plender Griffiths & Co., who handled our accounts, helped us to adjust our finance and to keep a record of the various and complicated payments we had to make, and steered us through many intricacies.

Messrs. Fry, of chocolate fame, as will have been seen, lent us one of their light aeroplanes that acted in many capacities, particularly as a scout for the big Westlands. We were armed with chocolates which travel seems to decree should be carried when on such a venture as ours; we found them an attractive greeting for those guests who dropped in on us at the base and elsewhere, besides helping to sustain us in the flights over the world's highest mountains.

No expedition would be complete without a record or impressions taken down on the spot, so that is why we carried a dictaphone. For this purpose we found it invaluable and dictaphones ought to be, like the fresh air, at every man's door.

There was the problem of motor transport, linking Purnea with the aerodrome, the advanced emergency landing-ground, and other points at varying distances, over rough and indifferent tracks, for which we chose the Vauxhall car. Some of us had used this car in previous expeditions and it had never let us down. Incidentally, some of the roads we went over were decidedly trying for long distances, and some that were quite indescribable. One can, however, regard these philosophically if you have a good car and good tyres, which with us were Goodyear and we did not have a single puncture or tyre trouble of any description.

Although we lived in luxury in a Maharaja's bungalow, we took certain camp equipment, choosing out of a number of firms that of Messrs. Thomas Black & Sons (Greenock) Ltd. Everything that we obtained from them stood the acid test of climate, unusual and strenuous conditions, and the wear and tear inseparable from travelling in rough and comparatively unknown corners of the world.

Closely allied to camp kit and equipment generally is the all-important question of stoves. Some of us had, as already remarked, been up and down and round the world, and knew what a priceless asset a good camp stove is, something that really *will* operate in a driving wind, in Arctic cold, and that "delivers the goods" when called upon to do so. We pinned our faith, after much anxious consideration and trial, to the Monitor supplied by Monitor Oil Appliances, Ltd. All our fears were set at rest, for this stove really did do its work, it never gave us any trouble, and we shall always treasure its memory.

We all kept in strict training; super-fit men were needed for the work that lay ahead. No Arsenal team preparing at some South Coast resort for their next cup tie could have taken themselves more seriously. The regimen adopted was helped by Sanatogen, a remarkably good food, especially for any altitude and mountaineering work, and under strained conditions its sustaining properties are amazing. One or two of the party who contracted complaints in India were greatly benefited by a course of it.

The general health and fitness of any expedition depends to a large extent on the clothes they wear and the material of which they are composed; it is so easy to get the wrong thing and all sorts of trouble ensue, apart from the invective that will be brought down on the organisation and administrative department. Gieves were the firm who saw us safely and comfortably through, and we never once had cause to regret any of the splendid material we took from them.

Came the matter of watches of which any number of grace and beauty were submitted for our approval. We wanted a watch that would tell the truth about time, a watch of lasting accuracy, and one that would go if we took it up to the stratosphere or deep down in the sea, a watch that would operate under all conditions. We recognised the exacting nature of our demands; many were called but only one was chosen—the Rolex, and it did all we asked of it.

One or two of the expedition were big game hunters, and in the hope of adding more trophies to their collections, Rigby Mannlicher rifles were taken out. Whenever we had an opportunity of using them they were found to be of the greatest use; indeed, we were definitely impressed with their accuracy and general excellence.

Finally, there was the matter of small hand cameras for taking subjects of general interest, apart from those in the air. Nothing is more disappointing than to return and find bad results, and any merit of the numerous pictures of general interest we took, is due to the fact that we were able to count on the accuracy of the shutters, the exposure, and, what is most important under tropical conditions, on the light-tightness of the apparatus. We chose the Six-Twenty Kodaks and never was there a more fortunate choice, although we anticipated their being up to form, having used Kodaks on many previous ventures into the wilds.

We hope we have covered the whole of the ground as regards equipment, concluding with a final word that we were extraordinarily lucky in all our selections, and if the description of our experiences in that direction leads others in a similar channel we shall have had our sufficient reward.

APPENDIX I

List of forty-six duties each observer had to carry out during the flight over Mount Everest. Each had these tasks in writing before him, as the rarefied atmosphere at extreme altitudes tends to loss of memory.

Before taking off:

1. Receive oxygen report.
2. Inspect pressure gauges.
3. Switch on oxygen heater.
4. Check levels of Eagle camera.
5. Check filter, stop and exposure of Eagle.
6. Check filter, stop and exposure of P.14 camera.
7. Check filter and stop of film camera.
8. Check electric connections to Eagle.
9. Check electric connections to spare magazine.
10. Check electric connections to P.14.
11. Check electric connections to film camera.
12. Check electric connections to spare film storage.
13. Check and count dark slides for P.14.
14. Turn off generator switch.
15. Turn off camera switch.
16. Wind and set clock.
17. Drift sight to zero.
18. Close prone position hatch.
19. Test telephone.
20. Uncap lenses.
21. Ink and set barograph.
22. Open prone position hatch slightly.
23. Turn on goggle rheostat about one quarter.
24. Pull out finder of ciné-camera.

At about 6,000 feet:

25. Turn on main generator.
26. Turn on camera switch.
27. Adjust rheostat to 13 or 14 volts.
28. Test body, hand and boot switches.
29. Ascertain drift and signal to pilot.
30. Check levelling of Eagle camera.
31. Check heating of P.14 camera.
32. Check heating of film camera.

251

Before reaching ground control:
33. Ascertain drift and instruct pilot.
34. Put drift on to Eagle camera.
35. Check levels of Eagle.
36. If light has changed re-adjust stops of P.14 and film camera.
37. Check main generator voltage continually.
38. Turn on camera switch, if not already done.
39. Watch Eagle camera and ensure its starting; if not, warn pilot to switch on control box.

During flight to summit:
40. Watch for change of drift, and adjust.
41. Note change of light values, and adjust.
42. Watch footage-indicator of ciné-camera.
    N.B.—Ciné-camera holds six runs of about fifteen seconds each on each spool.

On turning after summit:
43. Change Eagle magazine.
44. Ascertain drift and signal to pilot.
45. Put drift on to Eagle camera.
46. Change film spool as required.

APPENDIX II

THE MOUNT EVEREST CAMERAS

By COLIN M. WILLIAMSON, C.B.E., F.R.P.S.

By permission of the British Journal of Photography.

Eagle aircraft cameras are entirely automatic in action, and the type III, which takes photographs measuring 5 inches square, can be used either for oblique photography or vertical survey work. In this case it was decided to fix the camera in the floor of the aircraft for vertical photography only, suspended on an insulated gimbal mounting. A sectional drawing of the camera is given on page 255. It is constructed entirely of metal, chiefly aluminium and duralumin, and the mechanism, which is intermittent in action, is driven by an electric motor through a flexible shaft and worm gearing to the main gear-wheel shown at A.

The magazine B is detachable and is driven through the vertical bevel shaft C. Sufficient film for 125 exposures is carried in each magazine and along the edge of each exposure photographic records are made simultaneously of instruments carried in the receptacle in the side of the camera. On this expedition the instruments consisted of (1) a veeder counter for serially numbering the photographs, (2) a watch with centre second hand to indicate the time and number of seconds between each exposure, (3) an ivorine tablet giving the date and subject to be photographed, and (4) an aneroid. With regard to (4), since great variations in altitude were to be included in the photographic strip, two interchangeable instruments were supplied in order to cover the complete range with as open a scale as possible.

The first instrument registered from 0 to 17,000 and the second, which had to be changed in flight, from 15,000 to 33,000 ft.

Each instrument is photographed through a separate lens, and illuminated by small electric globes, the actual duration of exposure being regulated by the pneumatic switch F.

The 5-inch square ground photograph is taken by a special 5-inch focus Ross Xpres lens working at an aperture of $f/4$. The semi-angle is thus 35° and fully illuminates the picture with perfect definition. Immediately behind the lens is the all-metal Louvre shutter G, a comparatively recent invention but one which has made such a survey flight as this possible and the perfection of the results a certainty. This shutter consists of a number of thin pivoted metal blades which open and close at extremely high speed, exposing the whole of the aperture at once with a minimum loss of light and with great efficiency.

In view of the height (approximately 30,000 ft.) at which exposures had to be made, the chief precautions to be taken were against (1) low atmospheric pressure and (2) extreme cold.

Apart from the fact that the operator, besides having other duties to perform during the flight, could not expect to be able to do more than switch on the camera and regulate the intervals between exposures, the only part of the mechanism likely to be affected by the rarefied atmosphere was the pneumatic instrument switch.

Various experiments in a specially constructed vacuum chamber with electric-operating solenoids showed that a definite and too pronounced shortening of exposure of the instrument occurred half-way up the altitude scale, and in consequence a two-way switch was fitted which had to be operated when the high-reading aneroid was substituted for the low.

With regard to the drop in temperature it was thought originally that since the camera mechanism would function quite well without oil for the short period for which it would be required, suitable allowance in the fitting of spindles and bearings, and thermostatically-controlled electric heaters for the film chamber only, would overcome the difficulty. It was eventually decided, however, that temperatures in the neighbourhood of −50° C. might be encountered and the problem was, therefore, further complicated.

Luckily, it was found at this stage that a further supply of electric current was available from the aircraft generator for heating purposes, and internal heating elements and external electric blankets had to be made. Messrs. Hall and Co., of Deptford, most generously came to our aid by preparing and maintaining day and night, special cold chambers by means of which the actual conditions were reproduced and eventually overcome.

Strangely enough, the most delicate part of the whole photographic equipment, the electric control or intervalometer, which determined and regulated the time interval between exposures, was found to function with the utmost reliability after only minor alterations to the magnetic field. As previously stated, a 5-inch lens was selected with an extremely wide angle of view, which meant that a ground area of 4 square miles could be covered by each photograph at the average height above the ground at which it was arranged to fly. A calculation of the total area to be surveyed showed that two magazines each containing 125 exposures would suffice for the journey out to the mountain and back and provide

| Counter | Watch | Memo. Tablet | Altimeter |

A vertical photograph, taken with the Williamson camera from 32,000 feet, of the
high spurs and glaciers near Everest

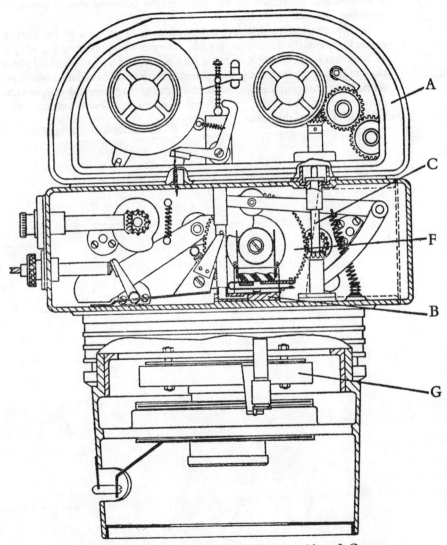

Sectional drawing of Eagle III Williamson Aircraft Camera.

overlapping pictures. Since a study of the contour map of the district, so far as is known, reveals vast and precipitous changes in ground level, a stereoscopic inspection of the photographs obtained should prove of immense interest.

Both aircraft were similarly equipped, and, in addition to the survey camera, carried two cameras for oblique pictorial photography, viz., a Williamson P.14, taking 5 inch x 4 inch plates, and a small standard pistol camera taking $3\frac{1}{4}$ inch x $2\frac{1}{4}$ inch plates. The fact that the latter was used without any heating arrangements or special preparation and was, in fact, delivered "off the shelf" at the last moment, speaks volumes for the value of Louvre shutters.

APPENDIX III

THE "BRISTOL" PEGASUS S.3 ENGINE

In the selection of engines the most important points to be considered were the power available at great altitudes and for taking off and climbing with a heavy load, the weight per effective horsepower under various conditions, reliability, and fuel consumption. The type of engine selected had also to be one suitable for the aeroplane obtainable, or such that the installation could be arranged with a minimum of structural alterations. As already seen the engine selected was the Pegasus S.3, manufactured by the Bristol Aeroplane Company.

Of the air-cooled, radial type, the Pegasus engine has nine cylinders of $5\frac{3}{4}$-inch bore and $7\frac{1}{2}$-inch stroke, giving a total swept volume of 1,753 cubic inches or just over 28 litres. It is fully supercharged to a rated altitude of 11,000 feet at its normal speed of 2,000 revolutions per minute, the rated power then being 525 brake horsepower. At its maximum permissible speed of 2,300 revolutions per minute the power is 580 brake horsepower at 13,500 feet, while for taking off at sea-level it is 550 brake horsepower. The airscrew is driven at half crankshaft speed through a reduction gear, and therefore gives high efficiency for taking off and climbing, as well as when flying level.

In regard to the principles of supercharging, it may be explained that the cylinders of an unsupercharged or naturally aspirated engine cannot be filled with combustible mixture at a pressure exceeding that of the surrounding atmosphere, while in actual practice the induction pressure is usually somewhat less than this. Such an engine will give its normal full power at sea-level, but as the aeroplane climbs the power drops off in proportion to the density of the surrounding atmosphere, until at a height equal to that of Mount Everest the power will be only about 27 per cent. of that at sea-level. Obviously, then, an aeroplane fitted with a naturally aspirated engine will have but a limited ceiling and is quite unsuitable for really high altitude work.

To increase the power at altitude it is necessary to force the mixture into the cylinders at a pressure exceeding that of the atmosphere in which the engine is operating, when the power will be increased in proportion to the difference in induction pressure. This difference is generally called the "boost," and for convenience is reckoned from the standard atmospheric pressure at sea-level. Thus, an engine supercharged to plus 1 lb.

257

boost is one in which the pressure of the charge in the induction system is 1 lb. per sq. in. above the normal pressure of 14.7 lb. per sq. in. at sea-level; while "zero boost" is just 14.7 lb. absolute pressure. When the engine is running throttled down the boost is, of course, negative, say minus 4 lb. or minus 2 lb.

A supercharged engine, then, is one provided with some form of air compressor, fan, or blower, by means of which the cylinder charge can be increased in pressure, and the rated altitude of such an engine is the height at which the induction pressure can be maintained at the rated boost, usually zero. The Pegasus S.3 engine has a rotary fan, driven from the crankshaft by a train of gearing, drawing the mixture from the carburettor and forcing it into the cylinders so effectively that the rated boost of zero (14.7 lb. per sq. in. absolute) is maintained up to an altitude of 11,000 feet at normal speed. Above this height the power falls off as in the case of the naturally aspirated engine, but not so rapidly; at the height of Mount Everest the power is just half that for taking off at sea-level, or nearly twice that of the naturally aspirated engine.

LA SCOLTA—WELCOME.

"Fall of Mount Everest"

On the occasion of Welcome of the Hon'ble Lady Houston's Expedition for the flight over the Mount Everest,
after their Final test at Yeovil, Somersetshire, England.

1st. Aeroplane :—*Houston Westland , Sq. Leader Lord Clydesdale & Observer Lt. Col. L. V S. Blacker.*
2nd Aeroplane —*Westland Wallace, Special R A. F. fitted with Bristol Pegasus, 580. Horse Power.*
Flight Lt D F Mc Intire, Officer No. 602. (City Edinburgh.) Squadron
Col. P T Etherton & Air Commodore P. F. M. Fellowes, D S. O.
(Captain C F Unwins—43976 ft. Sept, 32.)

May it please your Ladyship, Lordship & Etherial Honours :—

Fall ye Everest ! Bow beneath Air Com. Fellowes ! **F**ly ye Britishers ! Conquer Air altitude Zero
 Fight fearless Philosophic pinnacle, shower Flowery flags on bald head from windows !
Aviator Agasta's Vindhya discipleship ! **A**h, wish all "good morning" & God speed !
 Auspicious assault on stupendous front, golden Gauri Sankar gladly endures !
Leading Pilot, Krishna-Clydes Lord, **L**ured Lord Peel,Sanjoy profound !
 Lower O. snow-capped summit ! Let Lt. Kartic Mc.Intire's Wallace chariot clear !
Luminous Lady Houston's immortal generosity ! **L**iving goddess-Durga among demons & sprites
 Look-up Lamas snow-men, Saints dear ! Light signals of incense on Snow-Line lower !
O. mighty endurance of terrestrial tower ! **F**ar mightier Sir Simon's Foreign adventure !
 Objective obtain by obliques, dictaphone in Cock-pit, with oil oxygen, like' larks unseen !
Forbidden terrian by policy physical ! **F**ar reaching results to Sir Chetwood Marsha l !
 Fortunate Fliers get glorious blessings, on melodious wave-offering to deity Alpine !
Mount majestic, Himalayan Sunny soul ! **M**aharaja's permit, precious o'er Swiss-Nepal
 Meteor-like rise, mark Manas, & boundary, from Stratosphere like Piccard Professor !
Ethereal Etherton Col. Expedition Secretary ! **E**quipped by Courtesy of H. M.'s Air Ministry
 Establish record for Secy. Air, & Home Affairs, on Westland Air-wk's Cap, no small feather !
Victory to vertical Photo-Cinemas ! **V**eritable instruments of peace and passages !
 "**V**oice mighty of the Sea;" stretching hands of amity, grasp O , Sino-Tibetian mountaineers
Electric equipment in anti Zep Pegasus ! **E**xcellencies Willingdons' air-mindedness propitious
 Expedite Ruttledge's climb with Sherpa porters, by topography & wireless from Westminister !
Reward graciously, O, Majesties King & Queen ! **R**eprint, ho ! STATESMAN ! Cheer Chancellor Rankin !
 Really proud we with Scout Chief Sir Anderson, for risky rounding of the unconquered Lingam !
Eagle W**i**lson thermostats famous ! **E**xplorer Col. Blacker, bestowed Cross Victorious
 Engineers ingenious ! India's Innocents, Purnea's Planters, all Aero Clubs, do thee welcome !
Sun moon's docile descendants of south ! **S**alute Budhha's followers on Roof of Earth
 Submit ye for good, to British Pilgrims' Scientific Supremacy, in willing
Triumph of science over obstacle natural ! **T**hunder guns from H. M.'s Forts for feats supernatural !
 Tender we to Tourists "Bon Voyage," mapping, safety, health & happy Home-Coming.

Published by LITTLE BASUS of *Major* Judge Jameson's, COASTAL CORPS of S-W Bengal. C/o *Indu S. Basu* Senior Munsif, Contai MIDNAPUR. G —109. P —51 } The 11th February, 1933.	We have the honour to remain, with the profoundest veneration, your Ladyship's, Lordship's & Honours' most loyal & dutiful Servants, "SEA SANDS" of the Prov. Scout Secy. Mr. N. N. Bhose' LONE PACK of Coastal Cubs & Scouts.

INDEX

ABANA and Pharpar, "rivers of Damascus," 125

Abdullah, King of Transjordania, 122

Abraham, 124

Abyssinia, slaves from, 129

Accelerometer, loan of, 78; object of, 109; register by, in an aerial disturbance, 199

Accumulator cut-out, difficulty with, 184, 212

Accumulators, keeping warm of, 48

Aden, 129

Aerodynamic stress, investigation of, 109, 199

Aeronautical Engineering, the College of, 2, 231

Aeroplane lent by Messrs. Fry, 13, 111, 246

Aeroplane, Single-engine tractor, why needful, 56-7

Aeroplanes, choice of, factors influencing, 24-5; influence of, on antiquity, speculation on, 126

Afghanistan, military forces of, 175; mountains of, 137

African girls, attitude of, to slavery, 129

Agra, historical associations of, 218 sqq.; landing at, in a storm, 221-2

Air, the, new wonders of in relation to civil and commercial aviation in India, 229 sqq.

Aircraft, weather conditions for, 72

Air-liners, future, high-flying, 44, 230, 231

Air Ministry, the, help of, 3, 4, 6, 23, 103

Air Photographic Survey, details of, 50 sqq.; difficulties of, 56 sqq.; height at which to start, 59 sqq.; policy decided on for, 66; infra-red photography during, 66 sqq.

Aislu Kharka fort, 93

Ajodhya, mythical king of, a descent from, 163

Akbar, Emperor, and Fatehpur Sikri, 219-20; contemporaries of, 210

Akhwan tribe, the, 126

Alcohol, dangers from, 124

Alexander, the Great, 142

Allahabad, 132; aerodrome, the wrecked aeroplane at, 133, 143-4

Alps Maritimes, rough passage over, 114

Alpine Club and Mt. Everest Committee, 99

Altitude recorders, loans of, 78

Amlekganj, terminus, Nepal Government Railway, 149, road from to Bhimpedi, 150-1

Amman, R.A.F. Station at, 122

Anderson, Sir John, 216

Andes, the, 110

Anglo-Gurkha War, the, 157

Apennines, flight along, 111, 115

Aperture lens, loan of, 67-8; camera for, 68; flap for, 70

Appendix I, 251

II, 253

III, 257

IV, 259

INDEX

Appreciations of those who contributed to the success of the Expedition, 245 *sqq.*

Arabian Sea, shores of, 136

Arun river, gorges and valley, 88, 89, 91, 92, 164, 185, 190, 211

Asoka, 132

Assyrian Empire, the, 122

Atlantic Ocean, flight across in 1919, 7

Atmosphere, rarity of, at high levels, 107

Atmospheric pressure, decrease in at great elevations, 37; dangers from, 37, 38

Aviation, civil and commercial, the outlook for, 227 *sqq.*; with special reference to India, 226, 229 *sqq.*

Aviators, training of, for the Everest flight, 9; training college for, 231

BABER, Emperor, 102, 140, and polo, 171; conquests of, 218-9

Baddeleys, Messrs., 246

Baghdad, 111, 128, 129; a lost illusion, 127

Baghdad route, the, 122, 123 *sqq.*

Balkan aerodromes, 112

Balloons, use of, 76-7, 166

Baluchi tribesmen, 137, 175

Baluchistan, 130

Balukoti river, 89

Banaili, Raja of, cars lent by, 165

Bankipore, 144

Barkas, Geoffrey, Director, Cinematograph party, 15, 177, 178, 234; chapter by on filming the Flight, 232 *sqq.*

Barographs carried, 109

Barometric pressures, records of, 109

Barothermographs, loans of, 78

Barrackpore, 144

Bazaar, the, 176

Beauvais, the tragedy at, 136

Bedouin, the, 124, 125

Beharis at Shampur, 200-1

Benares, 132

Bengal, explorers from, 87; historic kingdom of, 102; landscapes in, 144

Bay of, 85

Bennett, Captain, M.O. of the expedition, 15, 177

Bethlehem, 121

"Bexoid" writing tablets, 70

Bhagalpur, 132-3

Bhagmati river, legend of, 152

Bhotia Kosi or Kosi river basin and plain, 85, 88, 90, 91

Bhutan, 148, 157, 158; Indian explorers in, 87

Bhutiya ponies, 171, 177

Bihar, 104; wild fauna of, 105; plains of, 132; seen from the air, 185

and Orissa, H.Q. of Government of, 146

Bikanir, the Maharaja of, 163

Bion, —, 131

Bithoor, 149

Black, Messrs. Thomas & Sons (Greenock), Ltd., camp equipment provided by, 248

Blacker, Colonel Valentine, C.B., first Surveyor-General of India, 79

Blacker, L. V. S., 8, 9, 11, 15, 16, 18, 130, 146, 167-8, 174, 177, 190, 191, 216, 243; plan devised by,

262

for aerial conquest of Everest, 1, 2, 3, and account by of the actual Flight, 183 sqq.

Bloch, —, 66, 67

Blood feud, the, 174

Blood vessels, bursting of, at high altitudes, 38, 107

Blumenfeld, R. D., 7

Bogaerde, —, camera for infra-red photographs designed by, 68; position of, 68-9

Bogdanovich, —, 98

Bombay, 226, 236

Bonnett, S. R., cinematographer, 15, 195, 197, 204, 233, 234, 236, 237, 240, 241, 242, 243, 244; acting observer on the Westland-Wallace machine, on the first flight, 191; photographing over Kangchenjunga, 198

Boost gauge, the, 32

Bristol Aeroplane Co., co-operation of, and thanks to, 2, 11, 14, 18, 19, 20, 21, 22, 257; advice of, on fuel, 15

Brahmaputra Valley, 96

Brahmins, and Sir Pertab Singh, 224

Brahui tribesmen, 137

Bristol Flying School, the, 18

British Aviators, debt of, to Lady Houston, 7

British Oxygen Co., 45

British-Thompson-Houston Co., Ltd., co-operation of, 21

Bruce, Major (now Brig.-General) the Hon C. G., attack on Everest planned by, 96; and use of aeroplanes, 99

Buchan, Colonel John, 4

Burma Shell Co., Ltd., help from, 20, 139, 246

Burnard, —, 15; lens flap devised by, 70

Burnham, Lord, Hon. Treasurer of the Flight Committee, 7

Burrard, Sir Sidney, 85, 86

Bury, Colonel Howard, 99

Business Firms, generous help of, 6, 8-9, appreciation of, by the authors, 245 sqq.

CAIRO, 111; desert flying to, 120; a rest at, 121; sandstorm on leaving, 122

Came, —, 15, 131, 168

Camera equipment, and lay-out, 5, 25, 26, 27 sqq., 51 sqq.; keeping the cameras warm, 57 sqq., 62; plate, why preferred, 62; essential precautions with, 183, 184

Cameras, practice with, en route to Delhi, 135

Camp equipment, 14, 15; excellence of, 248

Cape, the, Cobham's flight to, 233

Caravan route to Baghdad, the, 124

Carthage, 120

Catania, 111, 115, 117

Cawnpore, 132; massacre of, 150

"Ceiling"=altitude, 26

Chajong, hot-springs of, 89

Chamlang peak, 95; passing over, 187, 192

Range, 211

Chandagiri Pass, 151, 152

Chang Tang plain, 87

"Charly" and his spelling, 236-7, 241

INDEX

Chawla, —, Indian aviator, a 'plane generously lent by, 133

Chesil Beach, the, 13

China and Tartary, Indian explorers in, 87

Chinese General, a resourceful, 158-9

Chisapani Pass, 151

Chocolates provided by Messrs. Fry, 246

Choksun village, path near, 90-1

Ciné-cameras carried, 66; arrangement of, 27-8; at work on the first flight, 188-9, freezing of, 190

Cinematograph party, personnel of, 15-6

Cinematographer, the professional, equipment and duties of, 66

Cleopatra and Mark Anthony at Mersa Matruh, 121

Climbing capacity, essentials for, in 'planes, 19 *sqq.*

Clive, Lord, 102

Clothing, *see* Flying Kit

Cloud conditions affecting the flights, 72 *sqq.*, 182, 198, 199, 203, 213

Clouds, information on, furnished by the Indian Meteorological Department, 76; at foot of Everest, and inability to use drift sight, 213

Clydesdale, Marquess of, 4, 111, 114, 118, 128, 132, 146, 176-7, 202, 206, 209, 216, becomes chief pilot, 5, 15; training of, 9; Tiger Moth of, taken to India, 13; account by of the flight over Everest, 190 *sqq.*

Cobham, Sir Alan, flights of, 100, 233

Cockpit, Observers', closing-over of, 25, 26-7; Pilots', unclosed, 26; instruments in, 32

College of Aeronautical Engineering, the, 2, 231

Colour-values and gradation of light and shade given by infra-red photographs, 72

Compass bearings and correct courses, thinking out by drift reading, 33

Connochie, T. D., 234, 240, 243

Cook, Messrs. Thomas & Son, Ltd., appreciation of, 246

Coppersmith birds, 124

Coronation Durbar, the, 155

Cosmic rays, the, 63

Crocodiles, 168 *sqq.*; fishing for, Job on, 170

Croydon, 130

Curzon of Kedleston, Rt. Hon. Marquess, 2

DAGMARA, 93

Dain, J. F., 15, 132, 133

Dalai Lama, the, 90, 98

Dalgoma, P. & O. s.s., 13, 111

Damascus, 124; the Eye of Arabia, 125; trade and population of, 125-6

Danger, physiological, to high flying airmen, 38, 107

Dango Pass, 89

Darbhanga House, landing-ground by, 163, 165; loan of, and life in, 165 *sqq.*, 240, 248

Darbhanga, Maharaja of, 15; generous hospitality of, 165; farewell to, 217

INDEX

Darjeeling, 84, 86, 87, 105; balloon station at, 16; observatory at, 73, 75; wireless station at, 176; hill railway to, 215-6; tour to and photographs taken at, 215-6; a flight over, 238

Darling, Commissioner & Mrs., 217

Dasaratha, King, 163

Daukes, Colonel C. T., and Mrs., 153, 154

Daylong Pass, 89

Dead Sea, the, 122, 124

Delhi, and New Delhi, 131, 132, 133, 135, 237; from the air, 142-3; battles fought near, 142-3; the Viceroy's house at, 142, 163; legend concerning, 162; inspection at, by the Viceroy, of the two 'planes, 162

Delhi Flying Club, the, 142

Deloitte, Plender Griffiths & Co., Messrs., help of, 246

Dholpur, the Maharaja Rana of, airmindedness and hospitality of, 218

Dibang river, 79

Dictaphone, results with, 78, 246

Dihang river, 79

Dinajpur, forced landing at, 201

Dingboche Monastery, 65, 101, 102, 213

Dip-needle, liquid, 78, 109

Dorji (Dorijeff), in Tibet, 98

Douglas and Clydesdale, the Marquess of, see Clydesdale

Drift, adjustment for, of cameras, 54, 59, 60

Drift-reading in the air, 33

Drift-sight, 60; unusable on second Everest flight, 213

Drigh Road, 135

Dudh Kosi river, Valley of, 93

Dust haze, 73, 86-7; height attained by, 61, 136, 184, 185, 191, 204; impenetrable to infra-red plates, 72; survey photographs marred by, 192, 195

Dust storms, 207, a flight before, in a Moth, 221-2

Dynamos, thousand-watt, 45; position for, 46; trouble with, at start of each Everest flight, 184, 212

EARTH's magnetism near the Himalayas, investigation of, 109

Education of Indian women, 180

Egyptian Empire, the, 122

Electric heating arrangements, 5; for clothing, etc., 10, 46-7, 134, 183, excellence of, 49, 248; voltage of, 47-8

Electric installation, 5; dynamos of, 45-6

Elizabeth, Queen, 220

Ellison, R. C. W., 15, 173, 177, 195, 196, 198-9, 202, 204, 216

English Channel, flying across, 113

English Embassy to Jehangir, 220

English weather, and high-altitude flying, 10

Ephthalite invasion of India, 140

Etherton, Colonel P. T., 2, 8, 15, 146, 167, 173, 177, 239, 245, visit of, to Nepal, 2, 15, 133, 147 sqq.; on the visit to Darjeeling and the air tour of India, 215 sqq.

INDEX

Etna, Mt., flight over, 117-8

Euphrates, the, 127

"Everest" cloth, suits of, 46

Everest, Colonel Sir George, 80

Everest mail, the, 183; carried over the summit and despatched on landing, 192

Everest, Mount, inaccessibility of, 1; geographical position of, and diplomatic difficulties concerning, 2-3, 103, 148; air temperature above, 57; wind conditions and velocities near and on, 62, 72, 74, 75, 86, 210; cloud conditions around, 72 *sqq. see also that head*; story of survey and other expeditions to, 79 *sqq.*; the triangulation of, 80, 82, 87; discovery of its being the highest mountain in the world, 83; attempted determination of its height and errors corrected and possible, 83 *sqq.*, snow on crest as affecting, 85-6, preponderant height of, verified, 98-9; former name of, 82; why so long undiscovered, 86-7; various views of, 87, 132, 164, 238, during the first flight, 185, 186, 187, 191; lake near, 89; circuited but unseen by No. 9, 91, 97; the newel post of two worlds, 103; cliffs of, 187; colour characteristic of, 188; heart-shaped black patch on, 214; conquest of, from the air, 189-90, 192, 210, 243, and close range

photographs obtained of summit, 192

Expeditions against till 1932, by land, that of 1933 (*q.v. infra*), by air, 1 *sqq.*

Expeditions to, in 1921, 1922 and 1924, 99, 100; the epic of 1924, 96

Houston-Mount Everest Flight, the, anticipated results of, 226 *sqq.*; basic conception behind, 17; equipment of, 14, *see also details under names*; objectives of, actual, scientific, economic, and patriotic, 17, 106, 108-9, 205 *sqq.*; 226; obstacles surmounted, 6, Lady Houston's support secured, 7; permit from Nepal for first flight secured, 4-5, 148-9, and later, that for the second flight also, 206; personnel of, 1, 2, 8, 15, allocation of duties of, 173-4, 177-8; planning of, 2, 18 *sqq.*, and other preliminaries, 3 *sqq.*; preparations for, 8 *sqq.*, 245, the final, 183; problems before, 103; risks attending, 4, 106 *sqq.*; training for, 9 *sqq.*; unusual conditions of, 5; widespread kindness and help extended to, in India, 15, 16, 133, 165, 226, *et alibi.*

First flight, story of, 183 *sqq.*, 190 *sqq.*; the swoop over the summit, 189-90, 192, close-range photographs of the summit obtained, 192; difficulties with vertical

266

cameras and telephone gear, 195, the Kangchenjunga flight to adjust, 195; unsuccess of, 204, 205

Second flight, reason for, 205 *sqq.*; story of, 207-8 *sqq.*; the summit crossed, 210; the two minor hitches in, 213-4

Ice-plume of, 186, 187; passage through, of the aeroplanes, 189, 192; riddle of, 193-4; hurricane blast evidenced by, 210; length of, 210, 211

North Col of, 102

South Peak (Lhotse), 101, the swoop over, 60, 188, and passage through the "down fall" by, on the first flight, 192, 194; the second flight over, 210, 213, avoiding the "downfall," 210

South side, steep slopes of, 60; air survey of, planned, 108

Everest range, rivers bursting through, 88, 90

Exhaust rings, complete, 21

FAKIRS, 147
Farnborough, 9 *sqq.*, 16
Fatehpur Sikri, 219-20
Fedden, A. H., 18
Fellowes, Air-Commodore, P. F. M., 8, 111, 123, 128, 132, 146, 168, 177-8, 191, 195, 196-7, 216, 222, 226, 238, 239
Fellowes, Mrs. P. F. M., 111, 202
Ferghana, 102
Filming activities at Purnea, 178
Filton, 18

Financial questions, advisers on, 246
Fisher, A. L., 15, 195, 201, 233, 234, 236, 237
Flying, fascinations of, 112-3
Flying instruments, 23-4
Flying kit, 9, 10, 11, 31-2; electric warming of, 10, 46, 47, 134, 183; excellence of, 49, 248
Flying personnel, training of, 9 *sqq.*, 248; testing of, 38, 108
Forbesganj, 105, 131, 191
Ford, Henry, 230
Fox Moth, taken to India, 13
Framjee, 172
France, flight across, 111; aviation regulations in, 113
Fraser, —, 177, 212
French Air Company (Air Orient) 141
French and German flyers, plans of, for flying over Everest, 100
Fry, Messrs., aeroplane lent by, 13, 111, 246; chocolates provided by, 246
"Frying-pan of the World," the, 130
Fuad, King of Egypt, 121
Fuel, advice on, 15; that chosen, 20, 246; for extreme altitudes, 246
Fuel consumption as affected by force of wind, 24, 75, 181, 207
Fuel problems of the two Everest flights, 246
Fuel supplies, depots of, 14-5, 246

GABES, quickest get-away effected at, 114

INDEX

Gandarson Singh, explorations of, 92, 97, 101

Ganges, the, 132; affluents of, 88, 144; paddle-steamers on, 131, 146; basin of, 142; sanctity of, 146-7

Garhwal, 158; mountains of, 147

Gaumont-British Picture Corporation, and the making of "Wings over Everest," 191, 232 *sqq.*

Gaumukh, source at, of the Ganges, 147

Gaurisankar, 186

Gaya, landing-ground at, 132, 144

Gearing, —, 177

Geology, hopes to benefit, 109

George V, H.M., fine shooting by in Nepal, 155; the "Everest mail" sent to, 192

Gieves, Messrs., silk gloves by, 46, 248

Gilgit polo, 171

Goggles, electrically heated, 47, 48

Golwalla, 172

Goomti tea estate, 216-7

Graham, Rev. Dr., 176

Gravimetric observations, 77-8

Great Britain, height-record secured for, by Capt. Uwins, 20

Great Indian Desert, the, 104, 141

Great War, the, 2, 96, 98

Guides, the, 174

Gujar Singh, 101

Gupta, S. N., and the upper air sounding station at Purnea, 76-7; invaluable weather reports by, 166, 178, 191, 240, 241

Gurkha forces, in Nepal, 160

Regiments in the Indian army, 97, 158

Gurkhas, the, 103; invasion by, of Nepal, 156-7; relations of, with John Company the Gurkha war and settlement thereafter, 157-8

Martial nature of, 156 *sqq.*, 175

Wars of, with Tibet, 89, 157, 158-9

Gwadur, 130

Gyachungkang, 186

HALL, Messrs. J. & E., co-operation of, 58

Halliburton, —, flight of, towards Everest, 100

Hand-cameras taken for oblique photography, 28-9, 248

Handley Page slots, 21

Hangars lent by R.A.F., 15, set up at Lalbalu, 131, 145, 166

Hanuman, 176

Hardwar, festival at, 147

Hari Ram (No. 9), journeys of, 87 *sqq.*, 93 *sqq.*, 97, 101

Harman, Captain, 92

Haroun al Raschid, 127

Harpur, 83

Haslam & Newton, Messrs., dynamos by, 45

Hathwa, Raja of, a visit to, 217

Havelock, Sir Henry, 217

Hayden, Sir Henry, 86

Hearsey family, the, 102

Heat "bumps" in the air, 142, 144, 237

Hermon, Mt., 122

Heston, 122, 130

High flying, advantages of, 44, 230-1

Himalayas, the, 84, 92, 103; spirit-level accuracy affected by, 84; earth's magnetism near, investigation of,

109; parts still little known 148; as Nature's irrigation reservoirs, 164; seen on first Everest flight, 192; seen from Darjeeling, 216

Hindu Kush, tribes of, 175

Hindustan, Blacker's map of, 79; explorers sent out by, 87; plains of, battles on, 142-3; brownness of, 143

Hinks, A. R., 3, 61

Hittite Empire, the, 122

Holy Land, the, 121-2

Honourable East India Company, explorers of, 102; treaty of, with the Gurkhas, 157-8

House-stealing, 172

Houston, Lady, munificence of, to aviation, and support by, of the Schneider contest, 7; the Flight financed by, 7, 205, 206; telegram of, to the Viceroy on its behalf, 111; the "Everest mail" sent to, 192; cablegram from, advising against a second flight, 206

Houston-Mt. Everest Flight Committee, the, 4, 7, 99, 245

Houston Westland Aeroplane, tests of, 9, 11; crew of, on the first Everest flight, 191; crew of, on the Kangchenjunga flight, 195; flight of, to Delhi, 237

Hucks Starters, 23

Hughes, —, 111, 128

Hughes Drift Sight, the, 60

Hughes, Messrs. Henry, liquid dip-needle by, 78, 109

Humayun, Emperor, 102, mosque of, 142

Huns, white and yellow, Indian invasions of, 140

Hyderabad, "wind-catchers" at, 138

ILFORD, Messrs., Research Dept. of, and infra-red photography, 65, 66

Imperial Airways, the expedition's transport facilitated by, 13; and Jupiter engines, 18; desert houses of, 130; liners of, 130-1; the tragedy of its monster airships and their hangar, 136-7; travelling by, to, and in, India, 246

India, landing facilities accorded in, 6; route to, by Eastern Europe uninsurable, 111-112; route followed, aircraft and personnel of, 111 sqq.; Northern, invaders and invasions of, 140, 142; key to the world, 143; nationalism non-existent in, 175; predatory races along its frontier, 175; the aerial progress over, 215, 216 sqq.; aviation in, future before, 226 sqq.

India Office, the, and the expedition, 3, 4

Indian Explorers, 87 sqq.

Indian Government, the, 175-6

Indian Meteorological Department, co-operation of, 75 sqq., 106-7; accuracy of its reports, 207; see also Gupta

Indian Mutiny, the, 149-50, 217

INDEX

Indian Princes, the, airmindedness among, 142, *see also under individual titles*

Indian Women, life of, 178 *sqq.*

Indrawati river, 91

Indus, the, 111, 138

Inertia starters, 23

Infra-red photography, 66 *sqq.*, 109; haze penetrated by, 72; of Kanchenjunga, 212 of Everest for the film, 235

Instruments taken, 5

Irish Free State, Aeroplanes offered by, 25

Irrigation Canals, 137, 140

Irvine, A., 96, 109

Italian aerodromes, perfection of, 115

Italian Air Force, the, 115, 116

Italy, airmindedness in, 115; flight down, 111, 115

JANO, 91

Jaumotte meteorgraph, the, 109

Jehangir, Emperor, 219-20

Jericho, 122

Jerusalem, 121, 122

Jesus Christ, scenes of the life of, 121

Jirol, 83

Joafpati, 83

Jodhpur, the flight to, 135; air port of, 141

Jodhpur Flying Club, the, 141

Jodhpur Lancers in France, 223

Jodhpur, Maharaja of, airmindedness of, 222-3

Jogbani, 105

Jordan, the, 122

Jubang village, 94

Jumla, 94

Jumna, the, 142, 144

Jupiter engine, successes with, 18-19

K.L.G. type of sparking plugs, 21

Kabul-Termez, mountain flying between, 110

Kabru, 211

Kalimpong, Clydesdale's flying visit to, 177

Kangchenjunga massif, 86, 91, 92, 198; clouds besetting, 73, 193, 196, 197, 198, 199, 203; flights in the region of, 77; a sight of, 132 other sights of, during the Everest flights, 185, 186, 211; Barkas's first view of, 238; the flight over, objects of, 195 *sqq.*, the scene during, 197-8, results of, 228

Kapok inner suit of Flying Kit, 46

Karachi, 131, 226; arrivals at, 14, 130; flight to, of the Moth aeroplanes, 111 *sqq.*; Aircraft Depot at, the Westland 'planes erected by and tested, 131, 134; flight from, to Delhi, practice during, of photography, 135; film work at, 236; the tragic hangar at, 136-7

Kata, village, 92

Keprak, 94, 95

Khatmandu, 3, 160 *sqq.*; Etherton's visit to and its object, 133, 153, 154; a review at, 160

Khunbu Dzong, No. 9 at, 94

Khumbu glacier, from the air, 211

Khumu Changbo river, 94

Kipling, Rudyard, 104

Kite-flying, 172

INDEX

Kites and vultures, danger from, to aeroplanes, 143

Komaltar ridge, 185, 191, 192

Krishna and his aery chariots, 103

Kumaon, 158

Kumbh Mela festival, the, 147

Kurseong, 84

Kutab Minar, the, Delhi, 142

LADNIA, observations of Everest from, 83, 84

Lahore, 237

Lalbalu, landing-ground at, 104, 105, 145; the hangars at, 131, 145, 166; life at, routine of, 166 *sqq.*; the bathing pool and the crocodiles, 168 *sqq.*; safe landing at, after first Everest flight, 192; the Kangchenjunga flight from, 208 *sqq.*

Lalbir Singh Thapa, 101

Lambton, Colonel, and the trigonometrical survey of India, 80

Landing ground, advanced, choice of, 104, *see also* Lalbalu

Lawrence, John (Lord Lawrence), 87

Lawrence, Sir Henry, 217

Lawrence, Stringer, 102

Lebanon, 124

Le Bourget aerodrome, formalities at, 113

Legal advisers, 246

Lepcha Chief, and No. 9, 87-8

Lhasa, British military mission to, 96, 98

Lhotse, *see* South Peak *under* Everest, Mt.

Light, Indian, quality and intensity of, 135-6; on snow, brilliance of, 186; penetrativeness of at high altitudes, 210

Light filters, 63, 235

Light values in the upper air, 63

Listibhansar, 90

Lot, 124

Lubrication on the flights, impossibility of, 205; oil used when practicable, 246

Lucknow, mutiny memories at, 217; train journey to, 237

Lutyens, Sir E., 142

Lytton, Earl of, 7

MACEDONIAN invasion of India, 140

McIntyre, Flight Lieutenant D. F., 118, 128, 129, 132, 146, 177, 216, 226; training of, 9; nominated as second pilot, 15; and the flight to India, 111, 114-5, pilot of Westland-Wallace machine on first Everest flight, 191, account by, of the flight, 190 *sqq.*; plan of, for route of second Everest flight, 207-8; and the sand-storm, 221, 222

Macleod, Colonel N. M., 16

Madras City, "Blacker's Garden" near, 79

Magneto difficulties, 20-1

Mahabharat range, the, 212

Mahratta Wars, the, 79

Makalu, 86, 95, 101; cloud conditions near, 83; a distant sight of, 132; seen on the first Everest flight, 185, 186; whiteness of, 187

"Mall" or polo, at Damascus, 125

Mallory, G. L., and Irvine, fate of, on Everest, 96, 109

Manu, Raja, 163

INDEX

Map-making, importance of, Air Surveys facilitating, 17; method of using Air Survey photographs for, 55

Martlesham Heath, the R.A.F. Experimental Establishment at, help from, 6

Medical Services in India, doctor appointed to the Expedition by the Director of, 15

Mekran, 130

Mersa Matruh, 120-1

Mesopotamia, 124

Messina, 117

Methodist Mission, Shampur, hospitality of, 202

Microphone communication, arrangements for, 31, 43

Minai, observations of Everest from, 83, 84

Minam, No. 9 at, 90

Mirzapur, 83

Moab, mountains of, 122

Mogul conquerors of India, 142, 218-19

Mogulistan, 102

Mohammed, and Damascus, 125

Mongol invasions of India, 140

Monitor Oil Appliances, Ltd., stove supplied by, 248

Mooltan, s.s., 236

Morshead, —, photographic survey work of, 100-1

Moslems of the North and North-West Frontier, 172, 174 *sqq.*

Moth aeroplanes, flight of, to India, 111 *sqq.*

Mountain flying, 110

Mountains, eddy on leeward sides of, 107; unnamed by natives, 92

Murderers as servants, 172

Mussolini, Benito, airmindedness of, 115

NADIR Shah, 140

Nairobi, 120

Nana Sahib, the, fate of, 149-50

Narpat Singh, Thakur, 140

Naples, 115, and its Bay, 116

Natives, reaction of, to first sight of aircraft, 203

Nawanagar, H.H. the Maharaja Jam Sahib of, support of, 7

Nazareth, 121

Nepal, approach to, difficulties of, 2-3, 4; permission accorded to first Everest flight over, 5; people in, importance of not alarming, 40, load-carrying powers of, 162; Indian explorers in, 87; Tibetan frontier of, 92; alliance of, with the British crown, 97; closed kingdom of, why remaining so, 97-8; Bengal mutineers in, 104; physical features of, 106; Etherton's journey to, object of, 147, 149; Mt. Everest within the limits of, 148; Indian frontier of, 149, roads and routes in, 150-1, 162, 193; valley of, 151 *sqq.*; population of, an estimate of, 152; Gurkha rulers of, 154, social organisation of, 156, rise of, history of, 156 *sqq.*; motors and overhead rope railway in, 152-3; army of, a review of, 160; mountains of, seen from the air, 185

INDEX

Government of, permit of for the first Everest flight, 4-5, conditions of, for permit for second flight, 206; survey of, 65, 101, 148, 149; railway of, 148, 149

King of, 154, coronation of, 160

Maharaja of, Sir Joodha Shum Shere Jung Bahadur Rana, Prime Minister and Commander-in-Chief, 4, 154; permission accorded by to the Flight Expedition, 102, and for the second flight, 133-4, 148-9, 153, 156; approach to, by Etherton, 147, 151 sqq.

New Guinea, legendary peaks in, 98; and mountain flying, 110

Nichols, R. N., 215

Ninam, village, 90

Ningzi, 89

Nila Pass, 88

Nile, the, 121

Nobile, General, 206-7

Noel, Capt. J. B., reconnaissance of, S.E. of Everest, 96, 99; view of, on aeroplanes, 99

Norman, Dr., and meteorological data for the flight, 16, 75

North Africa, an impression of, 119; lost cities in, 121

O'Brien, —, of Goomti, 216, 217

Observers, duties of, during flights, 30-1, 48, 54, 66, 184-5, 186-7, 188, 251-2; difficulties of, 57

Ochterlony, General, 157

Oil, lubricating, 20; Wakefield's Aero C. used, 246

Oil cooler, type used, 22

Oil pressure gauges, 23

Oil thermometers, 23-4

Omar, Mosque of, 122

Omayyad Caliphs, capital of, 124

Oudh, 102

Outfit, old time, for climbing Mt. Blanc, 47

Oxygen, on the Everest flight, 5, 34 sqq., 45; small consumption of, during second flight, 213

for Aviators, how obtained, 35 sqq., how used, 37-8

Oxygen cylinders, number decided on, 39-40

Generating plant, portable, 39

Intra-venous or intra-muscular injection of, 39

Oxygen masks, troubles with, 11-12, 189, 190, 196, 200; bayonet joint for, 41; air hole in, plugging of, 42; inconveniences of, 42-3;

Oxygen supply, gear for, 5, 29-30, control of, 30-1, redesign of needed, 43; regulating valve of, 45; warming of, 44-5; importance of, 107

Palestine, from the air, 121-2, 127

Panchromatic film, the, 235

Pangji Pass, 94-5; rest house, horse-god image at, 94

Pangu Pass, 93

Parsees, the, 172

Pathans, the, 172, 175

Patiala, Maharaja of, 224

Patna, 132, 146; suburbs of, 144

Peel, Capt., V. C., 104

Peel, Earl, 4, 104

Pegasus S.3 engines, 1, 5, 9, 18-9, 24, 25, 40, 139, 141, 185;

273

INDEX

Pegasus S. 3 engines, supercharger of, 1, 5, advantage of, 19, height at which doing best work, 40; testing of, 9; *see also* Appendix III; engines, testing of, 9

P. & O. Steam Navigation Co., 146; transport facilities by, 13, 111, 233, 236; appreciation of, 245-6

Penrose, ——, first test pilot, 10

Persian Gulf, the, 129; slave-trade of, 129-30

Perim, 129

Permits to fly over countries *en route*, 14, 128-9

Persia, flight over, 111, permits for, 14, 128-9

Pertab Singh, Maharaja Sir, 140, 223-4

Petrol pumps, 23

Petrol supply, pilots' observation of, 32-3; *see also* Fuel

Photographic equipment, arrangement of, 27 *sqq.*

Photographic practice, 139

Photographs, Oblique, 16, value of, 61, success with, on both Everest flights, 214

Stereoscopic, 108-9, in pairs, 109

Vertical, over Kangchenjunga, 197; on second Everest flight, the black patch revealed by, 214

Photography, problems connected with, 13

Photography in the Aeroplanes, 26 *sqq.*; relative claims of the cinematograph, and of oblique and vertical photographs, 16, for Air Survey, 50 *sqq.*, vibration trouble with, 69; during the first flight, 186 *sqq.*, close range of Everest's summit secured, 192; the survey photographs not successful, 192; on the second flight, 209 *sqq.*, successful, 212, 213, *see also* Ciné-cameras, *and* "Wings over Everest"

Physiography, hope to aid, 109

Pilot, duties of, 32-3, 41

Pisa, 116

Pitt, ——, 15, 202

Plane-table, the aeroplane and, 82

Plotting machine, automatic, 55

Poles, the, flown over by foreigners, 7

Polo, antiquity of, 125, 170-1

Popte range, 92

Pratt and Whitney engine, 18

Prejevalski, ——, 98

Propellers, the, 21, 22-3, 24; factor desirable in, 44

Public Works Department, India, help from, 15, 131

Punjab, the, explorers from, 87

Purana Kila, walls of, 142

Purdah system, the, 178 *sqq.*

Purnea, the expedition's base at, 14, 15, 70, 71, 82, 145, 147, 163, 201, 233; aerodrome at, 15; balloon station at, 16; the journey to, 131; landing ground near, 104-5, 133 (*see also* Lalbalu), land temperature at, 57; observatory at, 73, 75; the expedition's home at, 165

Work at, routine of, recreations and visitors at, 166 *sqq.*; native life at, 172-3; weather-cycles at, 182,

274

INDEX

207; the snows invisible from, 238; farewells to, 215, 217

Purnea-Siliguri-Darjeeling road, the, 105, 215, interests of, 166-7

Puss Moth, loan of, 13, 111, 246

Pyramids, the, 121

RAGULONG PASS, 89

Rain-storms, 207

Rajput descent, claimed by the Gurkhas, 156

Rajputana, 140; desert of, 135, 141

Rajputs of Nepal, 97, 102-3

Raleigh, Sir Walter, 220

Rangit, confluence of, 197

Rawling, Capt., survey by, in Southern Tibet, 98

Raxaul, 147, 149

Read, R. L., 233, 234

Red tape, 113, 114

Reserve pilot lent by R.A.F. in India, 15

Rheostat, sliding, 68

Rhinoceros, Asian, Bihar, 105

Richardson, —, 176

Rigby Mannlicher rifles, excellence of, 248

Roberts, C. H., 2

Rolex watches, reliability of, 248

Rome, 114, 118

Royal Aircraft Establishment resources of, accorded to the expedition, 6, 23, 39, 43; and the microphone communication, 31, 43; tests of personnel at, 38, 108

Royal Air Force, experimental stations, tests at, 6, 234; school of photography, help from, 6; other assistance from, in India, 15, 131,

236; Jupiter engines used by, 18-9

Royal Dutch Air Line, Fokker airships of, 141, 144

Royal Geographical Society, approval by of the Flight Expedition, value of its support, 3, 4, 102; the Mount Everest Committee formed by, with the Alpine Club, 9

Rumba, the, as landing-ground, 105

Rutbah Fort, 123

Rutlam Cup, famous game of polo for, 223, 224-5

Ryder, Captain, estimation by, of the height of Mt. Everest, 95; survey by, in Southern Tibet, 98

SAHARA, the, irrigation of, 119-20

Saidjong, village, 89

Sakkya, monastery of, 89

Saladin, and Damascus, 125

Salim Chisti and Akbar, 219

Sanatogen during training, value of, 248

Sandakphu, 84

Sand, high-rising, 123

Sandstorms, 121, 123, 124, 127, 128

Saria village, 93

Sarzana, 115

Sasaram, 132, 144

Sayid Ali, 174

Schneider Contest, Lady Houston's support of, 7

Screw-driver, the, 209, 211, 212-3

Scythian invasions of India, 140

Sempill, the Master of, 4

Servants, Indian, 236-7, 241

Shaiba, 127

275

INDEX

Shampur, forced landing at, 200-1, 202

Sharma, —, 131

Sheba, Queen, 124

Sheka river, 89

Shell Anglo-Persian Oil Groups, advice from, 15

Shell Aviation Spirit, fuel like used in the flights, 20, 246

Shell-Mex Co., advice from, 14, 15, and provision of fuelling depots, 15

Shepherd, E. C., 111, 114, 128

Sher Shah, tomb of, 132, 144

Shigatze, No. 9 at, 88, 89

Shira village, 88

Sicily, 111, 112, 117

Siebe Gorman, Messrs., oxygen gas masks by, 42, 43
Electrically heated flying suits by, 46, 49, 134

Sifton, Sir James, 146

Sikkim, 86, 87, 96, 98, 148, 157, 158, seen from the air, 197-8

Siliguri, 84, 105, 215

Sinilochun, 211

Sinclair-Newman cinema camera, the 66

Sind desert, the, 130, 136, 237

Sisagarhi fort, 151

Siva, 152

Six-Twenty Kodaks, light-tightness and other points of, 248

Skinner family, the, 102

Slave trade, Persian Gulf area, 129

Smith, Tom, and Mrs. Tom, 171-172

Smith's Aircraft Instruments, Messrs., 23

Sodom and Gomorrah, 124

Solomon, 124

Somaliland, 129

Soucek, Lieutenant, altitude record made by, 18

Sparking plugs, 21

Sphinx, the, 121

Starters, "inertia" type chosen, 23, 139

Stephens, Messrs. James, electrically heated goggles by, 47

Stereogoniometer, the, 55

Stereoscope, use of, in plotting survey from air photos, 55, 56

Stereoscopic images, transmission of, 230

Still cameras, photographing with, 61, 66

Stratosphere, the, future traverse of, by air liners, 44

Stringfellow, —, and his monoplane, 82

Stromboli, 117

Suberkun, 84

Sun Kosi river, 93

Survey photographs oblique and vertical, methods of taking, 50 sqq.; supplementing of by oblique stereoscopic photographs, 109; taken on the first Everest flight, not successful, 192, 204, taken on the second flight, success with, 214

Sweeny, W. H. O., 233, 234

Sykes, Major-General Sir F., 146

Syria, 124, 127

Takdeo, image of, on Pangji Pass, 94

Tambar Valley, 92

Taskichriang, lake near, 88-9

Tashi Lama, the, 89, 98

Tassading, 197

INDEX

Taylor, Taylor & Hobson, Messrs.,
lens lent by, 67-8
Teheran, 128
Telephones between pilot and
observer, 49, 70
Television, 230; in colour, *ib.*
Telephoto lenses, 234
Temperature changes, records of,
109
Terai, the, 158, 162; flight over,
105-6; and the Nana
Sahib, 149-50, a royal
shoot in, 155
Tetra-ethyl-lead fuel chosen, 20
Thakurganj, 105
Thanglang Pass, 89
Thankot, 152, 153
Theodolite of Lambton, and those
of to-day, 81
Theodolite observations, 83, in-
accuracies in, 84-5
Tibet, 148; a hermit kingdom, 2-3,
98; closed to airmen and
all Europeans, 2-3, 97,
98, 106; Indian explorers
in, 87 *sqq.*, 92-3; Gurkha
Wars with, 89, 157, 158,
159; plains of, 90, moun-
tains beyond seen on the
first flight, 187; Southern,
Ryder's survey in, 148
Tiger, in Bihar, 105
Tiger Hill, Darjeeling, observa-
tions from, of Everest, 84;
filming from, 216
Tiger Moth, Clydesdale's, taken
to India, 13
Tigris, the, 127
Time, in the East, 176
Times, The, and the expedition,
16, 68, 111, 177
Tingri village, 89, 93; the Daipon
of, 95

Tingri Maidan, the, 89, 92, 95
Tingri river, 89
Tipta Pass, 88
Tobacco-smoking, beginnings of
in England and India, 220
Townend Ring, the, 21-2
Trading, native, 176
Training for the Flight, 9 *sqq.*, and
before the Flight, 247
Trapani Aerodrome, 118
Transport, present day, superses-
sion of, by air transport,
227 *sqq.*
Travel books, annoyances concern-
ing, 114
Triangulation, process of, 80 *sqq.*
Tripoli, air-mail to, 120
Tube wells, siting of, 131
Tunis, the flight to, 111, 118-9;
arrival at, 120
Turan plateau, the, 103
Turkey, permits to fly over, 14
Turkistan, a motor-cycle in, 167-8
Turubaz Khan, 101
Tutankamen's chariots, 121

Udaipur, the Maharana of, and
his descent, 163; a visit to,
by air, 225-6
United States Army Air Corps,
height record achieved by,
18, 19
University of the Air, the, 2, 231
Upper air, at 33,000 feet above
Karachi, temperature of,
134
Ur aerodrome, 128
Uwins, Capt. C. F., height record
secured by, 20

Vauxhall car and Goodyear
tyres, excellent service of,
248

INDEX

Veevers, V., 233, 236

Verne, Jules, anticipations of, on aircraft, 100, 227

Vespa Aeroplane, Uwins' height record made in, 20

Vesuvius, 117; flying across, 116

Vibrac oxygen cylinders, 38

Vickers Armstrong, Messrs., oxygen cylinders by, 38

Vickers-Potts oil-cooler, 22

Vickers-Vespa aeroplanes, 25

Victoria, Queen, 222

Vishnu and the Bhagmati river, 152

Voltmeter for observer's use, 48

WAKEFIELD, Messrs., provision by of fuelling depots, 15

Wakefield's Aero Castrol C lubricating oil, 246

Wales, H.R.H., the Prince of, 224, 225; "Everest mail" sent to, 192

Walker, General, 80

Wallace, Edgar, 135

War Office, Geographical branch of General Staff, help of, 16; suggestion of, on oblique stereoscopic photographs, 108-9

Watches used by the expedition, 248

Water-cooled engines, and altitude flying, 19

Waugh, Major-General Sir Andrew, 79, 82

Weather conditions for aircraft, 72

Weather cycles at Purnea, 182, 207

Weather forecasts, arrangements for receiving, 16

Wessex monoplane, 29

Westland Aircraft Co., 14, 25; thanks to, 11; Wessex monoplane of, 29

Westland P.V.3, the aeroplanes chosen for the Everest flight, 5, 25; tests of, 9, 10 *sqq.*; transport of, to India, 13, 111; fitting up of, 25 *sqq.*; assembly of, and trials of, at Karachi, 134; flying of to Lalbalu, 135 *sqq.*; the flights over Everest in, 182 *sqq.*; flying of, back to Karachi, 216; *see also* Houston Westland, *and* Westland Wallace

Westland Wallace aeroplane, crew of, on first Everest flight, 191; crew of, on the Kangchenjunga flight, 195 *sqq.*; camera practice in 236

Wheeler, —, survey work of, 100

Williamson's Automatic Eagle III survey cameras chosen for the Everest flights, 51-2; position for and for its spare spool, 27, a slight defect in, 213-4; control box of, 52; spirit levels in 53-4; adjustment of, for drift, 54; electric heating of, 57 *sqq.*; cold chamber tests of, 58-9; light filters used with, 63; observer's duties regarding, 55, 66, *and see* Appendix I; vertical survey photos taken with, supplementing of, 108-9

Williamson's hand-held cameras, 29

INDEX

Williamson's P.14 oblique plate camera, reliability of, 62; operating of, 64-5; Hinks's expectations from, 65; use of on the flight over Kangchenjunga, 210, good results obtained, 214

Williams's P.14 camera 5 × 4, oblique photographs taken with, 214

Williamson's Pistol Camera 3½ × 2½ as duplicate for the chief camera, 66; good oblique photographs from, 214

Willingdon, Earl of, Lady Houston's cable to, on behalf of the Flight Expedition, 111; review by, of the aeroplanes, 163; and Countess of, airmindedness of, 142, 162-3

Wind currents and wind velocities near and on Everest, 62, 72, 74, 75, 86, 210, information on from the Indian Meteorological Dept., 75 *sqq.*, 106-7

Wind velocity at start of first flight over Everest, 182, at start of second flight, 208

"Wings over Everest," production of the film, preliminaries to, 232 *sqq.*, equipment for, details of, 235; scenario for, 235; scenes for, filming of, 238, 240, with aviators in flying kit, 241; rehearsals for, 238-9, sound-production for, 232, 233, a *contretemps* over the sound-truck, 242-3; weather difficulties of the filming party, 239 *sqq.*; the actual making of the film, 243-4

Wodehouse, P. G., 135

Women of India, conditions of life of, 178 *sqq.*

Wright "Apache" biplane, 18

Yaks, problem concerning, 159

Yeovil, aeroplane trials at, 9-10, 11, 234

Younghusband, Sir Francis, 98

Zenobia, Queen of Palmyra, 124

MORE TITLES ON MOUNTAINEERING AND TREKKING FROM PILGRIMS PUBLISHING

- **Among the Himalayas** .... *L A Waddel*
- **Annapurna South Face** .... *Chris Bonington*
- **Attack on Everest** .... *Hugh Ruttledge*
- **Climbing the Fish Tail** .... *Wilfred Noyce*
- **Everest:** From the first attempt to the final victory. .... *Micheline Morin*
- **Everest the Challenge** .... *Sir Francis Younghusband*
- **Everest: the Hard Way** (The adventure story of the Decade) .... *Chris Bonington*
- **First Over Everest:** The Huston-Mount Everest Expedition 1933
.... *P F M Fellowes, L V Stewart Blacker, P T Etherton & others*
- **Himalayan Adventure Trekking Gear:** A Checklist for Women .... *Joyce A Tapper*
- **Lost in the Himalayas** .... *James Scott & Joanne Robertson*
- **Mansalu: A Trekker's Guide** .... *Kev Reynolds*
- **Mount Everest :** The Reconnaissance 1921 .... *C K Howard-Bury*
- **Mustang: A Trekking Guide** .... *Bob Gibbons and Sian Prichard-Jones*
- **Mustang: Un Guide de Trekking** .... *Bob Gibbons and Sian Prichard-Jones*
- **Nepal Die Far Western Region:**
Reisecompanion für Abenteurer, Trekker und Bergsteiger .... *M Lindenfelser*
- **Nepal Himalaya** .... *H W Tilman*
- **Nepal the Far Western Region:**
A Travelling Companion for Travellers, Trekkers and Climbers .... *M Lindenfelser*
- **Peaks and Lamas** .... *Marco Pallis*
- **Round Kangchenjunga** .... *Douglas W Freshfield*
- **The Assault on Mount Everest 1922** .... *C G Bruce*
- **The Epic of Mount Everest** .... *Sir Francis Younghusband*
- **The Fight for Everest 1924** .... *E F Norton*
- **The High Altitude Medicine Handbook** .... *A J Pollard & D R Murdoch*
- **The Himalayas** (An illustrated summary of the World's Highest Mountain Ranges)
.... *Edited by David Mordecai*
- **The Kangchenjunga Adventure** .... *F S Smythe*
- **The Land of the Sherpas** .... *Ella Maillart*

www.pilgrimsbooks.com

For catalog and more information, mail or fax to:

PILGRIMS BOOK HOUSE
Mail Order, P.O.Box 3872, Kathmandu, Nepal
Tel: 977-1-424942   Fax: 977-1-424943
E-mail: mailorder@pilgrims.wlink.com.np